FOUR GIFTS

GIFTS

of the

HIGHLY

SENSITIVE

Hay House Titles of Related Interest

YOU CAN HEAL YOUR LIFE, the movie, starring
Louise Hay & Friends (available as an online streaming video)
www.hayhouse.com/louise-movie

THE SHIFT, the movie,
starring Dr. Wayne W. Dyer
(available as an online streaming video)
www.hayhouse.com/the-shift-movie

***

*DODGING ENERGY VAMPIRES: An Empath's Guide to
Evading Relationships That Drain You and Restoring
Your Health and Power,* by Christiane Northrup, M.D.

*ENERGY STRANDS: The Ultimate Guide to Clearing the Cords
That Are Constricting Your Life,* by Denise Linn

*SUPER ATTRACTOR: Methods for Manifesting a Life
beyond Your Wildest Dreams,* by Gabrielle Bernstein

*THE UNIVERSE ALWAYS HAS A PLAN: The 10 Golden
Rules of Letting Go,* by Matt Kahn

All of the above are available at your local bookstore
or may be ordered by visiting:

Hay House USA: www.hayhouse.com®
Hay House Australia: www.hayhouse.com.au
Hay House UK: www.hayhouse.co.uk
Hay House India: www.hayhouse.co.in

FOUR GIFTS
of the
HIGHLY SENSITIVE

**Embrace the Science of Sensitivity,
Heal Anxiety and Relationships,
and Connect Deeply with Your World**

COURTNEY MARCHESANI

HAY HOUSE, INC.
Carlsbad, California • New York City
London • Sydney • New Delhi

Published in the United States by: Hay House, Inc.: www.hayhouse.com®
Published in Australia by: Hay House Australia Pty. Ltd.: www.hayhouse.com.au
Published in the United Kingdom by: Hay House UK, Ltd.: www.hayhouse.co.uk
Published in India by: Hay House Publishers India: www.hayhouse.co.in

Cover design: Howie Severson
Interior design: Julie Davison

Cataloging-in-Publication Data is on file at the Library of Congress

Tradepaper ISBN: 978-1-4019-5703-2
E-book ISBN: 978-1-4019-5704-9

11   10   9   8   7   6   5   4   3
1st edition, February 2021

Printed in the United States of America

For Thomas
This book simply wouldn't
exist if not for you.

CONTENTS

INTRODUCTION

While I don't know how or why you discovered this book, I suspect you experienced something extraordinary. If this is correct, then it is a dream come true for me as an author and fellow seeker. I began a similar journey to understand the unexplainable and found little in the way of science back then. What could be labeled as supernatural, I knew on a deeper level, was an innate part of the human condition. Now I consider it an honor to have a title in the canon of books published on topics like intuition and empathy. I didn't know at the start of my own search that it would transform into a lifelong odyssey. The upshot of realizing you are just one minor character in a much longer story, one that may seem more like an Homeric epic, are the colorful people you encounter, their place in your journey, and how they move you along the path of destiny.

If you find a piece of your own story within these pages, arm yourself with knowledge and recognize that all great mysteries have maddening and unsolvable elements. The phenomena written about in this book have serious real-world implications. Sensitivity and its powerful effects have caused divorce and driven obsessions. Even so, some elusive elements of sensitivity have a tendency to create an unwavering curiosity as you find new clues and breakthroughs along the way. Inevitably, as you draw closer to what you feel is an answer, a thousand different questions spring up in its place like a hydra. While this book could be considered a recitation on the origins of the gifts of *sensory intelligence* (empathy, intuition, vision, and expression) it is also a bridge into the future. Science fiction morphs into science fact before your eyes.

My aims were to champion the exciting science that explains the gifts while also addressing the real challenges sensitive people face every day. Sensitivity can be misunderstood, especially in doctors' offices, schools, and workplaces. Individuals who display the four gifts of sensitivity are equally miscast. The problem with misinterpreting sensitivity is that it leaves us feeling lost, lonely, and confused. The old way of thinking about sensitivity comes with a lot of unwanted baggage. As my daughter once said, "It feels like *sensitivity* is a dirty word."

Our society marginalizes sensitivity due to a pervasive fear of mental illness, a fear of being labeled *crazy*. Because sensitivity has such potent effects, there is a lot of inaccurate information that leads people to believe sensitivity is a clinical disorder like anxiety or depression. It isn't. It can bring on irritating physical symptoms and unusual pains. These symptoms may lead to the misconception that your sensitivity is an inherent problem you need to fix. This book dispels old-fashioned notions and embraces the new reality: sensitivity is an *advantage*. It is also the underlying "hidden" nature for healing the empathic, intuitive, visionary, and expressive soul. When gifted sensitives find their own healing path, they destroy outdated stereotypes: that creativity stems from madness, that psychics want attention, or that the only way to cope with pure raw talent is through substance abuse. If you've ever reached out to others to explain how deeply you think, feel, and perceive on such intense levels, and someone said you were being dramatic or exaggerating, you're not alone. This rejection has a deep and lasting impact. My hope is that by providing a new perspective about these fascinating gifts, I will help you feel less isolated by that intensity you may be drawing inward.

On the bright side, our sensory abilities shape our life experience through advanced perception. There are some sensitives who have developed their consciousness into advanced Buddha-like states of awareness and awakening. This conscious awareness gives sensitive people an edge. We don't just sense or classify information; we figure out how to use it. Sensitives are adept at solving certain real-world problems, like finding clues on a crime scene, performing an award-winning role, or saving someone's life. We also have a deep capacity to hold others' intense emotions (as a doctor or therapist, for example), detect threats, embody "genius," have creative insights, possess heightened kinesthetic awareness, and show deep compassion for others. As sensitives, we must recognize our gifts and protect our valuable senses so we can access our advanced states of consciousness.

ABOUT ME

I've spent the past 20 years passionately exploring the research gap that exists between what medical science believes and how the gifted sensitive feels. Through that process, certain life patterns took shape. Investigating these life patterns helped me identify the extreme edges of the gifts and focus more upon sensitivity's role in our conscious evolution. Cutting-edge studies illuminate different aspects of the phenomenon and lend credence to the gifts. Harvard Medical School and Stanford University have supported research on sensitivity. In this book, I draw from the foundational studies that led to sensitivity finally being recognized scientifically. More importantly, I share what I have learned firsthand in my health practice working with extraordinarily sensitive people for more than two decades.

I came to understand some of the mysteries of sensitivity through a life-changing personal experience. In 2002, I prevented a fire in a Seattle, Washington, brownstone. While on an errand with my friend Rebecca, my intuitive instincts begged me to return to her apartment. I had no proof, just a raw gut feeling. Back at her place, we found a three-wick candle burning on the living room windowsill beneath a bamboo shade. There was no doubt we had prevented a fire. We started calling it "the woo factor." Since then I have had more extreme intuitive experiences, and I have heard similar stories from my clients. They didn't know how or why they knew what they knew; *they just knew.* After a sensitive first experiences a profound empathic insight or intuitive vision, they are usually energized to search for their own answers.

When I started searching for answers as to why I was having precognitions and heightened intuition, and, on rare occasions, seeing auras, I found American physicist Russell Targ and healer Jane Katra's book *Miracles of Mind*. Then, like tiny breadcrumbs on the trail, I found the works of Rupert Sheldrake, Fritjof Capra, and Linda Kohanov. A few years later, I was referred to a Hollywood spiritual medium whose abilities were enhanced through a near-death experience (NDE). Her name was June DeYoung and she became a dear, invaluable friend. She was the first person who taught me how to understand messages and signs from the other side. At a horse farm in Olympia, Washington, I learned from therapist Leigh Shambo how subtle energy flows between individuals along communication channels by working with highly intelligent animals like horses. Several years later, I met a former FBI profiler who explained the phenomenon further. She taught me how to use sensory intelligence for safety by applying intuition for threat detection. Gary Swanson, actor, lifetime member of the Actors Studio, and founder of the Montauk Group, shared his insights on the nature of the creative artist. His teaching, knowledge, and experience working directly with Lee Strasberg has shaped my own coaching practice and understanding of expressive artists, expressive art therapy, and drama for healing. Strasberg was the original Artistic Director of the Actor's Studio in New York City. He created an American version of method acting based on Konstantin Stanislavski's work with the Moscow Art Theatre. Strasberg's method has been used by Oscar-winning actors Dustin Hoffman, Al Pacino, and Sally Field.

One of my favorite teachers, master herbalist and spirit medicine healer Joyce Netishen, taught me plant-spirit medicine. Plant-spirit medicine is the ancient practice of using the vibrational essences of flowers for healing. At her sanctuary Fire Rose Farms, I learned how sensitivity operates spiritually on an entirely unseen level. Hence, the "hidden" aspects of sensitivity that are accessed for spiritual growth. Whenever I felt uncertain or confused about the spiritual side of healing, Joyce always reminded me that no matter how I decided to use the knowledge about the spiritual realm, knowing it existed would always make healing work stronger. As I learned from Joyce through rediscovering the language of the soul, our best medicine is always within us.

HOW THIS BOOK IS SET UP

In Part I, I identify the four gifts, the studies that support them, and take a deep dive into their specific complexities. I bring these all together and describe how they help shape your personality. The descriptions of the gifts' inner workings are thrilling to explore. They bring into sharp focus how special you are. What this book also does like no other is touch upon the multifaceted influence sensitivity has on your mind, body, and spirit. I call this phenomenon sensory intelligence because it is truly a holistic understanding of sensory perception.

Part II discusses the Mind-Body Method. This integrative health program was designed to help sensitive people protect their mind, body, and spirit from overstimulation. Sensitives will learn specific strategies to reduce cognitive processing errors (perceptual and cognitive) so they may receive the benefits of the gifts more often.

As a coach, teacher, and health advocate with a master's degree in mind-body medicine, my position on coaching sensitivity is this: you will always be more successful when you work *inside* your strength zone. This book provides a fun opportunity to identify those talent zones. Then you can strengthen them with mind-body therapies explained in the Mind-Body Method (MBM). The beauty of learning the MBM is that you can design your own plan based upon your unique sensitivity processing style.

To provide some context, sensitivity is typically studied exclusively under the umbrella of personality psychology. This approach deals primarily with the mind, mental health, and mental disorders. While I have great respect for psychology, as a former mental health counselor who worked in the fields of trauma and mental health for more than a decade, I find deeper meaning in how the gifted sensitive's unique sensory experience influences who she is, how she feels, and what she can do to achieve success. This perspective falls within the field of humanistic psychology.

Sensitivity has been studied in other fields, such as occupational therapy and education. One of the areas where sensory intelligence appears most commonly as a measure of success is in different learning styles, executive function, and decision-making. Through this mind-body medicine approach, you'll see an emphasis on reducing sensory overwhelm to tap into the gifts more routinely. These gifts are extremely advanced and have unlimited potential, yet sensitives often feel they are unpredictable, only come in rare flashes or in emergent situations. The only drawback in developing the gift's potential is former trauma. Sensitive individuals are more deeply affected by these negative experiences. This book teaches you how to transform past trauma borne from sensitivity. We'll create a new mind-set together and gently reshape such triggers. When you believe you can achieve this transformation, your vivid dreams take shape and become reality. Using sensitivity to guide this transformation is called realizing your *omni potential.* In mind-body medicine this means healing yourself *in all ways,* which brings whatever you set your heart and mind on. That is true freedom. And it isn't magical; it's sensitivity's intuitive healing nature.

It is my belief that sensitive people are evidence of the next level of human consciousness. I also believe sensitivity can be a beautiful place of strength, a place of grace intertwined between our hearts and minds that fortifies, revivifies, and inspires us. Sensitivity has been, and will always be, our greatest asset. It helps us embody kindness, acceptance, and resiliency in the face of extreme challenge. My wish is that we take this journey together and discover how it not only benefits our culture and society, but you as well.

TAKE THE SENSITIVITY TEST!

Wouldn't it be nice if there was a genetic test like 23andMe to delineate the sensitivity gifts? There isn't, although let's hold out hope that that work may still be accomplished in the future. For right now, I designed the Sensitivity Test to help you get a jump start on identifying your gifts based on your own life experience. Before we dive in, I recommend you take my free Sensitivity Test online to discover your gift type. You will find the test on my website homepage, at inspiredpotentials.com.

Part I

THE FOUR GIFTS OF THE HIGHLY SENSITIVE

CHAPTER 1

THE SCIENCE
OF SENSITIVITY

There is nothing in the intellect that is not in the senses.

— ARISTOTLE

Trying to define *sensitivity* is a bit like herding feral cats. No matter
how hard you try, they won't be hemmed in. The word sounds
simple enough. We link sensitivity to a vulnerability, or a weakness: to our environment, other people, substances, or the food
we eat. However, the word *sense* has a much longer story. Historical records from the Oxford English dictionary in the 16th century show the complex underpinnings of its root word, *sens*. The
cultural pedigree of the word sense was so long and diverse, its
usage reflected shifting perspectives of different time periods. In
our modern vocabulary, sense remains one of the most commonly
used words to describe a complicated set of physiological and psychological experiences of mind and body. By the early 20th century, *sense* had been divided into several categories for clarity: faculty
of sensation, perception or feeling, and meaning (or significance).

In mind-body medicine we also apply this word three ways:
how sensitivity affects our mind, body, and spirit. In a discussion

with Cliff Smyth, a doctor of movement therapy, he explained an interpretation he once came upon, "In an old French version, the word *sense* carried with it a deeper meaning about movement and direction in life."[1] Dr. Smyth's version acknowledges a *sense of the self,* which involves our perceptions, feelings, and who we think we are in relation to our world. And, how we perceive the world with our sense of self is how the world touches us.

As sensitives, or individuals who are gifted with expanded sense perception, we need to take care of our precious senses. The senses are the first line of defense the mind and body use to help fight the bombardment of chaotic energy in everyday life. This symbiotic relationship between the senses, the sense of self, and one's relationship with the world influence the relative peace and calm, happiness, or pain we feel. It's no coincidence words infused with great feeling like *sentient, sentimental, sensation,* and *sensual* stem from their root word *sens.* When we feel less suffering, our body, mind, and spirit open more to bliss.

This book introduces a new concept, sensory intelligence, that may be new to you. Sensory intelligence deserves a new perspective within the traditional medical model. For many doctors, the modern word *sense* brings to mind a cartoon chart they've had to memorize. An artistic eye will see the same chart and perceive a surrealist composition reminiscent of Salvador Dalí. This cross-sectioned brain represents a nebulous blob in a half-moon shape. The anatomical slice depicts the sensory systems of the body. It's a classic medical illustration with one large eye and prominent big black pupil, strange and asymmetrical, affixed to the edge of the *sensory homunculus,* our brain's mapping system. Then a protruded tongue, lips, and so on descend down the half-moon with corresponding labels where sensory information flows into a master regulator called the *somatosensory cortex*. The sensory system's cortex is like the Library of Congress of sensory stimulation. It catalogs every sensation from the whole body.

Maybe you've seen this same anatomical chart in your doctor's office depicting where your body sends this sensory information to your brain's homunculus, or, in alchemical terms, the "little man." Alchemists dubbed this mysterious location "little man" as a symbol of inner selfhood. He was thought of as a metaphorical innerscape where sensations were carried into another dimension within the self. The alchemical functions of little man were similar to a sorcerer's stone, where our individual identity transported worldly perceptions within a hidden complex, converting them with revivifying spiritual energy. This idea may have been a holdover from Aristotle's notion that the brain was an ancillary cooling organ that supported the heart's spiritual functions. In Aristotelian anatomical terms, the heart's chambers circulated spiritual energy and one of its functions was a mixing place of all sensation known as *sensus communis*. The heart encapsulated spiritual energy and was a storehouse of physical sensations where they flowed together freely. This central location for all sense perception became the budding philosophy of common sense.

Neuroscientists have entitled the brain area tasked with perceiving all physical sensations the *sensory homunculus*, whose literal translation from the Latin is "little man." This area of the brain integrates sensory information from the outside world within the mind and body. It processes sensations from your environment automatically and mostly unconsciously. The way your brain processes this information determines how you think, feel, and move through your world. In the simplest of terms, a sentient being is one who is self-aware. When sensations coalesce into specific thought patterns, sensitive individuals use this awareness to find meaning. As our mind seeks to know the world outside of the inner self, it uses the senses to explore the nature of reality. The distinct perceptive faculty it utilizes is sensory intelligence. The four sensory intelligences, or gifts, detailed in this book are intuition, empathy, vision, and expression.

A CLOSER LOOK AT SENSITIVITIES

Within every culture there are special individuals who display the remarkable gifts of sensitivity. In discovering the abilities of sensitivity, you might be reminded of some famous characters, like Marvel Universe's Dr. Strange, who glimpses alternate futures, or *Twilight*'s vampiric Jasper Hale, who senses and controls the emotions of others. However, the four sensitive gifts are real.

In this chapter, I'm going to share stories as well as the science behind them. My hope is that you'll find a balance between compelling stories and authoritative medical studies. As a kindred spirit, I know your heart's true intention: to access the gifts of sensitivity practically so you can use them in your everyday life.

Now strap in and let's fly.

REAL-LIFE CASES INVOLVING SENSITIVES

In 1956, a manhunt was underway in New York City. Widespread fear and panic had taken hold from the man infamously known as the Mad Bomber. His pipe bombs had blown up in Grand Central Terminal, the New York Public Library, Radio City Music Hall, and many other locations throughout the city. The first pipe bomb attributed to the elusive bomber had been left on the windowsill at the Consolidated Edison building on West 64th Street. Over 16 years, he set 33 bombs. Twenty-one of these had exploded, injuring 15 people.

Anxious for leads, Captain Howard Finney from the New York Police Department consulted a unique source, psychiatrist Dr. James Brussel, a sensitive-intuitive. Brussel examined the snapshots of the obliterated crime scenes with discerning eyes. He pored over the meticulously written letters that outlined the bomber's revenge. They were all neatly signed with his initials "F.P." in slanted script. The measured tone and capitalization of the letters that described F.P.'s threatening plans suggested the bomber was careful and well organized. His language indicated an intelligence for methodical thought. Odd word choices, such as "dastardly deeds," indicated the bomber may have been raised abroad. Additional intuitions included his single status as well as the geographical region where he lived.

After carefully analyzing all the facts in the case, Brussels closed his eyes, imagining the mind of the bomber. He received several vivid images. He relayed the detailed information to Captain Finney's investigators: "I saw the Bomber: impeccably neat, absolutely proper. A man who would avoid the newer styles of clothing until custom had made them conservative."[2] He continued, "When you catch him—and I have no doubt you will—he'll be wearing a double-breasted suit. And it will be buttoned."

A month later, when George Metesky was arrested, many of Brussel's profiling facts about the Mad Bomber were confirmed. He lived in the predicted location, Waterbury, Connecticut. He was unmarried and lived with his two sisters. When he was asked to get dressed and come with the officers, George Metesky was escorted by authorities sporting an old-fashioned pompadour and a clean, double-breasted suit. It was buttoned up to the top.

Turn the clock forward 10 years and travel across the world to the unforgiving bushlands of Australia. In 1966 an eight-year-old girl named Wendy Jane Pfeiffer was stabbed and abducted a few feet from her family's farmhouse. When a search and rescue effort of 150 volunteers failed to find her across massive acreage of dense scrub brush, everyone assumed the worst. Fearing her dead after two days, local police enlisted two aboriginal Pitjantjatjara trackers to find her, Jimmy James a sensitive-empath and his relative Daniel Moodoo.

Jimmy James found Pfeiffer still alive in the Adelaide bushlands, a territory described as remote and wild.[3] Ms. Pfeiffer remembered surviving after her abduction: "I walked 12 kilometres [roughly 7 miles] over a 42-hour period, becoming more and more dehydrated and totally exhausted." At the time, Jimmy James's ability to detect the location of the young girl became well known in Australia. What these stories didn't report, since Jimmy James didn't speak English and held no interviews, was his ability to sense Ms. Pfeiffer's presence in the bush using his near-photographic memory of the place with which he had a natural and enduring bond. According to one interviewer[4] who studied Jimmy

James's life history, James had a deep feeling, connection, and sense for the land. This empathic connection manifested in his extensive knowledge of plants, interpretation of weather patterns, and the entire ecology he mapped from learning how to track game. When the story was finally featured in the documentary *Missing*, Ms. Pfeiffer was given the opportunity to reflect on her abduction and express gratitude for Jimmy James, who had since passed away, "Today, I'm lucky to be alive. . . . without [Jimmy] I simply wouldn't be here."

In 1990 Daniel Day-Lewis, one of the most accomplished British actors alive today, won his first Academy Award. It was a prolific time for Day-Lewis, a sensitive-expressive. He won his Oscar for *My Left Foot*. In the poignant film, the actor portrayed Irish artist Christy Brown who had cerebral palsy. The condition rendered Brown unable to control anything beyond his left foot. Day-Lewis revealed the intense mental and physical control Brown summoned to use his foot for routine tasks like feeding himself, and more complex ones, such as writing and painting. To embody Brown's resiliency, Day-Lewis stayed in character. He never left his wheelchair on set and had to be lifted and carried throughout the production.

Daniel Day-Lewis used this direct kind of physical experience to tap into his emotions so he could transform into Christy Brown. Using his gift of expression, he evoked the feelings Brown must have felt while enduring chronic disability. Gently, he invited the audience in to experience Christy Brown's colorful inner life.

A year earlier, Day-Lewis performed the title role in *Hamlet* at the National Theatre in London. Midperformance the ghost of his own, late father, Cecil Day-Lewis, appeared and stared back at him. No one else saw his father that night. On stage Day-Lewis's deeply personal experience quite realistically embodied Hamlet's own tragic loss. In the first act, Hamlet sees the former king, his deceased father, who is called "the ghost."

The unexpected sight of his own father shocked Day-Lewis and exacerbated a growing sense of nervous exhaustion. Shortly afterward fatigue struck his mind and body, affecting him for several years. He left in the middle of *Hamlet*'s production and has never returned to the theater.[5]

In 2011 Stephen Wiltshire, a London-based architectural artist and best-selling author, was contracted by Swiss bank UBS and their global advertising campaign. The project was titled "We will not rest" and commissioned Wiltshire, a sensitive-visionary, to draw a 250-foot long panoramic rendering of New York City after a single flyby in a helicopter. Wiltshire received public attention in 2003, when a retrospective of his artwork entitled "Not a Camera: The Unique Vision of Stephen Wiltshire" featured his massive cityscapes intricately detailed, which were drawn entirely from his photographic memory. These landscapes were usually viewed only once before he drew them.

When interviewed for a short documentary about his drawing of New York City for the UBS project, Wiltshire reflected on the visuals and his favorite structure, the Empire State Building. He paused, quietly capturing the details in his mind's eye, "It's a brilliant building." His sister explains Stephen's love for design: "I think drawing for Stephen is like air and water for us. He cannot live without it." After the New York creation was displayed at John F. Kennedy International Airport, many observers witnessed his aesthetic ability to depict every aspect of what he sees with near-perfect detail, including how many windows, doors, and floors there are, right up to the rooftops.

These are just four examples of famous sensitives. There are many more. People from all walks of life display a range of these abilities. Sensitive individuals can see, hear, and feel the subtlest level of reality. Often, they bring their insights back to benefit others. They are artists, designers, detectives, doctors, engineers, inventors, psychologists, scientists, and teachers. Sensitive people possess an innate ability to perceive sensory information that often goes undetected by others. This talent is directly linked with different kinds of *sensory acuity*.[6]

Acuity means sharpness or keenness of thought, vision, or hearing, such as *visual acuity* or *sensorimotor acuity*. There may also be an *emotional acuity* or a deftness for sensing through feelings. Depending on a sensitive's unique type of *sensory processing*, they will exhibit certain gifts, or intelligences, based on the skills they have inherited and developed. While all humans share this link between cognitive processing and sensory perception, sensitives have a genetic predisposition called *biological sensitivity*, also known as the sensitive survival strategy, which enhances these survival instincts. For example, discrimination of specific sensory information through temporal coding (alteration of time on acoustics), pitch, feeling, or visual-spatial sensory information directly influence the speed of sensory processing.[7] These different types of acuity make up sensory intelligence. We see the characteristics of emotional acuity, speed for processing language, and judgment of aesthetic quality develop into a particular processing style within the sensitive-expressive, one of the four main sensitive types. Sensitive-expressives will use these abilities and integrate them for a clear descriptive language to convey what they see, hear, and feel with an unparalleled intensity.

The four gifts of sensitivity are so tightly interwoven with an individual's central nervous system (CNS) that no two highly sensitive people (HSP) will respond to an environment in the exact same way. For example, take clairvoyants, mediums, or psychic channelers. They will tell you that the ability to read people is based on their unique sensory interpretations. As astute readers of energy, these sensitive-intuitives use the way someone's energy appears and moves (e.g., dense, fast, colorful, dull), vibrations they feel and hear, and other sense perceptions to discern and translate the intentions, emotions, or personalities of the people they read. There is a vast difference between an expert psychic channeler who knows how to interpret this energetic, spiritual, or emotional information, and someone who is first learning what their sense impressions mean.

Every sensitive has an innate talent for perceiving or detecting information. However, the development of consciousness or awareness of what is being perceived takes time. The gap between pure awareness and the analytical mind has been called *conscious overlay*, or perception filter. Conscious overlay skews perception through belief systems, emotional feedback loops, and personal biases. This gradual development of conscious awareness makes understanding how one's gift works challenging. Not everyone is blessed with a parent or teacher who can explain their particular gift to them or how to advance it.

Researchers have found 20 percent of the population are sensitive.[8] Sensitive people span all age ranges from young children, through twentysomething millennials, and into old age. In the United States alone, 20 percent of the population (328 million people) yields more than 65 million highly sensitive people. However, the phenomenon favors no one culture, appearing with equal proportion across the globe. While you are learning about the science of sensitivity, which explains your own gift, sensitive type, and how sensory stimuli directly affects you, keep this in mind: sensory processing depends on your specific *sensory modulation* or discriminatory abilities.[9] These are both explained in the second half of this book.

A BRIEF HISTORY OF SENSORY PERCEPTION

Historically and culturally, the medical profession has cast sensitive people as neurotic, shy, or hysterical. There was even a time in psychiatric care where famous doctors like neurologist Jean Martin-Charcot committed vulnerable women suffering from hysterical symptoms into psychiatric wards that in retrospect look a lot like sensitivity. Hysteria was considered a difficult disease with mysterious or unpredictable symptoms that encompassed a whole host of negative behaviors—tearfulness, anxiety, nervousness, and depression. Now we know more about the sensory regions in the brain and how they connect to the nervous systems. Sensitives' brain functions are unique in the way they perceive and translate sensory information. Thankfully, due to new types of medical im-

aging, pioneering researchers, and neuropsychology, we can transform shame-inducing stereotypes like hysteria and shed light on
what's *really* going on.

In neuropsychology, the study of the brain's influence on
behavior, we see major historical strides in understanding sensory
perception. Neuroscience has shifted the cultural norms. When
the gods once ruled, our souls were weighed by the good and evil
in our hearts. Gradually, through science, we have come to realize
how the mind works via sensory processing and conscious reasoning. We now know sensory processing areas are specialized
regions within our brain that integrate sensory information from
the body. Science has illuminated what was once kept dark and
stifled by the all-powerful gods.

Ancient Egyptian scribes thoroughly outlined the procedures
of sacred entombment. They specifically recorded preservation of
the heart and other important organs to prepare the soul for flight
to the afterlife. For ancient Egyptians it was the heart, not the
brain, that was considered the supreme seat of the soul. Up until
the 4th century, predominant thinkers like Aristotle still believed
the locale of human intelligence, or soul, flowed within the heart.
In his treatise on the rational soul, this ethereal nature could not
be found anywhere else in the body. As someone who believes in
an eternal soul, it is easy to romanticize a luminary like Aristotle. The remnants of his ambitious search for the seat of the soul
still reverberate through his elegant theories. Can we honestly
say modern science aims for such altruistic goals as Aristotle's
attempt to understand God's earthly design for housing our delicate and everlasting soul? As time marched on, the ethereal nature
degraded. The brain became more mechanistic and our human
soul lost its home.

Over the next four centuries, this philosophical paradigm
shifted to a more anatomical brain. Led by Greek surgeon and
physician Claudius Galenus, or Galen for short, scientists departed
radically from Aristotle. Through his observation of brain injuries,
Galen discovered that the brain was the center of mental activity
and categorized four vital humors: blood, phlegm, yellow bile, and

black bile. While the field of anatomical brain science advanced through Galen's discoveries, functional aspects of the brain remained crude and shrouded in mystery. Even into the 19th century, physicians recognized Galen's treatments for hysteria, which he attributed to demons. Astonishingly, one of his remedies listed was purification by fire.

Science moved slowly in treatment of mental disorders like hysteria. In the 1600s philosopher and mathematician René Descartes improved the biological science of human behavior significantly. He investigated reflexes that "bounce off" the pineal gland. This breakthrough linked the brain's physiological systems responsible for movement with behavior instead of an ethereal mind. Descartes determined there is a big difference between mere sensory functioning and an ability to think, feel, and perceive a sense of oneself. He distinguished a metaphysical separation between animals and humans. Due to our higher form of perceptive thought and the ability to deal with complex feelings, he separated the functions of sentience from the physical senses.

Descartes challenged the science of the day by claiming the nerves were mechanistic like a motor. He proposed they carried sensory information to the ventricles. In Descartes's theory, the fluid inside the ventricles resembled hydraulic fluid. Nerves were used for information transport by communicating sensory information about control of the body, thereby influencing physical behavior. His applications inspired a new model of sensory information delivery between the brain and body. He formally established the theoretical argument known today as the mind-body problem. Since Descartes still couldn't explain higher cognitive functions such as emotion, desire, and intellect he created a division between them. The mind, which is not the brain, must embody a person's ethereal nature, aka the soul. This powerful division still influences brain research today.

A century later, in 1780, Italian physician Luigi Galvani had a major breakthrough. Observing frogs, he discovered their muscles twitched using "animal electricity." While incomplete due to the insufficient technology, Galvani's foundational work established the electrical underpinnings of the nervous system.

By the 1800s German physiologist Franz Joseph Gall determined the brain had specific regions or localization of mental functions. He looked at the bumps and nodules of the skull and decided these revealed intelligence, features of character, and personality markers. Today Gall's pseudoscience known as phrenology has been discarded, but localization was adopted into the medical lexicon. The localization of different areas of the brain still shape neurology. By 1869 Sir Francis Galton published *Hereditary Genius*, which later led to a terrible controversy involving eugenics. He introduced the topic of visual acuity and hypothesized that sensory channels are a means of information input that form intelligence. He speculated that gifted people may have superior sensitivities. One hundred and fifty years later, his work was dissected and studied more extensively. Researchers found sensitivities are *not measures of intelligence*, but there are *specific links to intelligence through sensory modulation differences*, such as sensory speed, discrimination, and acuity levels. In the early 2000s, measurement tools like the Adolescent/Adult Sensory Profile were developed to test the differences of sensory processing.

The end of the 19th century was an exciting time for brain research. Carl Wernicke, the German anatomist, physician, neuropathologist, and psychiatrist, combined his fields of study. By observing and working with language deficits from patients who were unable to speak, he differentiated a specific area in the temporal and parietal lobes at the back of the brain. This region, where language deficits generate (known as aphasia), is still called Wernicke's area. The scientific evolution of sensory perception takes shape through psychologists' understanding of different neurological disorders, like Emil Kraepelin's discovery of manic depression, Wernicke's localization of language processing, and how the physiology of clinical mental disorders impact behavior. These touchstones are the scientific origins of modern neuropsychology.

In 1906 Santiago Ramón y Cajal won the Nobel Prize (with Camillo Golgi) for his work detailing the basic structure and function of nerve cells. Ramón y Cajal was the first brain researcher to isolate nerve cells and connect them to the wider processing functions of the nervous system. The invention of the electroencephalograph (EEG) both revolutionized understanding of brain functions and provided a new electrical model to represent the nervous system. Now scientists can record electrical activity in the brain.

The last 90 years are dizzying in terms of brain research. In 1932 neuron function was explained and we learned how nerves actually transmit different messages. By 1944 nerve fibers were explained. Then work begun on the hypothalamus and thalamus. These interconnected areas became formally recognized as an *interbrain*, which involves memory, sound processing, and emotions. Rapid eye movement (REM) followed, using EEG to track sleep patterns. Then the positron emission tomography (PET) scan was invented, which provided visual information about the activity of the brain.

In the 1980s research focused on the unique functions of the right and left hemispheres.[10] Then, the 1990s became the Decade of the Brain. Through these time periods we learned about ion channels, proteins' influence on brain receptors, and single transduction of nerve cells through chemicals called neurotransmitters. At the end of this period, sensitivity was formally identified through Drs. Elaine and Arthur Aron's development of the Highly Sensitive Person Scale (HSPS).[11]

Our modern understanding of the brain has been shaped by the growing fields of neuroscience and neuropsychology. Through scientific evolution, understanding of brain functions has changed markedly based on the technology available at the time. Sifting through extensive medical terminology, we see different analogies to explain neurological concepts in medical research. For instance, the senses are gateways to intelligence. Or, behavior is regulated like a thermostat. The brain is like a computer. Nerve cells communicate like the Internet. These analogies help us picture brain phenomena. But they also constrain our understanding of sensitivity, tying it to current models and technology. Several prominent studies into neurological sensory processes, like Dr. Elaine Aron's, broke free from the constraints that have defined investigation. Others like Rupert Sheldrake, Russell Targ, and Hal Puthoff completely transformed the field of study on sensory perception and how it informs consciousness.

MODERN SCIENCE AND THE DESCARTES MODEL

Sensory perception is the use of human senses (seeing, hearing, smelling, tasting, touching) to process stimuli or information from the environment. Our wide-open senses were how we explored the world before we could communicate. There is a crossroad dividing the science on sensory perception. On one side, widely accepted science, which is neurological and evidence-based, explains the specific anatomical and neurological functions of the senses and how they perceive information. It is then applied to how the brain connects sensory information within the body (motor neurons, reflexes, and sensory neurons). These fields of study investigate how brain function shapes human behavior. On the other side is the field of sensory perception research conducted by parapsychological investigators, which has largely been neglected by traditional science. These studies have become shrouded in conspiracy theories, which complicates differentiating the real science from the lore.

Many people, when they first hear the term *sensory perception,* believe it refers to *extrasensory perception* (ESP). While I am unsure how this association came about, there is an interesting connection. For starters, ESP would be considered a form of sensory intelligence. It falls within the range of human sensitivity as being a kind of intelligent perception and an intuitive mental faculty. Because it has been so difficult to research under laboratory conditions, ESP has been widely criticized. There are distinct viewpoints around ESP. It is thought to be a function of sensory perception. Alternatively, sensory perception is sometimes considered a bridge to nonlocal consciousness (mind). In terms of sensory perception, nonlocal consciousness may be the final frontier.

The most frustrating part of this struggle between traditional neuroscience and consciousness research is the very real separation between the two. The materialist viewpoint suggests the mind is generated from the organic biochemical processes in the brain. The relatively new field of consciousness studies leaves open the location of the mind, including a nonlocal model. These studies include traditional physical sciences that sometimes appear metaphysical (e.g., quantum effects, quantum mechanics, and particle entanglement). Scientifically, we are still at pains to change the Cartesian abstraction of mechanistic sensory duality (the senses versus a "self"). Nowadays, a collective immune system in the scientific community combats new knowledge about consciousness. A "seeing is not believing" attitude prevails. Dr. Rupert Sheldrake's morphogenic fields and Dr. Jacobo Grinberg's neuronal fields show support and evidence of a participatory mind with the ability to connect and influence the environment and others.[12] Yet these studies remain buried in obscurity and the discoveries wither rather than enrich knowledge and build on consciousness as a legitimate field of research.

Sir Roger Penrose, English mathematician, physicist, and philosopher of science, likely holds the current mantle for the most controversial theory of consciousness today. He calls it orchestrated objective reduction, or Orch OR.[13] Orch OR has been panned by critics. Due to Penrose's brilliance in traditional science, researchers cannot discount his theory completely. With the help of anesthesiologist and consciousness researcher Stuart Hamerhoff, Penrose designed the Orch OR hypothesis using microtubules in the brain to explain the possible quantum mechanical nature of consciousness.[14] With work by Japanese researchers on microtubules, there is some narrow support for Penrose and Hamerhoff's initial claim that consciousness is derived from a deeper level, on a finer quantum scale of activity, within brain neurons.[15]

Earlier research by parapsychologists Russell Targ and Harold Puthoff at Stanford Research Institute (SRI) in Menlo Park,

California, showed a positive correlation between subjects having higher than average positive (correct) responses on describing targets at a distance while under sensory shielding.[16] The researchers used EEG recordings to track participants' physiology while they sensed targets. Targ and Puthoff used remote scenes as targets on blind-guessing tests. Experimenters either used pictures of the target or were located at a distant site, many miles from the test location at the SRI research facility. Test subjects described or drew the target at the experimenter's location. They were able to detail the location conditions such as buildings, docks, roads, or gardens, including structural materials, color, and shape, sometimes with great specificity.

From this landmark study, Targ and Puthoff established a theory of higher cognitive functioning of what they originally called *remote perceptual ability*. Their subjects were able to describe the target or location while under blind conditions (experimenters also used visual, acoustic, and electrical shielding). The researchers concluded these perceptions were an extrasensory function of the mind. In their summary they noted, "It may be that remote perceptual ability is widely distributed in the general population, but because the perception is generally below an individual's level of awareness, it's repressed or not noticed." Targ has written several books about his research including *Miracles of Mind, Limitless Mind, The Reality of ESP*, and *Mind-Reach*.

Since ESP has largely been rejected by modern medicine and science, we must look to the forerunners in the field of parapsychology for insights. They form a kind of scientific subculture. Suppressed science includes the work of biologist Rupert Sheldrake, Ph.D., who modernized morphogenic fields, and physician Norman Shealy, M.D., who studied energetic healing.

The relevance of ESP to sensitivity was made evident through a groundbreaking 2015 Italian study published in the *Journal of Nervous and Mental Disease* on the links between telepathy, clairvoyance, precognition and trauma.[17] The Italian study was based on the earlier research of psychoanalyst Sándor Ferenczi, a neurologist who theorized that children who suffered extremely painful experiences, such as sexual abuse, might develop hypersensitivity to environmental conditions in order to avoid traumatic events in the future.[18] The results from the Italian study suggest that individuals who experience recurrent ESP phenomena report higher levels of past trauma compared to individuals who report no such experiences. Additionally, this study showed an association between anomalous events, uncommon events outside the normal range of human sense perception, and trauma.

The authors of the study propose that consciousness provides a regulatory function during emotionally and physically painful traumatic events: dissociation. This means when there is a failure or breakdown of normal dissociative defenses, the gifts of sensitivity emerge. This process is an automatic defense mechanism and we have little control over it during the cascade of nervous system responses (freeze, flight, fight, fright, fragmenting) that flow from a traumatic event. To understand how sensitive our nervous system is and how consciousness may serve as a regulatory function, we'll look at this more look closely when we learn about the sensory systems.

SENSORY PROCESSING SENSITIVITY (SPS) FORMALLY IDENTIFIED

The Highly Sensitive Person Scale was first designed by Drs. Elaine and Arthur Aron. Their work ushered in a new era of personality research on sensitivity. The HSPS delineated different kinds of sensory stimulation through subjects' answers on a 7-point rating scale from 1 (strongly disagree) to 7 (strongly agree). It included 27 questions and targeted a range of environmental stimuli such as loud noises, bright lights, emotions of others, and common substances such as caffeine. Sample questions from the HSP scale were "Are you made uncomfortable by loud noises?" and "Do other people's moods affect you?"[19] Modern personality psychologists characterized the highly sensitive person as having a unique organic brain processing function to handle more sensory information. Researchers label this trait *sensory processing sensitivity* (SPS) because sensitive individuals use a specific depth processing function to detect and interpret information. Sensory information streams through the senses and an acuity is felt such as brightness of lights, intensity of sounds, and differentiation of smells.

This recent formalization of sensitivity as an organic brain process was breakthrough science. Assigning clinical definition to SPS legitimized sensitivity. It moved from an easily dismissed generalization to a definable part of human existence. Clinically it wasn't considered a mental disorder, but a unique inborn temperament influencing the personality. Curious social science investigators repeatedly tested the validity of the HSPS questionnaire, cross-culturally as well, and have found it valid by four and five factor analysis.[20] The HSPS provided a consistent measurement of the unique qualities of SPS, now considered subprocessing types, such as ease of sensory excitation (EOE), low sensory threshold (LST), and aesthetic sensitivity (AES). Through these advances, psychologists could now quantify some of the negative associations attributed to sensitivity. The data dismantled the stereotype by identifying the specific subfunctions of sensory processing. Not all sensitives are created equal, nor are they all shy, tearful, sad, neurotic, or hysterical.

For a great many of us, this shift in psychological culture leveled the playing field. It validated new ways to describe sensitivity. With the knowledge that sensitives really do see, hear, and feel more, we could explore the possibilities and advantages rather than being negatively clouded by psychology's need to pathologize the unknown.

This field of sensitivity research informed open-minded doctors about the subtleties of sensory processing. It enabled them to focus on specific areas of the brain enhanced in sensitive individuals. More recent work expanded field studies, evaluating SPS and causal relationships between anxiety, depression, autism, and learning differences. While there is still a long way to go, these informative studies shape our understanding of SPS.

We now know SPS is not limited to mental function. SPS affects us emotionally and physically. Studying SPS through the different cognitive pathways for processing sensory information helps us understand its physical influences. The connection that stands out, the one you can witness yourself, is readily detecting when someone is lying. Many of us have experienced this innate knowing when confronted with a lie. If you have a high range of emotional acuity, like an empath or expressive, you may even discern the underlying reasons why. This prominent ability stems from the recognition of unconscious states, micro facial expressions, and body language, which reveal a deceptive pattern.[21] Psychologists and movement therapists who work in the field of trauma and somatosensory therapy call this deceptive pattern inauthenticity. Human lie detection gives you a significant advantage in your relationships. Detecting truth from falsehood is felt physically as a pang in the gut we call instinct. When a wave of uneasiness, nausea, or discomfort passes through, it is your body's *somatic awareness* warning you. It's your bullshit detector.

SPS also includes aesthetic sensitivity (AES), or the heightened awareness to one's surroundings and a facile ability to perceive beauty. This gift allows you to harmonize with and synthesize visual information from your environment. It yields a highly inventive creativity. Empaths who have AES may have the distinct ability to feel someone else's feelings through their aesthetic awareness and eloquently describe what those feelings are.[22] Your sensitivity will always help you perceive advantages and detect potential pitfalls faster than others.

There are different kinds of research on sensitivity, which include sensory awareness, sensory processing, and sensory disorders. I have quantified what I have studied and applied it by helping the sensitive clients I serve in my health practice. In both psychology and psychiatry, there is a general premise that exists that is important to mention as we wade into the gifts. When someone is referred for a persistent symptom or physical complaint, it is always best to rule out the physiological nature of an illness. For example, diagnosing disorders like attention-deficit/ hyperactivity disorder (ADHD), autism, or other serious medical conditions such as Lyme Disease infections or Lupus autoimmune system responses, that increase sensitivities can help rule out other contributing factors attributed to sensitive reactions. Sensitivity is linked to all of these conditions: ADHD/rejection sensitivity dysphoria, autism/sensory processing disorder (SPD), and Lyme sensitivity. Having extreme symptoms of sensitivity (such as photosensitivity to bright lights, explosions of anger from contact with an environment, or fear of loud sounds) cannot be attributed to sensitivity alone. There is an overarching reason why the sensitive reaction exists. That is why I am so adamant about the incorrect public perception that sensitivity is a disorder or condition. It isn't. This confusion arises from sensitivity's appearance as an adverse behavior pattern in several medically diagnosable conditions such as sensory processing disorder, or post-traumatic stress disorder (PTSD).

Scientists and doctors have defined sensitivity by its negative influence on diagnosable conditions. There is a very real field of study that shows the positive aspects of sensitivity too, albeit there are fewer publications about them. These are what I call the benefits or multiple intelligences of sensitivity. If we pull these positive aspects out of the medical picture frame, magnify them, and work within their nature, a whole different landscape takes shape. We start to see how an inherent intellect shapes these benefits of sensitivity. Connections are forged through routine encoding of sensory information into long-term sense impressions infused with meaning. This process, which directly influences wider neural networks, molds the multiple intelligences of sensory awareness.

Medical studies have definitely informed my general knowledge about sensitivity, and so have the people who display the gifts through sharing their experiences. From these two sources, science and sensitive individuals, I have defined four specific sensory intelligences (gifts) that run in typical patterns or types. After categorizing these four distinct patterns, I created a characterological typing system, or archetype, that describes the gift and how it influences the personality.

THE NEWEST FIELD STUDIES

Pioneering researchers have begun to seriously study sensitivity. One discovery, mirror neurons, has exciting potential. Using functional magnetic resonance imagery (fMRI), researchers examined the entire brain. They found a wide network of cortical areas showing specific motor neurons that help us translate the movements of other people into our own movements—that is, to *mirror* observed actions. Simply, mirroring action is when a specific brain area observes and repeats an action from the environment. The action does not have to be executed by the brain in order for the brain to feel a response. This phenomenon was first uncovered in studies of primate behavior. In a study of macaque monkeys, it was found that the same mirror neuron fired regardless of whether the monkey ripped a piece of paper, watched a person rip it, or heard paper ripping (without visual cues).

From the mirroring properties in these studies, researchers concluded that mirror neurons become encoded for abstract concepts related to actions like ripping paper. It doesn't matter who performs the action. Scientists believe mirror neurons are the brain's sentinels, or helpers. They discern and translate for the observer what it feels like to act, move, or speak in an observed way. Some psychologists theorize that highly sensitive individuals have more active mirror neurons or a larger mirroring system than people in the less astute range of sensing. This increase gives sensitives the feelings of enhanced empathy, greater depth processing, and a stronger ability to read a range of emotions from facial expressions and body language. You can test this yourself. When you're in a meeting or any kind of social setting, make yourself yawn. If you see others start yawning in your vicinity, you've successfully engaged their mirror neurons. If you see someone in the crowd who doesn't yawn . . . well Houston, you might have a problem.

Mirror neurons were only identified a few decades ago and news of their existence has attracted the attention of neurologists and social scientists who are exploring their implications. In humans, mirror neurons are not as well understood as in monkeys because human behavior is more difficult to study. The heavy reliance on animal test subjects has created some controversy. Thus far mirror neurons have been found in the *premotor cortex* (involved in planning and execution of voluntary movements), the *supplementary motor area* (involved in control of movements), the *primary somatosensory cortex* (which receives information from nerve cells located all over the body), and the *inferior parietal cortex* (which helps us interpret facial expressions).

Researchers speculate that mirror neurons help us pick up cues in the environment so we can make good decisions, like finding safety. They may also participate in higher cortical processes (reasoning, communication), such as abstract thinking. An example of this type of cortical abstraction is how we learn to translate and interpret messages through visual cues for decoding different styles of communication. Using mirror neurons to understand the symbolic meaning in communication helps humans understand the multifaceted language of emotions. Although scientists have not uncovered a direct link between mirror neurons and sensory processing sensitivity, many researchers believe a relationship exists.

Amazingly, sensitives who are gifted with intuitive sensory intelligence can predict future events and see mini snapshots of the future. This intuitive ability can take multiple forms. In one of the main areas studied by researchers at Stanford, subjects intuited correct information in a forced choice experiment with limited time available.

A study by Dr. Garry Nolan, the Rachford and Carlotta A. Harris professor of pathology at Stanford University School of Medicine, explored the link between genetics and highly intuitive people. Dr. Nolan and Dr. Kit Green observed that individuals in the group they studied, who had high intelligence and tested for increased intuition, were physiologically and neurologically different than the control group. His co-researchers found a high correlation between extraordinary intuition and an area of the brain called the *caudate putamen,* which is involved in decision making—and is a known center for intuition.

In a conversation about his research, Dr. Nolan reported aspects of his study, in preliminary form, had already been confirmed by a postgraduate student at Harvard. He also suggested that research studies validate the genetic link between highly sensitive people and the expanded sensory intelligence of intuition, since they observed the same neurologic feature in families. He underscored, though, the preliminary nature of the findings and insisted that much further work is required before any firm conclusions are made.

Famous neurologist Dr. Oliver Sacks once said, "Whatever is intuitive must have an underlying method." I asked Dr. Nolan about finding a direct physiological connection (caudate putamen) to this organizing structure of the mind and whether intuition could be trained through critical periods of intuitive development. He replied, "Well, you can't train what's not there." Since highly sensitive-intuitives might be genetically predisposed for more intuitive thought through higher caudate putamen activation, this new research has proven neurologically what many of us have felt as sudden flashes of insight.

THE FOUR GIFTS

The four gifts of sensitivity are intuition, empathy, vision, and expression. When these gifts are developed to their potential, you can tap into them freely and employ their strengths. The unique forms of sensory acuity are what drove me to explore these fascinating features of sensory perception. As I worked with sensitive individuals through my career as a mental health counselor, I was fondly referred to as the person who handled "the weird stuff." I felt like the central operator in my small corner of the world fielding questions about the woo factor.

If someone got called an oddball when a sensory anomaly presented itself, I drew closer. I've enjoyed this role in my community, and I'll keep turning over new stones in the medical literature to support what we sensitives feel on a regular basis while perplexing others. As our knowledge about sensitivity grows and expands, my hope is that sensitive people will help the scientific forerunners bring these connections together in the new field of consciousness studies. By providing a strong voice for sensitives, my aim is to make sure we get a spot at the table when scientists link these incredible gifts with breakthroughs in advanced states of consciousness.

As a sensitivity health coach, I discovered my clients had specific sensory abilities that were quite extraordinary, like exceptional intuition, hyperawareness, and visual-spatial reasoning to solve problems. Skills like these could be observed through their personal experiences, such as receiving sudden intuitions, feeling other people's feelings, and strong emotional expression that left no confusion about their passion. Knowing these qualities were somehow connected, I dug deeper, looking for the answers into how and why.

Most of these abilities draw on the interconnections between the perceptive and emotional functioning of the brain. The perceptive brain experiences the world through the senses. Seeing, hearing, tasting, smelling, and feeling come in through the somatosensory cortex (that area receiving sensory information). Sensation brings an internal awareness of an external stimulus through *interoception*, whereas emotional processing relies on several regions, including the left and right hemispheres and temporal lobes. Our emotions are the most difficult states for our brain to process and that's why there are overlapping systems involved. These subcortical areas of the brain, which encompass the hypothalamus, brain stem, and ventromedial prefrontal cortex, receive and send information through the neural networks responsible for forming memories, imagining, language, emotion, and discrimination of sound (musicality, rhythm, pitch, and tone).

The gifts develop from these neural networks and their interconnection between the sensory cortex as it feeds sensory information into the cortical regions of the brain.[24] Think of this process as tire tracks in the sand. Sensory tread marks help forge stronger neural networks . The more they are reinforced, the deeper they sink in. The remarkable capacity of the sensory cortex and its sensory function is the ability to evaluate external stimuli according to the context in which this sensory information is received. It is called *context dependence* of sensory perception, and it helps our brain predict environmental outcomes based on these representations. Scientific proof of this amazing process is found in the cortical representations of sensory stimuli as they stream inward and how network states rely on this moment-to-moment feedback loop to influence sensory processing.[25] Cognitive states modulate these sensory representations.[26] Since we don't know how these cortical representations influence the feedback loop between contextual cues, influence on sensory perception, and their effects on neuronal inputs into other regions, scientists are left to hypothesize until they can eventually target and test the exact components involved.

What we do know is sensory perceptions directly influence their targeted cortical regions, producing what are called network states. These network states and their influence are broken down into specific facets of sensory processing such as arousal, attention, increased precision, temporal coding, and modulation of neuronal correlations.[27]

Empathy, intuition, vision, and expression are correlated to these facets of sensory processing as they have their own specific types of sensory acuity and discrimination functions. These functions contribute to *global sensory processing*,[28] which in turn affects the *global cognitive function*. We know these two factors exist and rely upon each other because as aging populations were studied, age-related decline of the five classical senses (vision, smell, hearing, touch, and taste) showed a marked shift in cognition. As sensory functions decline, so do mental abilities.[29]

Mirror neurons help us understand empathy and the ability to relate and share the feelings of others. Through Stanford's research on intuition, we now know the ability to acquire knowledge without conscious reasoning is enhanced through activation of the caudate putamen. Vision in this context relates to the interconnectivity of visual-spatial awareness, the inner mental visual field, and imagination. Expression through the use of language helps us find meaning in one's own thoughts and emotional processes as they relate to the outer world.

THE GIFTED SENSITIVE

While there is often overlap in different styles of processing sensitivity, generally one type becomes dominant. Let's look at the four types of sensitive people now, one by one.

Empaths. Sensitive-empaths have great compassion for others due to their ability to read emotions. When this trait intensifies, empaths can sense and process others' feelings in their own bodies. Those who choose to cultivate this gift develop a caring and responsible nature that motivates them to help others. Empaths make excellent advocates, communicators, doctors, healers, negotiators, peace makers, and therapists.

Intuitives. Sensitive-intuitives perceive clues that enable them to detect important information that would otherwise be ignored. They are usually extremely bright and highly aware of social dynamics due to their high-functioning perception. They are experts at sensing the interconnectivity between relationships due to their adroitness for reading body language and microexpressions. When intuitives take leadership roles, they can accelerate important social trends. Because they can anticipate consequences, intuitives can become highly influential people. They excel at planning by seeing interconnections and are exquisite pattern finders, especially in business.

Visionaries. The sensitive-visionary can perceive the world holographically, from different angles, with visual acuity and spatial awareness. They have a clear, colorful inner vision. Dreams are remembered with incredible accuracy, detail, and clarity. Sometimes they are doubly blessed with photographic memory. They usually have a great eye for detail with the ability to design, envision, innovate, and imagine what might be possible. Those who cultivate it often excel in the fields of architecture and design. In combination with their emotional acuity and compassion, they can perceive solutions that will make the most of the environment for living and functionality.

Expressives. Sensitive-expressives are highly creative and use expression to embody the beauty, comedy, and tragedy they perceive in the world around them. They communicate their bold ideas and strong emotions with a high degree of artistry. Whether as actors, dancers, painters, singers, or writers, expressives can use their gift to create compelling works of art that guide us into a deeper understanding of ourselves as human beings. They help us find shared meaning in our collective experiences and bring us together through their vivid imagination, inspiration, and creativity.

The gifts of empathy, intuition, vision, and expression are needed now more than ever. In a world facing the difficult challenges of climate change, inequality, overpopulation, food and economic insecurity, and rapid technological advancement, sensitives can offer guidance and help humanity make sense of this world. Albert Einstein (sensitive-intuitive), Oprah Winfrey (sensitive-empath), Steve Jobs (sensitive-visionary), and Carlos Santana (sensitive-expressive) are prime examples of highly evolved sensitives who developed their gifts and used their sensate abilities to make monumental and beneficial impacts on our world.

The science of sensitivity is complex due to the multiple physiological systems involved in processing sensory information. A sensitive's need for understanding their functions is simple enough. Sensitives must learn how to process excessive stimuli during sensory overload. *Sensory overload* is a commonly used term that actually refers to the inner feeling of reaching your maximum sensory threshold. Think of it as intensity. It is known clinically as *sensory overwhelm*. Sensory overwhelm describes the massive influx of sensory information that floods into a sensitive's awareness as they perceive their environment. The terms can be used interchangeably, and sensory overload often traumatizes us if not identified early enough.

Sometimes due to our extreme sensitivity, called *hypersensitivity*, we have an overpowering fear of rejection. When we feel we have disappointed someone, even if the perception doesn't match the reality, we feel an unbearable vulnerability. Clearly there are individual differences between this feeling of rejection sensitivity, early-life trauma, and sensory overload. There is much we still don't know and understand about these differences. In my own work I have found early-life trauma has a certain wordless quality. When using counseling and mind-body therapies to work with a traumatic memory, a counselor or healer uses the lack of verbal communication to magnify where overwhelming sensations were once felt on the body. I discuss this in detail in Part II: The Mind-Body Method. Remember this: when you can learn how to heal your own trauma, you can thrive and enjoy the benefits of your gifts.

By becoming highly aware and attuned to subtle cues in your surroundings, you will be able to wield your sensitivity with strength rather than being wounded by it. Think of a machete cutting through dense weeds. These weeds of information are like tangled vines of meaningless material that must be sorted through. When we kick into high gear and access extreme states of hyperawareness, sometimes we perceive too damn much.

By learning your current level of awareness, you'll be able to discern what you need to develop and surrender. Consider Italian Renaissance artist Michelangelo pairing his artistic aesthetic awareness and tactile sensibilities, which guided him through a sublime interpretation of beauty. With the finest sense of touch Michelangelo knew what to cut away and what to play up in his version of magnificence. We can only look back as bystanders and marvel at his devotion to shape since he absolutely broke the mold. He channeled an original perfection unseen in other artistic eras. By tapping into his transcendent senses to creatively guide him Michelangelo carved one of the most impressive sculptures the world has ever seen, his masterpiece *David*. Sensory intelligence is the gift that creates such works of art. No wonder his nickname was *Il Divino*, "the divine one."

SENSORY AWARENESS

As a rule the five classic senses shape our overall experience of sensory awareness, though some scientists, educators, and researchers also include the sensory systems of *proprioception* (sense of relative movement), *vestibular* (sense of balance), and interoception (sense of internal bodily states). The combined perceptions of these sensory channels create sensory awareness. Sensory awareness is direct attention paid to sensations flowing inward into the mind-body and how our own thought processes shape them. It has also been called *neuroception*. Sensory awareness is a filtering process, a manner of sorting information provided to the brain and nervous system through the senses. We take this information in and then we make cognitive judgments or interpretations.

By the 1990s, the decade of brain research, clinical psychologists found that highly sensitive individuals, or sensitives, more quickly process and respond to external environmental cues, such as noise and bright light, and internal cues, such as hunger and thirst. Along with observing more sensory input, sensitives also have a higher emotional reactivity to the stimuli they perceive. This means they feel an emotional response faster and more intensely than others sensing the same stimuli.

This heightened processing ability is now recognized as a function of sensory processing sensitivity and the *subjective experience* or *felt-sense* that the mind-body receives and translates from the signals of the five senses. The nervous systems of individuals who have SPS amplify these impressions, increasing both their ability to perceive information and their susceptibility for sensory overload.

Sensory overload can be painful and traumatic. When any kind of pain is perceived by the mind or body, it is interpreted as danger. When the body perceives any kind of danger it activates the CNS. There is even some newer research that suggests sensitivity may help us mediate or cope with painful experiences.[30]

Another area where modern research on sensitivity has been done is from the perspective of many complementary healing modalities. These alternative therapies aim to help modulate the sensory issues that create physical and mental distress. The concept of sensitivity is also known to clinical and behavioral psychologists. When strongly linked with other kinds of inborn temperament such as introversion, some of the more powerful aspects of sensitivity impact us behaviorally, such as increasing anxiety, the acute fear of something bad happening. Another is rejection sensitivity dysphoria, which overlaps into clinical diagnosis of ADHD and borderline personality disorder. When rejection-sensitive dysphoria is in a magnified state, it is felt as an overpowering feeling of vulnerability and fear of failure. This is not just an average sense of someone not liking us; it feels like being sucked into an obsessive emotional vacuum and not being able to pull oneself out. SPS has been incorporated into research studies on temperament, facial recognition, cultural differences, body language recognition, reading emotions, and decision making.[31]

As a health educator, I take a holistic approach with my clients that includes mind, body, and spirit. Research has shown that sensitivity is a mental processing function that connects to the physical body. Some sensitives display a suprasensing *transcendent function* as well. I have found this suprasensing ability or transcendent function helps sensitive people who have an innate ability to use higher states of consciousness to perceive nonlocal reality. This is an expanded state of mind that feels entirely different from everyday consciousness. Sometimes it may be an ecstatic state with embodied feelings of joy, connectedness, and new knowledge (noetic downloads). Readers versed in the ancient teachings might liken this transcendence as a *samadhi* experience, the illuminated mind, or meditative consciousness. We can look to 20th century Swiss psychiatrist Carl G. Jung's profound body of work to understand the suprasensing function and why I draw on this premise of nonlocality.

Many people use the popular adage, "Where attention goes, energy flows," to explain how conscious awareness and attention shape their personal reality.[32] Carl Jung, founder of the psychoanalytical movement, proved attention flows where psychic energy runs between different states of awareness (conscious and unconscious thought) and synchronicity. Jung coined a similar phrase, "What you resist persists." These two phrases are often said in the context of transforming negative experiences into positive ones because they capture the woo-like essence of integrating sensory awareness from the deeper unconscious into the conscious mind quite accurately. It feels magical. I doubt you'll find anyone, regardless of whether they are sensitive or not, who hasn't experienced this phenomenon as a synchronicity. For sensitives the attention-energy game has serious impact on quality of life. Once you can observe the way energy streams inward and how you've chosen to translate it perceptually through your beliefs, biases, and filters, you can shift your perspective on life and create anything you need. The subtlest sensations we can perceive are movements of energy. Perception creates your reality.

SENSORY ANOMALY

Humanistic psychology defines a human *anomalous experience* (AE) as an unusual experience outside the typical range of human thought, behavior, emotion, and perception that is difficult to classify by normal standards.[33] AE is any uncommon human experience that is hard to quantify but still remains, such as psi phenomena and NDEs.

I define experiences of sensitivity outside the range of normal human perception as *sensory anomalies*. These rare events are directly connected to the heightened acuity of our physical senses. The 20 percent of the world population who has a genetically inherited trait of high sensitivity, however, experience sensory anomalies more often.

The extreme range of sensitivity, or hypersensitivity, which overlaps into sensory anomaly, is where the phenomenal abilities like intuition and expression come from. Common examples of the gift of expression include feeling the beautiful qualities of life more readily as aesthetic sensual awareness through magnetic colors, harmonious sounds, and pleasing textures. When a visionary's interest arises, flow states occur which magnify a peaceful fluidity between the mind and body. Full mental and emotional absorption create an unwavering concentration of focus. Time seems to fall away. For empaths the emotions of others are not only perceived but deeply felt through their grounded sense of feeling. Along with enhanced feeling, empaths receive direct knowledge of the intention of someone else's motivation, struggles, and passions. The gift of intuition may cross over into several areas of cognition. It might be received upon cogitation as a vivid image seen as a flash in the mental field, through lucid dreaming, or a gut-level answer to a difficult problem.

Sensitives perceive sensory stimuli both positively and negatively. Positively, they get sudden insights, feel fully encompassed in the beauty of nature, have a loving connection to their pets, observe the rich interconnectedness of life, access hidden information, and use sophisticated mental processing to solve difficult problems. Negatively, they feel tension between themselves and the world, the toxicity of others, and a general discord.

While sensitivity has only been scientifically accepted since the late 1990s, this innate ability to sense threats and ensure safety likely manifested much earlier in human societies like indigenous communities. I learned the ancient healing art of Huichol plant-spirit medicine (the Huichol tribe of central Mexico) from my teacher Joyce Netishen. In Huichol perspective, an inner cosmos resides within each individual that connects the soul to the divine universal. Through our sensations and introspection, we can gather the soul's light and reinforce this spark of divinity through sacred rituals. Ceremony and sacred rituals help illuminate and reinforce our spiritual core by deepening our connection to the creator, or all-that-is.

Under this cosmic umbrella, heightened sensitivity is not an anomaly, but a unique primeval force provided to us by universal spirit as an evolutionary survival mechanism. Practically, it helped tribes track and hunt wild game and anticipate harsh environmental conditions, like weather changes, so they could choose opportune times for travel and ideal locations for settlement. Their civilization was one of the only tribes in Mexico that remained undisturbed in the central mountainous regions in the modern era (up until 2012).[34] These highly aware indigenous peoples used their enhanced senses for survival. From their oral history about medicinal plant usage, their visual acuity helped them identify nonpoisonous plants, their empathy to connect deeply to the medicines of place, and they also received intuitive insights (gut feelings) on how to use medicinal plants through their direct access to the spiritual plane. Even today some societies still revere these abilities.

In a traditional medicine and holistic perspective such as the Huichol tribal view, sensitivity evolved to help humans stay in contact with the spiritual world, including for healing illness. Other traditional tribal leaders have expressed this same sentiment. One shaman who came to the United States publicly expanded on this idea. In an article on Uplift, Malidoma Some stated that he believed many of the individuals he encountered while traveling stateside who were labeled "mentally ill" were actually experiencing a spiritual emergence, or "the birth of the healer."[35] He described this rapid shift as a significant transformation in consciousness while an individual self-actualized the manifestation of their inner healer.

For these reasons, looking through a more native lens, those special individuals who've inherited the sensitivity trait often feel out of place in technologically advanced societies, sensing they don't belong. Sometimes their lightning-fast emotionality is interpreted as mental illness. Before they realize they are sensitive, individuals who are unaware of their gift endure a disproportionate amount of internal pain. This pain can stem from feeling the unfiltered intensity of living in high-density urban centers, near pollution, amid "toxic" people, and working in noisy and hyperactive offices or interacting with angry and aggressive people. Sensitives feel pain more frequently if they shut themselves off from nature, which is one of their primary healing sources. Coping with such deep emotional forces without collapsing requires great strength and is in no way a weakness. Witness Daniel's strength as he navigates the difficult waters of emotion.

DANIEL'S STORY

Daniel was a 55-year-old stay-at-home dad who had recently lost his brother Eugene to terminal cancer. Daniel helped Eugene transition through his illness by moving him into his family home and tracking all his pain management. When the time came, he arranged hospice care and executed all of Eugene's final wishes. Spiritually, Daniel felt honored to help his brother's peaceful transition while also providing an intimate healing connection with the support of his two daughters, Kate and Heather. While this fragile dynamic would be a challenge on its own, I came to understand how difficult a decision this was for Daniel to make considering his tumultuous relationship with his wife, Grace.

Daniel found me through a local newspaper. When he reached out, I learned he had already made some major strides in his health and wellness. He had lost over 20 pounds and healed chronic back pain he suffered since college using Dr. John Sarno's *Mindbody Prescription.* While Daniel had already made the connection between his emotions and debilitating physical pain, he wanted to understand how his empathic sensitivity was still affecting power dynamics in his volatile relationship with Grace and their two daughters. He thought he might be able to effect some change in their difficult dynamic.

According to Daniel, Grace had a tendency to reject his feelings before he could even express them. Adding fuel to the fire, he felt dominated in an unhealthy way since she was the financial breadwinner. He likened many of her behaviors to gaslighting or challenges to the way he believed he felt. If he tried to discuss emotional discomfort, usually not about his own needs but his children, she would ignore him or tell him "you don't really feel that way." This rebound of fear came back in full force when their oldest daughter returned home after her first year of studying abroad. Daniel recognized Grace's narcissistic tendency to verbally abuse Kate by making overt comments about her weight gain. This tendency to draw negative attention to their daughter's body started at an early age. Kate loved ballet. Grace always pushed her daughter to slim her body down and perfect her performances. She demanded a near-impossible training schedule, with endless classes, and a rigid, high expectation for achievement.

Daniel relayed his concern over Kate's inability to form positive romantic relationships. He felt this was a result of his own dysfunctional marriage. Daniel jokingly reported he needed more beers to deal with his wife and daughters as he prepared their nightly dinners. He felt he had to numb himself to cope with the pressure as a social leveler for this emotional tension.

Daniel first learned about the explosive coupling between narcissistic people and empaths at one of the workshops he had attended in the past for back pain. When he was undergoing specific physical therapy for his back, one of the facilitators identified him as an empath. At the time, he reported, he thought the woman was somewhat crazy for trying to establish a connection between empathy (a personality attribute) and his pain. He didn't see a relationship between his chronic pain and what he referred to as "a character flaw."

Daniel exhibited the classic traits of an empath. He loved his role in their family as the primary caregiver of their girls. He took painstaking efforts to ensure their safety, protection, and comfort. He often volunteered for odd jobs at their school. One time, he took the low-paying, noon duty position and had a hair-raising experience. While working on the playground at school, he saw a young boy get bullied. It unleashed a rash of unexpected anger. We explored what this experience meant through his perspective as an empath. Why was it that younger children being bullied by more privileged kids kicked off an emotional tirade? Over a period of several weeks, Daniel repeatedly reported child-on-child violence on the playground. The lack of action of the school's administration angered him. He perceived this ineffectiveness as failure on his part and it led him to quit the noon aide position. We worked together to identify his emotional trigger.

Reluctantly, he agreed to commit to some expressive writing to observe his sensory patterns. As we discussed the incident at school, his body visibly locked up and he started trembling. By tracking his body sensations through a clear dialogue, Daniel made a connection between volunteering at his daughter's school and linking it with a larger feeling of being intimidated by people in authority. I encouraged Daniel to stay present with this powerful emotion. When he slowed down and tracked these physical sensations, Daniel realized his feelings were related to marital disempowerment. At the close of our coaching session he agreed to write a letter that would express these feelings safely. I hoped to bring his inner thoughts into his conscious awareness, rather than let them fester.

> *Writing to myself for myself has never worked, has never felt right or good. Writing in general for me is slow and hair pulling. The starting issue was "why does thinking about Kate incite the strong and unique sensation of neck hair raising/face/body tingling?" Um, rattlesnakes and earthquakes do the same thing. Reliving other similar incidents from being at my daughter's school does the same thing. By and by, it became very apparent that I'm scared of people that treat the disadvantaged as throwaway, base a lie on them to protect themselves or an institution. I'm scared of people with authority that knowingly mistreat defenseless people. I'm scared of people-in-authority who willfully neglect/abuse others and lie about it.*
>
> *The letter resulted in the best possible outcome. I left the letter I originally wrote for myself on our bedroom dresser for Grace to read. For the first time, she took the subject to heart with minimal defensiveness, seemingly none in fact. I finally felt heard and we seemed to really talk. This immediate change was startling. I'm very cautious because of the*

past. Grace acknowledged that we've negatively affected our kids. For the first time, I feel relieved that she got what I had been trying to convey for so long. She seemed genuinely curious about the "work" I've been doing and wasn't threatened by it. Indeed, all this stuff about empathy is admittedly serious. More than I ever imagined.

The letter resulted in a positive outcome for Daniel and he made the connection between his empathic abilities and his physical sensations and emotions. For the first time, Grace took the subject to heart. She wasn't defensive, and they began to really communicate about Daniel's true feelings. It was a huge relief for Daniel to get these issues out in the open, and he felt validated.

PROMISING RESEARCH AND SENSITIVITY

Neurological research of genetic sensitivity is still in its early stages, though what has emerged in field studies on highly sensitive people shows incredible promise. Interestingly, research on an extreme subset of the population has led to an understanding of some of the specific traits of sensitivity. Alvaro Pascual-Leone, M.D., Ph.D., a professor of neurology at Harvard Medical School, is one of the principal researchers in the field of transcranial magnetic brain stimulation (TMS). He helped develop a research study to test TMS and subsequently shed light on some of the brain areas that are also activated in highly sensitive individuals.[36]

To be crystal clear, although all the patients in the study were autistic, highly sensitive people are *not* autistic. The preliminary results of Dr. Pascual-Leone's research have shown that when certain areas of the left prefrontal cortex are stimulated, patients with autism who were formerly unable to pick up on emotional cues from others experienced an "emotional awakening." They reportedly felt the brilliance of life, could easily read the language of emotion, and experienced a "magical" empathic connection to others.[37] These behavioral effects lasted for thirty minutes in a lab after the autistic patients received TMS.

These abilities to read emotions, feel deep connection with others, and experience empathic awareness are how sensitive people feel most of the time. John Elder Robison, an autistic patient who participated in the Harvard experiment and the author of *Look Me in the Eye* and *Switched On*, described feeling other people's anxiety and sadness after he received the TMS treatments. In an NPR interview with Terry Gross, he tearfully reflected how he felt his wife's depression as "overwhelming and painful."[38] Throughout the interview, he further detailed how the TMS treatments activated and heightened his emotional resonance and altered many of his relationships as he integrated a new perspective that was infused with emotion. With an articulate poignance he detailed the emotional awakening that occurred, how it affected him personally, in his relationships with others, and in his career.

When floods of sensory information are properly interpreted and integrated, the resulting sensitivity and corresponding extraordinary sensorimotor acuity[39] help sensitives interpret cues through nonverbal intelligence with a high degree of accuracy. These benefits depend on how much a person can cognitively process while simultaneously receiving sensory information. Basically, this hypothesis means perceived mental effort, such as demands from increased processing of stimuli from the environment, affect cognition. This cognitive load theory directly relates to sensory integration and learning.[40] If cognitive capacity in working memory is limited due to processing a greater influx of sensory information, it will make it harder to learn and focus.

The cognitive load theory was originally developed by John Sweller[41] in the 1980s as it applied to learning. Theoretically it has gained ground in research areas of problem solving, the aging population, and stereotypes.[42] It applies to sensitivity as a model for understanding the balance of functioning between different types of nonverbal intelligence (visual, hands-on, experiential), analyzing sensory information, and reasoning. In other words, the massive amount of sensory information a sensitive takes in through their sensory perception affects cognitive processing speed and efficiency. As more sensory stimulation flows inward, it will affect how information is parsed, translated, and integrated into cortical functions (accurate decisions, memorization). We can modulate the sensory information that is being received and apply it cognitively by increasing the working capacity of available memory during sensory processing. The balance of this function (called sensory modulation) helps sensitive people strengthen their perceptions. This is how we access the gifts—by mindfully attuning to the highly activated perceptual areas of our brain and relying upon our sensory discrimination for quicker reaction time. This can be applied to decision-making, imagining novel solutions, and increasing speed in problem-solving.

THE BENEFITS AND CHALLENGES OF HSP

Right now you may not feel blissed out by your high sensitivity. If you've been extremely anxious in a large group, couldn't take a pain reliever because it made you nauseous, had fluorescent lights trigger a migraine, or have been terrified by the prospect of watching a horror movie, you've already been affected negatively. There are four common symptoms of sensory overload or burnout: abdominal pain, anxiety, depression, and distraction. In Part II of this book, I go into these symptoms in detail and suggest different healing strategies. Sensitivity challenges us because our brutal and uncaring world can feel like it conducts a painful assault on our wide-open senses. It can be so crippling that many sensitive people build their lives around dampening sensory stimulation.

When managed and self-regulated with the right kind of health care, the trait of sensitivity can help us become more perceptive, introspective, warm, caring, attuned to others, creative, and innovative. Sensory intelligence reveals itself socially as the ability to discern accurate information about others through perceptual pathways. Due to this ability, we become trusted advisers to our friends and family. We're the people at the office whom other people go to for advice about life direction, big decisions, and important relationships. We go out of our way not to hurt other people. Infliction of pain is viewed as a cardinal sin. For example, we can feel the tension within relationships, how our friend's new lover might not be as perfect as advertised, or sense the right timing for a difficult business decision. In response to these perceptions, we'll make a concerted effort to diffuse tension in a social dynamic by making a joke, we'll gently warn our friend about our intuitions, and we'll advise a business partner to be patient.

However, *you require time and space to process the subtleties of your daily interactions.* Let this fact seep into your conscious mind; it can change your perception of reality. Given the time needed to relax and engage in calm introspection, the intensity from your expansive sensitivity will settle down into a relative calm where you can observe and use your sensory intelligence to tap into your creative genius and receive stunning insights.

In the next chapter, on the sensitive-empath, we will explore this notion through the different ways our intense feelings influence our perception and relationships with others.

CHAPTER 2

SENSITIVE EMPATHY

*I think we all have empathy. We may not
have enough courage to display it.*

— MAYA ANGELOU

Sensitive-empaths (empaths for short) are complex, deeply emotional, and attuned human beings who are extraordinarily in touch with their surroundings. And not just once in a great while when something particularly moves them—always. They tend to be self-aware, kind, and accepting of others and their struggles.

There are a few different types of empathic awareness, including:

- *Cognitive empathy* (telepathic)
- *Compassionate empathy* (care within feeling and a motivation to help)
- *Geomantic empathy* (environmental awareness)
- *Physical empathy* (responsive to place)
- *Plant/animal empathy* (perception of plant and animal consciousness)

- *Emotional empathy* (emotional intelligence)
- *Spiritual empathy* (transcendent sensing)

Empaths are also usually highly intuitive. There is some clear crossover with empathy and the gift of intuition through cognitive empathy. They can be differentiated by thinking and feeling modes of processing or foresight (intuition) and feeling (empathy). The underlying trait connecting all these characteristics is the ability to share the felt-sense. Felt-sense is the terminology used by sensorimotor psychologists to describe emotional embodiment, or awareness within the body. Sensations through feelings are connected to interoception (an internal sense of the states within the body) as the focus upon these internal feelings, sensations, and vibrations. The body uses this information to communicate about regulation of overall inner states. Thoughtful feelings are expressed internally through images, sensations, textures, and colors of a person's holistic inner experience.

JUSTINE, THE FBI PROFILER

I first met Justine when I was going through a challenging time with my then-13-year-old daughter. Justine was referred by a mutual friend. Because people didn't recognize what Justine did, there were a lot of rumors whispered around our small town about her work. Tall tales like she lived out in the valley near a commune, wore only certain colors of clothes depending on the day of the week, ate only one kind of food, and could talk to animals. Based on my friend's recommendation I knew most of these stories weren't true and went forward with making an appointment.

Justine was, in fact, an expert rider and animal communicator. She used to work for the FBI in the Behavioral Analysis Unit and suffered a near-fatal injury on the job transporting a dangerous prisoner.

When I walked into Justine's house for the first time, I realized I was in the presence of an extremely intelligent *sensitive-empath*.

I consulted with her to work with my daughter using a specific type of equine therapy that addressed early-childhood trauma. What I actually received was my first energetic diagnosis. For the next year, she trained me on how to perceive energetic information through the felt-sense. After quizzing me on several different "targets," she sent me home to try to perceive information about someone she didn't know personally. She didn't really have any sage advice about the selection process, only requiring that I "pick someone." The friend I chose was another mom whom I had gotten close with and whose daughter was the same age as mine. The girls were good friends. As parents we had bonded over theater practices, music, sports, and school functions. As instructed by Justine, I closed my eyes and imagined my friend. I went into the relaxed state and several impressions came to mind. The first was a plaid sash colored red, white, and green in a classic Scottish tartan. In my mind's eye, I saw the crisscrossed vertical and horizontal bands. Then I heard a woman speak. I couldn't see her, although I made out the strong sounds, "D-o-n-a."

It took me a few days to summon up the courage to contact my friend and ask her if she was Scottish. When I eventually did, she confirmed it. After sharing my intuitive insights, I told her about my work with Justine and how she was helping me learn the empathic-intuitive gift. When I told her I heard a woman say the name Dona, she drew a blank. I replied, "That's okay," and left it at that. I learned of her Scottish heritage, which was pretty cool on its own. After having received a "hit," I called Justine and told her. She reassured me, "Just give it time. Sometimes people have a little amnesia and they forget names and people."

Justine was right. A few days passed and I heard back from my friend. She said it dawned on her when she was doing laundry. Her grandmother's name was Idona. Justine taught me to trust my aural sensory ability to receive sensory information through hearing. I'll delve into this more in the next chapter.

COMPASSION EMPATHY

Empaths with the gift of compassion have laser-accurate emotional awareness. They feel their way through life and their surroundings. By the time they reach adulthood, they know just what to do to make others feel comfortable and at home in their presence. Concern is the backbone of *compassion empathy*. This empathy is the ability to feel what others are feeling and adapt to help them to experience comfort. It is feeling concern for another's state of mind, mood, or emotions, and then acting. This feeling may widen beyond concern for a single individual's needs. Empaths may have an instinctive drive where they are concerned about humanity, including community health and safety. This doesn't necessarily make compassionate empaths cordial or "nice." As an empath I feel great umbrage when the uninitiated call us "doormats." What it does mean, however, is that compassion-empaths will usually give someone the benefit of the doubt if they find themselves drawn into a confusing or conflicted situation with a difficult person. Because they can read other people's emotions easily, they learn to comprehend the subtleties of feeling states and to respond appropriately. I firmly believe it has been your friendly neighborhood compassion-empath who has prevented dangerous outbreaks of violence due to their ability to quell an inflamed conflict. Their neutralizing effect happens by seeing the good in people.

All empaths have *emotional intelligence*, the ability to be aware of, control, and express one's emotions accurately. Individuals who use emotional intelligence have the capability to recognize their own internal emotional drives and discern the slight differences between their feelings and others'. They have clear insight into others' current moods and motivations. Their ability translates as a critical judgment into how moods and feelings influence the way other people react and relate. For example, Justine was a military-trained empath who was extremely sensitive. Make a slight gesture, touch your face, or mindlessly stroke your hair and she would discern the reasons why. Justine was tough and followed the rule of law as a consultant to law enforcement officers. Her gift as an empath was having the ability to investigate the complex dynamics of unsolved cases, many times perpetrated with gruesome violence. Since she was able to detach from her own emotions, Justine was highly adept at understanding the inner workings of the criminal mind. She could compartmentalize images, information, and scenes that would make others flinch, while also connecting them to a larger pattern of behavior. Many times, she found the victims of crimes, even in cold cases. Like Justine, empaths can train their emotional acuity. They can become more aware of how their emotional intelligence works and how to use it.

Empaths must develop considerable inner strength and energy to cope with the strong emotional undercurrents they perceive all around them. The capacity for great feeling requires equal measures of stamina, strength, endurance, and resilience.

Nationally and internationally we are witnessing a divide in public opinion. Whole cultures are working to sustain their way of life. Political lines are being drawn. The dividing lines include new levels of violence worldwide, even in our schools. As such, empathy is critical in our world right now. However, no one suffers more emotional pain than the compassionate empath. They perceive the discord and discontentment of these widening divisions on a visceral level. *Compassion affects empaths because they not only feel everything, they care about it too.* This is a virtuous quality. Legal advocates, counselors, theologians, and emergency responders must care for another. This ability can be misunderstood or mismanaged when not coupled with the awareness of other people's pain process, how they project it outward, and how to detach from it.

Emotional intelligence can be felt not only in the shift of feelings an empath feels; they home in on in the images, colors, and textures they receive. These inputs inform them about the general state of someone they meet. It depends on how they perceive energetic information. Often it is through the felt-sense. They may receive flashes of information through their mind's eye as well (cognitive empathy). A sensory impression, or emotional concept, may stimulate personal associations within the empath. Depending on how their sensory intelligence perceives the energetic information, sensations could trigger one of their own memories as energy is stimulated in their body. A trigger is a sensory cue that evokes a past traumatic experience. Empaths may also feel an urge to act, to give a spontaneous hug, or share an insight.

DRAWBACKS OF COMPASSION EMPATHY

Emotional exhaustion can quickly overtake a sensitive-empath who has not developed the ability to detach. Sensitive-empaths who score very high on the emotional sensitivity scale can sense subtle energies from other people and environments and absorb them into their own mind-body-spirit. This ability can be positive, as when viewing the magnificent beauty of a colorful sunset, or negative, as when feeling the troubled emotions of others. There are many reasons for this absorption of energy, but by and large it relates to disruptions in early childhood attachment. Every empath is different, and it requires determination, self-care, and patience to discover why an empath gets triggered emotionally.

Research emerged in the early 2000s that investigated empathy in educational and health-care settings. The best-selling books *Emotional Intelligence* by Daniel Goleman and *The Age of Empathy* by Frans de Waal are two of the most popular for describing the empathic nature. One of the more obscure theories, the theory of *emotional contagion*, might help make sense of the triggering aspects of emotional sensitivity. Emotional contagion is when one person's emotions trigger similar emotions in other people. It has also been called *projection*. This triggering effect could be due to the presence of mirror neurons. Remember how the brains of monkeys were firing signals whether a monkey was ripping paper itself or watching another monkey ripping paper? But there may be another explanation as well that has to do with unconscious motivations, such as the projection of hidden thoughts and feelings on the actions of another person.

Perceiving someone else's unconscious feelings and identifying with them could also be viewed as emotional projection. When emotional contagion occurs through a process of unconscious reasoning, it may serve as a healing mechanism to help empaths confront unacknowledged aspects of themselves and resolve the associated feelings. In terms of emotional sensitivity, like compassion empathy, empaths use emotional awareness to pick up on the feelings of others. I believe the biological purpose of this may be as a social-neurological developmental mechanism. Feeling others' hidden emotions may help empaths realize their own underexplored thoughts and feelings, which helps them heal and evolve to higher states of awareness. This is a form of cognitive-emotional intelligence (cognitive empathy).

Due to their ability to read the emotions of those around them, compassionate empaths care deeply about the well-being of other people. If this trait intensifies, a sensitive may report feeling in their own body sensations another person feels. Sometimes they must process emotions as if they were their own to release any discordant thoughts and feelings. As a result, their central nervous systems are doing double duty. An empath learns this skill early in life. Processing other peoples' emotions brings with it a responsible nature that motivates the empath to help out. Empaths are born to be activists, advocates (such as lawyers), doctors, healers, feng shui practitioners, naturalists, therapists, teachers, and social justice workers.

Research on empathic sensing has been done in clinical settings to study its connection with movement and learning. Western medical science does not fully understand this enhanced capacity to sense through feeling. It is considered a prosocial behavior, and we know that the empathy trait is not solely a human genetic inheritance. It has been found in many different animal species such as ravens, elephants, and mice.[1] Behaviors throughout the animal kingdom show that some animals can detect pain and suffering in others and respond to different emotional states such as excitement, fear, and anger. Orangutans have been shown to "take on the moods" of relatives. Service dogs are trained to read the different emotional and physiological states of their human partners. What we do know is empathic sensory awareness allows empaths to experience the energy around them, not only through emotions but also through the physical sensations of others (physical empathy). What sets compassion empathy apart from other forms of empathy is the innate ability to perceive the emotional states of others coupled with a motivation to care for their well-being. Let's hear from Anna, who found out the hard way she was a compassion-empath.

ANNA'S STORY

Anna was a college student who first experienced the phenomenon of compassion and empathic physical sensing in her relationship with her first serious boyfriend, described as follows.

I was always told the intimate relationship I imagined having would be when I matured enough. All I had to do was wait. Except my generation has a different mind-set than mine and is focused on hooking up. During college this reality left me ostracized and alone. I even tried doing what they were doing to satisfy my longing. After a few failed hookups, I felt horrible about myself, resigned, and lonely. I had standards for the person that I wanted to date. I wasn't going to let just anyone into my life. Then, in a newly formed study group, I met a handsome student who was studying film direction. I let myself fall. It was easy to fall in love with him because I wanted it so bad. I didn't realize that just feeling you could trust someone didn't mean they were the right person for you.

He made me laugh every day and I formed a relationship bubble with him. We moved in together and I shut out everyone else. At first I was blissful. Soon I found myself falling into some bad habits. My boyfriend had anxiety, which I didn't understand at the time. I skipped classes to stay in with him and hide so he could feel better. My grades slipped. I gained weight. I didn't care because I was so in love.

Over time I realized these strange habits and feelings weren't mine. I was picking up on his feelings. Inexplicably my mood would plunge whenever I was around him and it would be fine anytime I was at work or in class. I felt crazy. It was like our minds were enmeshed; our thought processes were becoming the same. I could verbalize his thoughts. Unfortunately, I was going further and further down a self-destructive path by allowing myself to feel his anxiety and depression as my own.

I started having migraine pain, which my boyfriend told me had plagued him as a child. Never in my life had I felt such pain; it was like my eyes were being stabbed from the inside. The migraine pain started to happen even when I was away from him. The pain became a trigger for me to text him to ask what was wrong. I knew the pain wasn't mine. It got so bad that I shut myself in the house until I threw up to make it go away. Later I found out he was dealing with chronic depression. He had repressed emotional issues he didn't want to face. Frankly I was terrified to learn that I could be violated through my emotional vulnerability; I learned that is what empaths unconsciously do when they love someone. They want to take away their loved ones' pain.

Now I understand that it is not my job to save others. I have to save myself. This was a powerful experience because it revealed my empathic nature.

Energetically, empaths can silently internalize the feelings of others if they are unaware that these feelings are not their own. Distinguishing someone else's discomfort from their own is the empath's challenge. There is a critical difference between sensing the emotions of others and letting them in. When under stress empaths tend to become fragile, getting maxed out from the intense sensations and pain they pick up on from the world around them. Empaths experience the most stress when in social situations.

SENSING FROM THE HEART, SPIRITUAL EMPATHY

On the brighter side, some empaths have profoundly spiritual, transcendent, and divine experiences due to their ability to perceive different energetic states. This spiritual empathy allows the individual to pierce the veil of ego, or humanity's illusory nature. The human ego is a defense mechanism which protects the internal aspects of the mind-body by creating an external illusion of separateness. This separation is a dualistic thought pattern that creates feelings of control over one's environment through a division between the self, world, and others. It's a good coping mechanism because it helps keep us safe and grounded. Spiritual empathy helps the spiritual-empath go beyond the survival level of the ego (personal), the mundane or material level of reality, to a supreme expanded consciousness that might be called supramundane through transcendent sensing. Transcendent sensing is the elevated aspect of sensitive-empathic awareness. It has been described as astral travel, expanded consciousness, NDE, out-of-body flight, spiritually transformative experience (STE), lucid dreaming, and veridical perception.

Being a sensitive-empath comes from having a highly attuned nervous system. This type of awareness directly affects the CNS, hormones (especially adrenaline, cortisol, and norepinephrine), and the fight-or-flight response. The variability in the sensing ability of empaths stems from their diverse physical, mental, and emotional felt-experience. Some empaths are more attuned to emotions, others to physical pain. Sometimes empaths are attuned to both. Spiritual empaths are attuned to an expansive reality through all their senses. They have described this selfless attunement as awakened consciousness through a deep, loving connection to the preciousness of life through their heart-center. You could say they sense with their hearts and this love pierces through the defensive ego as higher perception. Spiritually awakened empaths have a consciousness that can transcend mental anxiety and fear. They are able to create and hold positive states of bliss and joy. Their playful attitude shouldn't be mistaken for a Pollyanna perspective. It's not that they don't see human suffering, they do. They have learned how to transcend it like Amma, the hugging saint. Spiritual empaths don't need rose-colored glasses to enjoy freedom from worry. They have achieved a state of higher grace through compassionate love. Their elevated feeling states connect heart and mind, and are truly infectious.

DRAWBACKS OF SPIRITUAL EMPATHY

Spiritual empaths describe the positive aspects of their empathy as being "stimulated," "lifted up," and "energized" by exposure to positive people. The evolved sensitive-empath is an individual who can perceive these differences in other people, accurately discern them, and adapt without internalizing another's attitudes or emotions. The main drawback to spiritual empathy is not immediately recognizing narcissistic people or energy vampires. This sounds heavy-handed, except the energetic exchange is real.

Narcissists are usually glamorous, charming, excellent conversationalists, magnanimous, and effusive. These traits attract spiritual empaths because of the expansive energy pattern narcissists run. Narcissists are also singularly focused on themselves. One surefire way to tell if someone is a narcissist is that they often bring the focus of a conversation back on themselves. They are highly focused on their image, influence on others, and how they are being perceived. These relatively harmless symptoms are a warning sign of a much larger pattern. It includes placing blame on others (rather than accepting responsibility for their actions), manipulating for personal gain, and exploiting the weaknesses of others to inflate or magnify their own ego. It seems counterintuitive that spiritually empathic individuals who have the innate ability to transcend the ego's limitations, who are also kind and feel so intensely, would be attracted to narcissists. There is an invisible web that binds them: energy.

The narcissistic energy pattern can be a big, wild, larger-than-life, expansive experience. They run a lot of energy. It could be described as indomitable or fearless. At first spiritual empaths admire these qualities, feel the intense energy the narcissist carries, and are magnified by the expansiveness of being near to them. Likewise, narcissists feel the depth at which a spiritual empath connects to them and they thrive on this energetic attention, a capacity for being held and cared for, and the strong compassion with which empaths love and accept others.

Since empaths are naturally deep, loving, and caring individuals, narcissistic people will always be attracted to them. This very magnetic attraction takes place subconsciously between the two as spiritual empaths enjoy being with fun, interactive, charming, and high-energy people too. When they meet it can feel like two very powerful forces coming together, almost as if the meeting was meant to be or predestined (from the spiritual empath's perspective). As any recovering empath who has dated or been married to a narcissist will tell you, getting involved with a narcissist was one of the biggest learning lessons of their life. It takes time to uncouple from a narcissist when you are constantly being blamed for everything, made to feel like the problems in the relationship are all your fault, or that you are crazy. The term *gaslighting* has often been used in the context of narcissism. It is exhausting and empaths will find themselves drained if they stay in the company of a narcissist. Empaths are conscientious deep thinkers. When highly self-aware, they consider their internal feelings as a gauge between themselves and the external world. When they are in a relationship with a narcissist, constant negation confuses the empath. It impedes their ability to trust their own internal thoughts, feelings, and instincts.

Gavin de Becker is one of the best examples of an empath who analyzes emerging situations, including narcissistic tendencies, and other individuals who lack empathy. His business guides and teaches people how to understand when threats escalate into real-life violence.

GAVIN DE BECKER, THREAT PREDICTION EXPERT

I remember hearing about Gavin de Becker for the first time from Elaine. Elaine was a deeply empathic woman who lived in the same small town where I met Justine. She recommended I read Mr. de Becker's book *The Gift of Fear*. After I had told her a scary story about my ex-husband showing up at my remote property in Montana, she told me urgently, "Read it right away!" I drove over the mountains to the closest Barnes and Noble and started reading Mr. de Becker's work. It was like finding an oasis in the high desert. Through his expertise and writings, I felt as though I were looking in a mirror, but through a man's confident eyes. After reading his story about how he protected his sister throughout their childhood, I suspected he was an empath.

In the book he described his childhood growing up in a violent home with his mother.

A woman was pointing a gun at her husband, who was standing with his hands out in front of him. She was anxiously changing her grip on the small semiautomatic pistol. "Now I'm going to kill you," she repeated quietly, almost as if to herself. She was an attractive, slender woman of thirty-three, wearing black slacks and a man's white shirt. There were eight bullets in the gun.

I was standing off to the side in a doorway, watching the scene unfold. As I had been before and would be many times again, I was responsible for predicting whether a murder would occur, whether or not the woman in this case would keep her promise to kill. The stakes were high, for in addition to the man at risk, there were also two young children in the house.

Threats like hers, I knew, are easy to speak, harder to honor.

Mr. de Becker describes his vantage point and calculation of his mother's deadly threat: "I then saw a detail of great significance, though it was just a quarter-inch movement. . . . The fraction of an inch her thumb traveled to rest on the hammer of the gun carried the woman further along the path to homicide than anything she could have said."

In *The Gift of Fear*, Mr. de Becker explains pre-incident indicators that are detectable before the outcome. He writes, "People do things, 'out of the blue,' 'all of a sudden,' or 'out of nowhere.' These phrases support the popular myth that predicting human behavior isn't possible. Yet to successfully navigate through morning traffic, we make amazingly accurate high-stakes predictions about the behavior of literally thousands of people. We unconsciously read tiny untaught signals: the slight tilt of a stranger's head or the momentarily sustained glance of a person a hundred feet away that tells us it is safe to pass in front of his two-ton monster."[2]

Reading about his childhood experience and later application of interpreting the "untaught signals," we get a view of why Gavin de Becker is an expert on threat prediction and quite possibly a sensitive-empath. His sensory acuity is zeroing in on the gestures, movements, subtle body language, and precise words being used, and making accurate judgments about these combined impressions. To survive such a turbulent environment, he had to learn to read his mother's unique language. This lifetime of experience led to a career as a skilled safety expert and the design of a system called MOSAIC threat assessment systems (MOSAIC). MOSAIC is a prediction method created for assessing and screening threats.

Like Mr. de Becker many empaths learn early in life that their empathic gift is a survival mechanism. Empaths are deeply impacted by the negativity of others. The empath's ability to feel emotions accurately gives them an edge in processing the dynamics of relationship issues, tapping into unconscious meaning, and extracting detailed information. If stress levels are high, an empath is on heightened alert. They will be distracted, fidgety, and restless. They may even mirror the intensity from the environment through their own body by increasing the volume of their voice, displaying more physical body movement, or acting in nonhabitual ways. Feeling the turbulent emotions of others can influence an empath's overall psychology, causing eating and sleeping disorders, weight gain, and anxiety. This stress response has been learned through their environment, and while they can't change their empathic nature, they can reduce the empathic survival mode they're in and feel relaxed more often.

All empaths attune to energetic imprints (energy patterns within the body), from animals (plant-animal empathy), groups, and even vibrations of specific locations (geomantic empathy). Being an empath means picking up some of these types of sensations. In addition, gifted empaths may be adept at identifying emotions in someone else (emotional intelligence) and not well attuned to understanding how their own feelings are being triggered (self-awareness).

Review the empathic subtypes listed at the beginning of this chapter to help you identify your type of empathy. Recognize it may be a combination of several subtypes.

If you have taken the Sensitivity Test I offer online and received a high score for sensitive-empathy, congratulations! The latest research shows you are more aware of opportunities and threats than other people. Because of this heightened awareness, you are more responsive to developing situations.

This acuity for judging emerging situations is an evolutionary defense mechanism. It allows the empath to determine the intentions of a person or the safety of a place or situation. There may be some pain involved in sensing malice and danger. The benefits of heightened perception for the individual and the collective (a family, a tribe) usually outweigh the costs. The costs could be physical and mental. For example, there is an increased cognitive and metabolic demand placed on the mind and body. Empaths need to be resilient to handle this burden of excessive processing. They also need more down time to integrate these complex experiences.

Due to their advanced perception, sensitive-empaths are likely to require more time than "normal" sensors for their observation and reflection. An empath must take the time needed to process the flood of sensations. If they cannot ascertain what has influenced their mood, they will be prone to internal distress and uncertainty. They may appear somewhat erratic—through displays of procrastination, tardiness, and anxiety—to friends, loved ones, and co-workers. It is their powerful sense of emotion that is behind these behaviors.

A big drawback is the need to be cautious about entering new places, as empaths may experience anxious feelings in active social settings. Typically for an empath, when there is anxiety there is also a flood of sensation that feels like an emotional undercurrent. An empath will be reactive, either positively or negatively, depending on the situation and the people involved.

This natural balancing act between identifying anxiety and managing flooding from emotional undercurrents is an inherent function of sensitivity. It helps us recognize situations where there is a high influx of sensory information. This is neither positive nor negative. Sensitivity will always increase when there is more sensory information to process.

EPIGENETICS, ATTACHMENT, AND IMPRINTING

Epigenetics is the study of hereditable changes in our genes that are not caused by changes in the actual DNA sequence. This relatively new field of science examines environmental factors like pollution, nutrition, and trauma. The main questions researchers are asking are: How do our genes get turned on or off? And how do these changes get passed down from one generation to the next? A large body of epigenetic research evaluates the link between heredity, stress, and disease. Epigeneticists are searching for specific susceptible genes and studying their relation to disease.

Hypersensitivity may be a genetic inheritance. Scientifically we know if trauma was experienced during an ancestor's lifetime it can be passed down to their children through short RNA molecules.[3] Whether we are aware of it or not, intergenerational trauma may have switched on gene expression for heightened sensory acuity. If so, perhaps it could be turned off again by the individuals who inherited it and felt it too profoundly. It may be possible to change gene expression during a sensitive's lifetime.

Understanding epigenetics has enormous implications for sensitive people, including the empath, in achieving health and wellness. Let's look at trauma through integrative medicine and health science where much research has already been done on sensitivity and environmental vulnerability. In integrative medicine and health sciences, a general hypothesis exists: if environmental factors impact genetic makeup, then patterns of gene expression are influenced by diet, reduction of stress, elimination of toxins, and physical exercise. Although research is mixed, there are several evidence-based studies that show the impact of stress, trauma, and toxicity on gene expression. Trauma transmission may be due to a family suffering a tragic loss brought on by war, unexpected death, violence, or a shared response to a societal disaster.

In the Adverse Child Experiences (ACE) Study done by Kaiser Permanente and the Centers for Disease Control and Prevention (CDC) from 1995 to 1997, more than 60 percent of the 17,000 middle-class American studied showed that adverse childhood experiences impacted physical and emotional wellness. It was one of the first studies to evaluate the risk factors of traumatic experiences such as death, divorce, neglect, and violence on study participants that could be passed on intergenerationally to their children. This research showed that a parent's adverse experience negatively impacted epigenetic markers, increasing their child's risk factors for heart disease, diabetes, and hypertension.[4] The results revealed a pattern that reflected predictive factors from these negative experiences. Further research has shown that the environment in the womb influences adult health. In other words, our health is not only determined by what we experience, but also by what our parents experienced.

Dr. Garry Nolan's Stanford research study showed that genetic changes in the caudate putamen run in families too.[5] In magnetic resonance imaging (MRI) scans subjects with faster intuition had more fibrous connections running from the head of the caudate into the putamen. In our conversation he attributed these changes to gene expression. We discussed how intergenerational trauma may be a factor in this increase of fibrous thickness in white matter and their higher activation of intuitive thought. Speaking in hypothetical terms, Dr. Nolan reported that these mutations may have happened through post-traumatic neurological growth. During post-traumatic growth, through a technical process called neurogenesis, new fibers may have been created by an influx of new neurons. These neurons rewire the bridge from the caudate to the putamen with greater connectivity. His researchers didn't have proof of a causal link between trauma, this increased connectivity, and expanded intuition. However, theoretically, it would be possible through such neuronal regenerative processes.

In terms of hypersensitivity, embracing that the sensitive-empathic genetic markers, or changes in the gene expression, were likely passed down through heredity explains some aspects of sensory processing sensitivity. This may give us a clue as to how to cultivate this trait. If we view it as a form of social and emotional intelligence, a neurological advancement that helps attune empaths for survival, we might be able to devise practical regimens that would enable us to rely on it. As a survival mechanism, the trait gives empaths invisible "feelers" for sensing and perceiving what conditions, people, and relationships are beneficial or harmful for them. This ability is hardwired into their nervous system and acts as a warning system.

AN EMPATH'S PERCEPTION OF REALITY

Your sensitive-empathy trait may have evolved through evolutionary forces (nature). Let's consider how it could develop through environmental forces (nurture). Certainly, people inherit their genetic code from their parents, but they also inherit a system of pattern recognition after being born. Identifying patterns helps make sense of the world. We are taught abstractions both by direct and indirect instruction, which are coupled with instincts. The nervous system contains the hardwiring for certain types of behavior. The brain uses these established programs and patterns to understand and interpret reality.

Legendary acting teacher and director Lee Strasberg (artistic director of The Actor's Studio) called these abstractions *stencils*. In his interpretation, stencils are the overall impressions passed down from our parents that help us order our worlds. He theorized that we fashion models of perception based on the belief systems of our parents. The schema we each inherit and then develop through behavioral interactions with our parents is our unique imprint.

Imprinting is a term I have borrowed from learning and behavioral theorists that explains the first critical stages of associative learning that occur after we are born. Nobel Prize–winning ethologist Konrad Lorenz discovered imprinting. In his research newborn animals instinctively identified the first thing they saw and experienced as their mother. A baby giraffe in Africa sees a zookeeper's Jeep and begins to follow it as if it was his mother. Animals can also exhibit fixed-action patterns, which are associated with imprinting. Fixed-action patterns are specific behaviors an organism uses to respond in an instinctual way. For instance, when baby herring gulls are born, they have an innate pecking instinct. They peck on their mother's beak to get fed. The mother has a red stripe on her beak (stimulus) which allows her babies to find their source of food. Science tells us that depending on the species' genetic code certain behaviors are truly instinctive. After birth and through childhood, imprints can be relearned.

Imprinting is also directly connected to our attachment bond with a parent or parental figure. If one of the empath's parents was emotionally unavailable or not physically present during the empath's early years of life, it likely affected their intuitive and emotional bonding experience. This may have occurred with one or both parents. When attachment is disrupted, I contend that a child becomes more empathic.

Infants and children must have a parental figure to bond with to feel safe, loved, and cared for. If this bonding does not take place with a caregiver, young babies fail to thrive. Empathic awareness is already common in childhood. During stages of early development, children naturally and intuitively seek out and explore their environment with their feelings and all their senses. This is how we discern the self versus the environment. The senses are what develop first because they help us to define our identity or perception of self. Forming an imprinted bond with a mother or other nurturing figure gives a child sense of security.

Imprinting is an internal construct that helps us make sense of the world. We can understand these complexities through the first experiences in life. Imprinting affects every child's mind and emotions as they perceive and construct different thought patterns based on their experience within their families. For example, when a sensitive child approaches a new situation, if they are securely bonded to a parent, they will feel free to explore that environment. If not, they will stay near their parent due to a feeling of insecurity and use their sensory awareness to detect more information from their environment.

Imprints are genetic abstractions that are activated by how we connect with our parents or authority figures. Attachment creates a specific sense of belonging. When a sensitive lacks attachment, hypersensitivity kicks in. As I mentioned, lack of an attached parent develops a higher sensing mechanism to perceive whether a parent is attentionally present or absent. This sensing for a parent's attentional presence puts undue pressure on the child to become hyperaware. They learn they must be hypervigilant, monitoring the environment for their own safety. Besides attentional attachment, hypersensing may also develop when one parent has an illness, is emotionally compromised, or is unavailable. We see this in the example of the *empath-healer.*

EMPATHS AS HEALERS, PRIESTS, AND SAGES

Empaths are the greatest advisers of our time. Whether they take leadership roles in spiritual communities, work in medical settings as healers, or are sage-like in their ability to forecast future events, they are in tune with their environment at a profound level. If you have an empath in your life, you are lucky to call the empath your friend, as empaths can detect lies without effort. Their senses are so highly attuned that they put the galvanic skin response—the physical basis for lie detectors—to shame. Nowhere else do we see such a strong display of the gift of empathy than in the empath-healer. Their extraordinary felt-sense, which enables them to perceive nuanced emotional states, emotional incongruence, and turbulence within the hidden, subterranean shores of the personality, makes them insightful counselors, doctors, medical-intuitives, and psychic readers.

As we've already discussed, empaths feel the energy of their surroundings intensely. When that energy is positive, it is exhilarating and blissful. Empaths love with an incomprehensible depth. Their love is an emotional force that brings their whole heart, mind, body, and spirit to bear in their relationships. They have also described their feelings of love as a sense of *transcendental bliss*. Transcendental bliss is the heightened feeling-state of ecstatic joy. This sudden and intense flood of overwhelming emotion can be positive when achieving flow states. In positive psychology, a flow state is also known as "the zone." In ancient Eastern traditions like Buddhism, this full absorption into trance states does not happen in a vacuum. Through attainment of higher states of consciousness, there are different levels of *transcendent awareness*. Feeling transcendent bliss can happen during any focused activity. We hear about it most often during peak states of physical performance such as dancing, running, or yoga.

Empaths feel these peak mental states more often as a result of complete immersion, or hyperfocus, into their activity of choice. It could be an artistic pursuit like painting, sculpting, or knitting. Many chefs, gardeners, and artistic performers have described this state as being so utterly engrossed in their talent that they completely lose track of time. For the healer, sage, or minister, flow states are achieved through a deep attentive focus on another's health, well-being, or spiritual needs. When these states accelerate through prayer, advanced energy work, or movement meditation they lead to more frequent peak states.

Due to their enhanced capacity to process emotions and feeling, empaths achieve euphoric moments. Ministers might feel such deep and powerful emotional reaction to societal injustices that they take community action such as setting up soup kitchens, crisis centers, and homeless shelters. When empaths are counselors or healers, they have a deep capacity to transform personal or spiritual pain by helping others transition through illness, death, or loss. Undoubtedly many highly evolved spiritual empaths commit to chaplaincy (in prisons or hospitals) and hospice work. This form of religious ecstasy may feel mystical and godlike. Peak states can happen spontaneously or through advanced states of consciousness in empaths who are highly developed in their self-awareness. An empath does not have to be religious to feel transcendental bliss states. Such states can be achieved during any activity the empath finds extremely enjoyable through total immersion of their emotional connectedness. This includes providing spiritual care, health care, or falling in love.

BRENDA'S STORY

I don't think people realize how hard it is to work with spirit. The stamina, energy, and work required is intense. I think some people have an extra capacity for this kind of work to attune with spirit, like empaths. See, I receive mental messages, sometimes through archetypes, and then use the pictures that form in my mind, or thought forms, to understand the spirit guiding me. This is because spirit communicates the way I can understand or empathize. I also use my knowledge of the tarot to channel spirit's directions. I interpret spirit's guidance for the person I'm reading for. There is a certain amount of healing that comes through these spiritual messages too. I can feel it by the energy that releases in a reading. I teach people how to change their life by giving them the steps spirit says they need to go through. Usually it comes through higher ideas and suggestions about a life direction they need to take. Jung taught that spiritual messages could be received from angels, symbols, and archetypal images. I believe that too. I think a lot of psychologists use this same kind of spiritual work for healing. Although I'm not sure they would consciously accept that.

DEEP AND POWERFUL EMOTIONS

There are a few "sand traps" empaths can get stuck in when they are head-over-heels in love. Their kind of love sometimes overwhelms others. If their love goes unrequited, the empath will start to feel discomfort, irritability, or heaviness in the body. This heaviness is indicative of the mind-body-spirit's exhaustion from carrying the burden of unexpressed emotions. Conceptually one can view the physical body as a container for past emotional experiences. Empaths can learn to use the body as a guidepost to understand unconsciously held emotions, which show up as sensation in their joints, musculature, fascia, and other soft tissues and structures of the body. The tool that will help them get out of the sand trap is somatic awareness, or the ability to feel the body.

Living as an empath is not easy. An empath's somatic awareness can be off the charts. Until the empath's consciousness is equally well developed, they cannot use the nuanced insights of the body to their highest potential. A jittery nervous system makes it difficult to manage complex sensory experiences. As they feel everything (they literally cannot filter out other peoples energy), they will be in a constant state of flux between nervous tension, doubt of their feelings, and a deep need for love and affection until they learn to "metabolize" the sensory information that's flooding in.

The most common example of this flux can be experienced in their work and home environments. When they work as healers, empaths feel a wide array of emotions in their clientele that they need to filter out between the client and themselves. They feel the illnesses that take shape from avoidance of deep-seated emotions that manifest on the body. The brain only has so much capacity to handle intense emotions, so the body does most of the suppression of emotional states that haven't been energetically processed. All empaths feel the different suppressed states originally born from anger. Empaths describe anger as a "hot" emotion, like aggressive disgust or rage. They also feel when anger is turned inward as a sad disappointment in a lowered mood. The empath senses what is hidden under the depressed energy of melancholy. Whatever is embedded within the energy of those emotional states of the people they encounter or treat, an empath will be able to sense it. If they haven't done the energy space-clearing work in their office or their own homes, the negative energy lingers. In their own living space, it could be from a difficult fight with their spouse or child. Coercive, controlling, or competitive environments are their enemies. These emotionally charged conditions are the antithesis of the peaceful settings and solitude necessary for empaths to restore their balance and equanimity.

Not only do empaths feel deeply, but sometimes they feel they must respond to whatever they are feeling and sensing like the compassion-empath. Empaths generally are conscientious, responsible individuals who carry other people's emotional baggage until they learn to surrender on a regular basis—daily letting go is ideal, especially for the empath-healer who is interacting with multiple clients each day. Depending on the circumstances, life situation, and moods of their loved ones and healing clients, these feelings might run from joy, passion, anger, to sadness, and grief.

As we heard from the young empath who experienced migraines from total loving immersion with her boyfriend, unmanaged sensitivity due to an untrained mind creates a dangerous and painful emotional cycle. Since sensory processes are different for every individual, no two empaths will experience an environment in the same way—with one exception. A common thread weaves through the empathic experience: transference of energy that triggers self-protection. When an empath feels insecure, an automatic self-protection mechanism kicks in. This coping mechanism is developed in childhood to shield the young empath from the pain of feeling the negative thoughts, emotions, and intentions of others.

The double-edged sword for healers and ministers is that the same receptivity that enables them to be compassionate with their clients and spiritual communities triggers their own nervous systems. This receptivity has consequences. This comment from Margie, an empathic woman who teaches Reiki, explains the importance of self-care to heal former trauma:

> *If I feel threatened, I often rush to say something negative about myself before others could. That gut-level defense mechanism felt far better to me than getting picked on by others. Only in rebuilding my self-image as an adult, particularly through utilizing positive self-affirmations to transform my mind-set, have I felt growth away from self-objectification. As an empathic healer, I believe that finding common ground with others begins within yourself. In any energy class I teach, our first several lessons are always about self-care.*

If, when empath-healers were young, they had a parent who was emotionally compromised, ill, or detached, this would have left a gap in their ability to consistently attune to a loving presence. Loving care from a positive influence has the power to stabilize a young empath until the empath has matured enough to manage their gift of sensitivity. As children witnessed and received sensory stimulation in their own body related to their parents' suffering, they may have subconsciously decided to take the illness on. The empath would have looked for the reason why the parent that they had imprinted on was emotionally unavailable for bonding.

If the reason is an illness, the empaths develop the awareness to discern how to mitigate it. This is not a conscious decision.

If an empath is highly evolved, the empath will become self-aware and realize they are trying to heal their parent, usually into adulthood. They ultimately gain great fulfillment from using the same type of empathic awareness to help other people. Putting this gift to work for the betterment of humankind makes them feel fulfilled and more whole.

SIGNS AND SYMPTOMS THAT REVEAL YOU MAY BE A SENSITIVE-EMPATH

First, don't let anyone else determine or compromise your health, dear empath—the world needs you. Empaths have a considerable self-healing mechanism built into the CNS. Mother Nature gave empaths a gift; she wouldn't hobble them with it. The first task as an empath is to learn the sensory emotional cues that will discern *me* from *not me*. This comes from testing and discovering boundaries. Medically, when empaths tax their nervous system, they experience fight or flight more often, and this impacts their hormones. Hormones are powerful predictors of the types of symptoms that will arise depending on how an empath's body perceives and deals with stress. Empaths usually struggle with candida (yeast overgrowth), chronic fatigue (loss of energy), getting stuck in emotional states (moody, irritable), irritable bowel or gastrointestinal distress, skin rashes (breakouts), headaches, unexplained weight gain, and loss of confidence. Chronic fatigue and loss of energy are the most common signs of imbalance in the sensitive-empath. When there has been a long-term loss of vitality for maintaining an empath's daily routines, their stress response has disrupted their hormonal balance. Chronic fatigue means their nervous system has been taxed in an unhealthy prolonged state.

Empathic sensitives are also at greater risk for developing sensitive states in response to gut inflammation or injury. This risk is dependent upon how the brain processes sensory information received from the gastrointestinal (GI) tract. For example, the gastrointestinal tract has *dual sensory innervation*. This means the GI tract has a unique pattern by the way nerves connect to the stomach, intestines, and to the spinal cord (CNS) and parasympathetic nervous system. Dual innervation means the nerves connect to and from viscera (organs). Most visceral sensory nerves and fibers end in the spinal cord, except the GI tract, which also has vagus and pelvic nerves.

The major issue associated with sensitive states from gut inflammation, or *visceral pain hypersensitivity*, is irritable bowel syndrome. Visceral hypersensitivity is when we experience pain from the visceral organs, in this case the stomach. Visceral pain is usually felt by highly sensitive people through a hypersensitive awareness or perception of pain in the abdomen. This kind of pain perception is commonly diagnosed as a functional gastrointestinal disorder. If you feel you have experienced emotional upsets, inflammation, and sensitized states from acute sensitivity, you can treat difficult gastrointestinal conditions related to your sensitivity. Talking with a gastroenterologist about sensitivity will help identify specific issues that might be related to gut health.

Famous empaths include dog trainer Cesar Millan, Princess Diana, physician Deepak Chopra, spiritual teacher Eckhart Tolle, primatologist and anthropologist Jane Goodall, psychiatrist Judith Orloff, social activist Mahatma Gandhi, poet and memoirist Maya Angelou, Mother Teresa, television host Oprah Winfrey, yogi Paramahansa Yogananda, and philosopher and social reformer Rudolf Steiner.

CHAPTER 3

SENSITIVE INTUITION

The intuitive mind is a sacred gift and the rational mind a faithful servant. We have created a society that honors the servant and has forgotten the gift.[1]

— ALBERT EINSTEIN

The best decisions often come unbidden. An answer arrives in a flash and we inherently know it's right on the money. Great decision makers, like business developer Richard Branson of Virgin Galactic, Beauty Pie founder Marcia Kilgore, and Marcus Henderson of Black Star Farms, are people who don't need to process tons and tons of information to arrive at an answer. Rather, they have perfected the subtle and invisible art of filtering out everything but the few important factors needed to decide. In other words, they have the gift of intuition. Sensitive-intuitive individuals make correct decisions using a fluid mode of thought, which depends less on analysis, rationality, logic, and intellectualism. It operates as a sudden instinct or flash of knowledge, very much a part of our ancient survival system. Intuitives who showcase their savvy business sense in the projects they champion are usually industry disrupters too. If they have a deep commitment to fair practices and social accountability, they work tirelessly to create unity where they see disparity or injustice.

Garry Nolan, Ph.D., gave an innovative lecture at the Harvard Medical School 2018 Symposium on Space Genetics entitled "Can Genetic Differences in Intuition and Cognition Drive Success in Space?"[2] In this talk Dr. Nolan discussed the genetic attributes of individuals his research team studied who exhibited extraordinary intuition. Those in his study with high intuition were labeled *experiencers*. They shared anomalous mental phenomena perceived through the senses. Family members were included in the study so researchers could track and observe genetic markers through DNA and rates of incidence. According to Dr. Nolan, "We had groups of patients who objectively had a higher density of neuronal connection between the head of the caudate and the putamen."[3]

To refresh our neurology chops, the caudate-putamen is in the interior region of the brain. The putamen and caudate together make up the dorsal striatum. It is a complex region that composes the basal ganglia, which is involved in voluntary movement, emotion, and decision-making. The basal ganglia are collections of nerve cells that extend down the spinal cord and are intricately connected with the cerebral cortex and brain stem. Most neurologists attributed the function of these areas of the brain with voluntary motor control. More recent discoveries connected them with higher cognitive functions, such as learning cognition and decision-making.[4] Intuition is considered a higher cognitive function. As we know, the CNS is the most important regulating function for sensitive people due to sensitized states. The CNS contains the brain and spinal cord, which are the complex of nerve tissues that control the systems of the body.

Nolan studied a test group of 105 people. Sixty percent were male and 40 percent female. They were evaluated by MRI scan. In comparison with the control group of 100 randomly selected people, those who exhibited exceptional intuition had a higher density and greater connectivity between nerve cells in the caudate and putamen. The density ranged from slightly above normal to *up to eight times the control range.*[5]

The intuitives with higher connectivity in their caudate-putamen processed information at remarkably faster speeds than those individuals in the control group. When family members were scanned, the same thickened white matter that increased caudate-putamen connectivity was found. Researchers concluded that the individuals with enhanced connectivity could be classified as hypermorphs.[6] *Hypermorph* is a medical term for a mutant gene having a similar but greater effect than the corresponding gene in the broader population. The hypermorphic genes in the individuals in this study showed higher intuitive functioning, which is often called *psychic thought.*

Personality traits shared by the individuals in the study with higher caudate-putamen connectivity included higher rank of performance (called high performers), more susceptibility to paranormal experiences, and enhanced intuition. They reported anomalous phenomena. Visual and auditory phenomena included seeing orbs of light, hearing voices, and observing noncorporeal entities. The researchers dubbed these anomalies hallucinations.[7]

While the researchers stressed these data are preliminary at best, Dr. Nolan emphasized, "Objectively, the connections in the caudate-putamen are real. What these connectivity patterns mean in relation to intuition and cognitive function will need to include neurological studies that involve disciplines of neurophysiology such as functional MRI and more."[8]

Interestingly he also speculated that certain kinds of intuitive processing are involved in nervous system components that read, sense, and transmit information and interact within the immune system. In his research study on intuition, Dr. Nolan also examined subjects' immune system injuries (illness, disease). Hypothetically, Nolan suggested that *sensory components within nerves* may be heightened in a certain group of people whose nerve centers are configured to be more attuned than the average person to sight, sound, or feelings. These individuals connect to their sensory nervous system in unique ways. As an example, some experiencers sense more through feeling, or psychic thought, or with their subtle hearing. Avid researchers who scour the Internet searching for meaning in field studies on intuition feel that it is not too far of a reach to assume this new science is the beginning of an explanation for ESP.[9]

Dr. Erik Davis, astrophysicist and peer of Dr. Nolan's, explains dispositional intuitive awareness as a sensitive's unique type of perception (anomalous cognition) that chips away at the wall of illusion. He theorizes that this particular heightened cognitive awareness might be connected to a supersensitive immune system that increases anomalous events. He further theorizes the immune system of HSPs might communicate in different ways. In an OpenMinds podcast interview with radio host Alejandro Rojas, Dr. Davis commented on Nolan's Stanford research. Davis explained his perspective of inherited super sensitivity in physiological terms, "The immune system is a separate organ in your body. It's not just a system of chemicals . . . [In Nolan's work] the immune system acts like a brain and it's responding in a psychic way. It does behave as if it has its own mind."[10]

Science on intuition stretches across multiple disciplines and aims to discover the processes behind the many modes of human thought. We know that during the normal process of thinking, the brain functions are mostly automatic, engaged in a mindless processing of information. Due to biases and other perceptual issues, there are also often cognitive errors in these judgments. In these instances, your analytical mind is not your friend. For example, your senses don't lie. It is through the deciphering and filtering of sensory information, when the analytical mind wants to jump in and interpret this information, that errors are made.

There are several modes of thinking including unconscious (hidden reasoning), conscious (cognition), and survival instinct (intuition). Consciousness is embedded within cognitive comprehension. Our conscious thoughts represent a small fraction of the entirety of our information processing. The brain selects the information needed in any given situation mostly on a need-to-know basis. This filtering helps maximize cortical activity, making information easier to manage. Intuition stands out from normally automatic brain functions as the ability "to know" quickly and with certainty.

SHARON'S STORY

I have been practicing for over 20 years as a clinical therapist, working my way through various agencies following graduate school. After working at one particular agency for 14 years, I made a decision to leave. I felt I was not living my truth and was put in the position to frequently betray myself. I understood my ability to process information was different than my colleagues. I felt things quite deeply and intensely. I needed more time to process all the nuances of my clients and the issues they presented. This agency had a one-size-fits-all framework for both the clients and the therapists, and it wasn't working for me.

I went to visit some friends in San Diego, and during the visit I had a dream that I was watching my colleagues being crushed under a big concrete wheel. I coaxed them to get out and focused on one particular nurse practitioner. A manager tried to whisk me away and was scolding me. Upon awakening I realized this dream was inspired by a book I read as an adolescent, Beneath the Wheel by Hermann Hesse. This author helped define who I was through his other books such as Demian and Siddhartha. I made contracts with myself regarding my spirituality and how to live my life at an early age. I realized this dream was telling me that I was being crushed beneath a large corporate wheel and I needed to be true to my early sacred contract.

Within a week after returning to the agency, I handed in my resignation. My plan was to take most of the summer off to learn the business end of my private practice, including credentialing and billing. I joined various groups for therapists, both clinical and business oriented. It was in one group when someone mentioned the HSP. She directed me to a group for highly sensitive therapists. At that point my whole life made sense and snapped into place. How could it be that a therapist with 21 years' experience would not have heard of this personality profile? I fit the profile of HSP, or sensory processing sensitivity, to a tee! Yet it was never mentioned by my colleagues and managers. In fact, I got the sense I would be mocked if I shared this with colleagues.

After I found this group, I flashed back to the early scenes in my life when my feelings, intuition, and imagination were in full mode. I remembered, for example, living in an apartment with my family in New York City. When it came time for us to move, one apartment stood out for me: it was on a tree-lined street and it felt so fresh and alive. My whole being—my body, mind, and spirit—felt calm and refreshed. I looked forward to a home that was surrounded by nature.

So many other memories came forth, like using visualization to ease disturbance in my body when I was a 9- or 10-year-old. Though therapeutic imagery was used as far back as ancient Greece, it was unheard of in my professional circle. I think back on my childhood imagination and realize visualizing these connections was intuitive on my part. I put my attention on the disturbance (mindfulness) and used my imagination to effect healing. I believe it was no accident that I gravitated toward the healing field as a clinical therapist.

Working as a private practitioner allowed me to lean into who I really am. I no longer need to sit at meetings where other therapists are jockeying to prove their power and show how brilliant they are. My work is so much more meaningful and richer. As the research shows, a significant percentage of people who seek therapy are HSPs themselves and can weed out the therapists who are attuned to them. I have found this to be true in my work.

SENSITIVE-INTUITIVE KNOWING

As a sensitive-intuitive, you need to learn about the gift of intuition from several vantage points: as a survival mechanism, interpersonal tool, and the divine connection. Many people who experience sudden insight or intuition for the first time explain it as a "flash of truth." They don't know why or how they knew something. They just knew it. Gavin de Becker explains intuition as a journey from A to Z without stopping at any other letter along the way, "It is knowing, without knowing why."[11]

Sensitive-intuitives perceive clues, make accurate guesses, and detect important information that might otherwise be ignored. They are usually exceptionally bright and quick-witted people, who get sudden flashes of insight when solving problems. In leadership roles they can accelerate important societal trends by seeing the interconnectedness, or larger patterns, within a system. Sensitive-intuitives excel at influencing others, planning (once again by seeing interconnections), finding patterns, and therefore are usually quite adept at business. They follow their hunches and often land on their feet due to their subtle intuitive intelligence for knowing who to partner with, when to make a savvy business move, or when to cut their losses.

Sensitive-intuitive people tend to be detectives, business executives, consultants, and entrepreneurs. In the health and medical fields, they are doctors, social workers, and forensic psychologists. Poker players benefit from sharp intuition because they can read tiny body movements and subtle facial cues, or the tells of their opponents.

THE SUBCONSCIOUS

The subconscious mind processes an extreme amount of data that the conscious mind does not immediately understand. It is also where we develop habits, where memories are stored, and it is responsible for many of our emotions. That means the bulk of cognition happens beneath the surface of our awareness. As a result our thought processing can be imperfect. Our conscious mind is considered the rational, analytical part of our brain—essentially our willpower. Intuitives are spectacularly gifted observers, skilled at parsing the overwhelming amount of information they subconsciously receive.

The brain is a reductionist filter. It blocks most sensory information. None of us consciously realize how much information we are taking in, nor do we immediately comprehend it. Accordingly, we do not consciously observe this invisible and fluid process that pulls information from the subconscious mind to make the immediate judgment calls we label gut feelings. Very simply, intuitives have powerful instincts. They observe, track, and parse information too quickly to logically process. When an intuition arrives, it can feel magical. It just may be a product of super-quick reasoning.

The inner balance of cognitive consciousness occurs at light speed. It helps an intuitive bring the necessary information forward fast to make accurate and prompt decisions. This phenomenon is personified as a predictive ability, sometimes as an actual foresight or snapshot of future events. Intuitives can see, hear, or observe something in the environment before it happens.

It is not only genetic expression, imprinting, and environmental vulnerability that influence our sensory awareness; psychophysiological mechanisms influence it as well. Field studies done in the former Soviet Union prior to Dr. Nolan's study linked intuition to the density of the nerve clusters in the caudate-putamen region of the brain. The Russian interpretation of intuition is that it is "an overexpression in the caudate-putamen that participates in higher integrative activity for synthesis of single (sensory) signals for programing future activity."[12] This genetic overexpression literally helps intuitive people foresee, predict, and visualize future events. No one yet understands why this psychophysiological genetic overexpression exists. Some theorists believe intuition is an evolutionary function preparing humans for a time in the future when we may need telepathic thought.

The evolutionary origins of intuition strike a more general cultural question as to why humans do what they do (think, behave). Social scientists have tried to explain the influence of genetic expression on human behavior. Let's alter the question slightly for sensitivity and ask: Why do sensitive people perceive what they perceive? We know both genetic expression and imprinting connect to cognition and behavior (the abstractions we are born with). They may also be the root of the intuitive phenomenon. Generally, trying to understand intuition, a higher form of thought, dives into the philosophical root of being human versus something else, like animals without rational thought. In his animal studies, evolutionary biologist Charles Darwin differentiated between humans and animals, since human species were the only ones that blushed with embarrassment, revealing self-conscious awareness. Consciousness is the main yoke linking together different philosophies on reasoning and intuition. Understanding intuition through consciousness and theoretical physics has exciting implications.

THE HARD PROBLEM OF CONSCIOUSNESS

Sensitive-intuitives generally roll their eyes at people who disbelieve that intuition is real—including skeptics who label intuitions as hallucinations. Even reading the word *hallucinations* makes a sensitive cringe. It is what it is—even if the rest of the world can't perceive it.

That doesn't stop the nonbelievers from trying to discuss it and label the experience, as if intuitives need people's permission to be as they are. Well, they sort of do. There is a cultural bias against anything that seems magical or nonscientific. To some degree any kind of consciousness is mysterious. Its existence, though, is self-evident. René Descartes famously observed, "Cogito, ergo sum" or "I think therefore I am," which means *consciousness is the one undeniable fact of our existence*. It is what makes us human.

Questions about consciousness have lingered and been asked by prominent philosophers throughout recorded history. These questions predate the discovery of advanced scientific methods to study brain activity. Socrates, Plato, and Aristotle tried to resolve humanity's hard problem of consciousness, which is the question of the origins of higher cognition and intuitive thought.

Descartes was one of the linchpin transformers who shook up the old-world order with his notions about how our senses perceive reality. He felt they couldn't be trusted. His insecurity and fear about the falseness of human perception led him to develop the scientific method, which changed the way science has been conducted ever since. The scientific method uses empirical observation to explain phenomena. It has become a mainstay of Western culture and discovery for more than four hundred years. This method continues to influence the debate about consciousness.

There are a few main schools of thought. The first is that consciousness creates the mind through cortical processes and activity located inside the brain. The second and more controversial school is that consciousness resides outside the body. In this second hypothesis, the mind controls brain function from outside the body. The critical difference between these philosophies is that in the second hypothesis the mind influences perception rather than the brain. This theory takes more of a quantum consciousness view, where consciousness is nonlocal. Many proponents believe that it solves formerly mysterious intuitive phenomenon such as precognition, psychic thought, and remote viewing. Scientists such as Edgar Mitchell (American astronaut), Jude Currivan, Ph.D., (author of *The Cosmic Hologram*), and David Bohm (physicist) theorized that perception is based on a quantum reality, where human consciousness is nonlocal and perceives information in a quantum field through quanta.

The hard problem of consciousness, which was formerly known as the mind-body problem and is sometimes alternately known as the meta-problem of consciousness, was defined by contemporary philosopher and neuroscientist David Chalmers. It is the analytical answer to the question, "Why does the *feeling* that accompanies awareness of sensory information exist at all?"[13]

British philosopher and Zen Buddhist Alan Watts described this concept of conscious feeling. He labels the function of feelings which accompany sensory perception as the *observing mind*. In his view the observing mind senses the differences between the external world and the self. These inseparable differences are fundamental to all humans. In simplistic terms the two ends are different: at one end are humans, and at the other end is our world. In Watts's opinion when our consciousness responds without any interval or interruption (not stopping to think about thoughts), we are using intuition to realize the true physical relationship that exists between man and his environment. I extrapolate this even further using intuition as a form of intelligence, which uses conscious awareness to discern the differences between our mind and the world, our mind and another's, our mind and God.

Within these contexts of human intuition, it is easy to wonder whether consciousness is a state of awareness generated within the brain or if it is nonphysical and located outside the body. *Veridical perception* may yield some important clues to bridge this gap. According to University of California, Los Angeles, professor of psychiatry Louis J. West and his colleagues, this form of sense perception is the direct perception of stimuli in an environment.[14] Russell Targ, Caroline Watt, and Ian Teirney have also done studies on veridical perception and connected it with ESP.[15] One of the first clinically documented examples of veridical perception was of a woman named Maria. She had a near-death experience (NDE) in Seattle, Washington, at Harborview Medical Center.

MARIA FINDS A SHOE

Maria is one of the most talked about stories that led to understanding veridical perception. According to medical records from 1977 and through witness accounts now cataloged by the International Association for Near-Death Studies (IANDS), Maria was a migrant worker who suffered a serious cardiac arrest while she was visiting friends in Seattle. During her resuscitation she felt herself float to the ceiling where she watched medical staff work on her body. During the NDE she felt her consciousness float further outside the Seattle emergency room. Later, after she woke up, she told an ER social worker she saw a tennis shoe on a third-floor window ledge on the north side of the building. Maria explained where she saw the ledge and gave directions to where the shoe could be found. She told the social worker what it looked like, how the laces were stuck beneath the heel, and that the little toe area was almost worn through. Maria begged her to go find it to make sure she had really "seen" the shoe. The social worker followed her directions to the third-floor window ledge. Not only did she find the shoe, but it was in the exact location Maria described; there was no possible way Maria could have seen all the details she related from inside her hospital room. Kimberly Sharp, the now retired social worker, shares her story about Maria at IANDS conferences. Unfortunately for the researchers looking to verify Maria's side of the story, she disappeared shortly after her hospitalization, and no one has been able to track her down.

In his book *Life After Life*, Dr. Raymond Moody first coined the term *near-death experience*, which sparked a wider debate about empirically studying consciousness. In his book Dr. Moody told the stories of more than 100 people who had survived clinical death and undergone an NDE. When they returned, or were brought back to life through resuscitation, some survivors provided verifiable facts about their environment while they were clinically dead (e.g., doctors' and nurses' conversations, what someone was wearing, conditions in the hospital outside their room). Due to the popularity of his claims about patients seeing, hearing, and witnessing events outside their own clinical death, consciousness scientists and doctors zeroed in on *nonphysical veridical perception* as the primary function that could prove consciousness survives beyond clinical death.

Veridical perception is a form of sense perception that may exist while being unconscious or in altered states. *Veridical* means *not illusory*, and in this context it means having an experience in which you see, hear, or witness events in the environment while being unconscious or during clinical death. If scientists could prove the existence of an aspect of consciousness survives outside the body, it would be revolutionary and may help us understand other forms of psychic phenomenon like intuition.

SENTIENCE AND INTUITION

Greek historian Herodotus believed human sentience was shaped largely by culture. He once said "culture is king."[16] We interpret this idea in modern times as society having the largest influence on our minds and behavior. Herodotus believed societal structures held the power to direct how we intuitively think and act. Many advertising executives would probably agree.

A sensitive-intuitive advertising executive named Gilbert Clotaire Rapaille is the author of over 17 books on psychology, marketing, cultural anthropology, and sociology. He refers to the connection between the triune brain, individual behavior, and culture as "breaking the cultural code."[17] In his successful 1979 Michelin tire campaign, he tapped into our nurturing instincts to sell us "safer" tires. You may recall the imagery of the now-famous television commercial that featured a cute baby resting inside a thick rubber tire and a narrator's soothing masculine voice saying, "Because so much is riding on your tires." Our brains intuitively interpreted this combination of words and imagery to mean *Michelin tires will keep my family safe*. We instinctively knew within seconds just by looking at the innocent baby resting inside the rubber circle of the tire that we could trust the Michelin Man.

In interviews he's done over the years, Rapaille explained how he draws on Carl Jung's cultural archetypes and different modes of thought to help corporations intuitively crack cultural codes and increase buying behavior and brand loyalty. He has consulted with Fortune 500 brands such as Boeing, L'Oreal, General Motors, and AT&T, sharing with them his interpretation of modern archetypes that could be used to position their companies through cultural influences. Understanding the cultural codes Rapaille relies on, we must operate on a distinctive premise which informs his work. One of the main evaluators of the cultural code and intuitive thought is the brain and central nervous system.

The nervous system evaluates the world and fires over 100 billion neuronal signals in the brain per minute. These neurochemical reactions determine reality for each person. Since the nervous system can't evaluate this much information or the entirety of the space-time continuum, the brain constructs an internal model, or schematic, of the world. This internal construct of reality connects to intuition through the Bayesian neurological principle called *predictive processing*. Predictive processing or predictive coding is a theory of cognition that explains that the mind generates and updates a mental model based on sensory input. This model is broadcast through the network of sensory processing regions in the brain. Then it interprets sensory information and learns how to confirm or deny (external stimuli filtering in) its own expectations about reality.[18]

Sensitive-intuitives may have an enhanced function for predictive processing. For efficiency our brain constructs a model of reality and uses sensory information to interpret and predict outcomes within the environment. Intuitives may make sense of the world using this sensory model inherited from their parents through three functions of cortical processes (instinctual, emotional, and rational). This may be where the cultural code we share and intuition—a form of thought unique to everyone—intersect.

Carl Jung, one of the founders of the analytical psychology movement, brought a breadth of knowledge to his theories about the inner workings of our conscious and unconscious minds. Jung was devoted to dream analysis. Many of his hypotheses have withstood the test of time, including the concepts of archetypes, extroversion, introversion, the collective unconscious, synchronicity, and the psyche. He defined the psyche as an executive organizing function that balances three distinct levels or modes of thought: the unconscious, conscious, and transpersonal. Jung's concept of a collective unconscious held that everyone within the human species carries hidden memories of an ancestral past. He said,

"The form of the world into which [a person] is born is already inborn in him as a virtual image."[19]

According to Jung a universal human memory existed in our genetic blueprint as a result of human evolution.[20] He believed intuition was a mode of thought intertwined within this complex, serving as a sensory function. He also outlined several other psychological functions that are now used in the criteria for personality testing. The main psychological types he originally included were extroversion/introversion, sensing/intuition, and thinking/feeling. Modern depth psychologists (doctors who use psychoanalytic methods) theorize that these inherent dispositions shape who we are. They are hidden influences on us. In the example of the Michelin tire campaign, Rapaille intuitively knew the shared human motivation of protection of our young would be a cultural win—the idea of a baby in a car accident is universally upsetting.

Rapaille's ad campaigns were successful because he knew symbolic imagery and language could influence and guide our purchasing decisions. In this context his intuition told him which images would be the most affecting. In other fields, including the arts, business, psychology, and criminal justice, professionals use their intuition to understand and predict why humans behave the way they do.

Although I personally believe far too much money is being spent on influencing the behavior of the population (more than 190 billion U.S. dollars were spent on advertising in 2016), advertising is one of the fertile testing grounds for the gift of sensitive-intuition. As a mental faculty, intuition stands out. Executives like Rapaille who gather in expensive boardrooms are using intuition to uncover the patterns and interconnections that influence humanity. These intuitives get paid well to tap our unconscious desires.

As consumers intuition can help us cut through the propaganda. It does so in concrete albeit nonverbal ways. The challenge is learning how to *listen to the wisdom*. The chips are stacked against us in terms of information overwhelm, technology, and every kind of advertising trying to catch our attention. Our subtle, intuitive sensing, which is a felt-sense, often gets washed out. Cognitive processing errors can occur if we are bombarded with stimulation.

COGNITIVE BIAS AND PROCESSING ERRORS

In *Thinking, Fast and Slow,* Nobel Prize–winning economist and psychologist Daniel Kahneman, Ph.D., shares decades of insights from his research on two different modes of thought. System 1 is fast and instinctive and includes the emotions. System 2 is much slower, more deliberate, and logical. Through his fastidious research, Kahneman focuses on the cognitive biases of these two systems of thinking. He uses a theory called *framing*, which explains our tendency to replace difficult questions with ones that are easier for us to answer. A way of subconsciously cherry-picking favored information we feel more confident about judging. He points out clear cognitive biases that we create so we can feel better about our world. Our intuition helps us cut through biases. It bypasses our typical analytical processes with lightning-fast speed.

Cognitive biases can be problematic. We use what we think we know or a specific train of thought to make decisions based on learned behavior—even if those thought patterns are false. In psychology there is a considerable amount of research associated with cognitive biases called *attentional bias*. Attentional bias is the natural tendency of our recurrent thoughts or thought processes to focus on typical patterns of perception. In this context of attentional and cognitive bias, we may fail to consider alternate possibilities because of unconscious thought patterns. In short it is an effect that works like magnetic attraction. It draws our conscious attention to our own recurrent thoughts and beliefs—reinforcing what we believe. It could also be thought of as confirmation bias or a self-fulfilling prophecy. We are confirming our preconceived conclusions or projecting the patterns we expect onto the world. This is based on the premise that fixed perception (or projection) helps us build the world we believe it to be.

As mentioned earlier, Lee Strasberg called these biases stencils. In his sensory exercises, which are an advanced part of the creative method, he helped actors observe their sensory responses to their environment. As part of the sensory work he guided actors into an emotional memory and helped them break through their fixed associations of an experience by using sensations (taste, touch, sight, sound, and smell) to explore what was seen, heard, and felt. The power of the method to break through the stencils or repetitive patterns of thinking is what Strasberg achieved. He called them *actor problems* versus *acting problems*. Actor problems are hidden within the depths of an actor's own internal character, including their habits, thoughts, emotions, unconsciously stored body tension, and routine behaviors. Acting problems are more technical and involved with the craft of acting. Strasberg believed that stencils (biases, snap judgements, learned behavior, and unconscious reasoning) limited the actor's performance in distinct ways, sometimes in the extreme (stuttering, forgetting lines, and habitual movements). During emotional memory work he was famous for repeating this phrase, "Don't tell me what you think it was. . . .Tell me what you saw, what you heard, what you felt!" Regardless of how redundant that may seem, he was an expert on guiding his students into the mysterious terrain of their internal memories. By exploring vivid sense memories, he helped students learn how to identify and break through their own stereotypes, labels, and judgments. The sensory exercises allow discovery of new realizations by freeing up a more intuitive mode of thought. His protégé Gary Swanson, a lifetime member of the Actors Studio and founder of the Montauk Group, calls it "freeing an actor." It is a process that helps actors relieve stored tension and fosters inner growth so they may be more spontaneous, unrestricted, and less influenced by social norms. Sudden intuition helps an actor translate the meaning of emotions on stage, through their highly attuned sense of expression, as a palpable force that audiences can feel.

Sensitive-intuitive people, including actors, have a facile ability to navigate through different modes of thought using an intuitive acuity. They are not immune to cognitive biases, attentional biases, and repetitive patterns in their environment. But by freeing up stored tension or stress in the mind-body, using focus and intention, they may experience the wider sensory expanse using intuition. Whether through physical mechanisms like a highly connected caudate-putamen (which allows for intuitive insights that occur eight times faster than the average) or outside the mind-body through veridical perception, this expanse brings new detailed information, higher forms of learning, and sudden genius. Sensitive-intuitives have an advanced sense perception to navigate between what has been forgotten or is hidden in the unconscious mind and an ability to bring forth the information they need in any given moment.

THE FIVE TYPES OF INTUITION

As with empathy there are different types of intuition. Intuitive abilities may be classified in the following five ways.

- Felt-sense, delivered through sensations in the body, such as having the hair on your arms stand up, shivering, and feeling a sudden change in vibrations

- Visual sense, when sensory information comes through images seen in the imagination or in the world around you through the mind's eye

- Aural sense, when vibrations are perceived through music, sounds, or through hearing an inner voice

- Lucid dreaming, when you are aware while you are asleep and in a REM cycle

- Internal knowing, a gut feeling, or strong pull sometimes accompanied by a thought process or hearing messages like "Dona"

Now let's look at each intuitive subtype after a brief story from a sensitive-intuitive, Anita, an intuitive health coach.

ANITA'S STORY

If you are reading this, it is meant for you to see in some way, perhaps to help you gain insight or perspective. My whole life, from age 2 to 42, has been about change, moving, love, fear, and loss. I was a military child, an Air Force member, and then the moving continued. This was normal to me, all I knew, and I considered it good.

After many years of that lifestyle, in my late twenties and early thirties, it brought me anxiety and depression. I became noncommittal. My isolation drove me to dig deeper inside myself. I was depressed. It is the scariest thing imaginable to feel so low. I went through years of emotional pain, stress, isolation, and loss. I developed panic attacks, and I was hospitalized to address them. The reason why is complicated; suffice it to say that I was different and didn't know it. I was extremely intuitive. Not knowing or understanding this caused a lot of turmoil. I picked up on everything said and unsaid, to the point where I told myself I must be crazy, because "why else isn't everyone else seeing and feeling what I am?"

What got me through that terrible time was my tenacity and resilience. Building a relationship with my intuitive ability in subsequent years has been the most enlightening, wondrous, and mind-blowing journey I could have ever imagined. With such laser-sharp intuition, you question everything and everyone, looking for the truth. You learn how to find the answers in the most loving and painful ways. Sometimes you question your own sanity.

And then you regain balance. You learn who you are and that you are responsible for creating your own reality.

The Felt Sense

Sensitive-intuitives who use their feelings (physical sensations) to guide them have a knack for discerning the felt-sense. This type of sensory intelligence has been applied in the fields of animal communication, sensorimotor psychology, bioenergetic analysis, and mind-body medicine. It works through the intuitive's attunement with the environment or another being (for example, a plant or an animal). It presents largely through the body as an energetic form of communication that may be fleeting. Sensory impressions may be felt in different areas of the body. For this reason it can sometimes be problematic for intuitives. They may not be aware of the meaning of their own subtle feeling states that carry information. Like interoception, which helps us know what the body needs, such as when we are thirsty or hungry, the felt-sense is an internal bodily awareness—except that it reveals subtle energetic information as a response to something exterior to the intuitive.

Many emotional intelligence teachers suggest that sensitive-intuitives use authenticity as a guidepost to help them identify the felt-sense. Authenticity is the ability to discern your true emotional state. By not hiding, suppressing, or covering up feelings, intuitives learn how to know themselves. Like a tranquil pond and sensing the quiet, then throwing a stone into it and watching the ripples of water, an intuitive learns how to observe and track these emotional states in themselves so they can discern patterns or specific fluctuations of energy they encounter. Intuitives who can perceive their own emotional states use the felt-sense as an intuitive mechanism. It cuts through the sensory noise in an environment by feeling or mindfully attuning to their own body. When intense emotional states are projected from others, like aggression (anger), frustration, or sadness, the sensitive-intuitive encounters them. In social situations where people often present a facade or tell fibs for the sake of getting along, an intuitive will sense the inauthenticity by the latent tension they feel. Sensitive-intuitives must learn to trust these intuitive impulses to discern authenticity. The bodily recognition, or felt-sense, of these states may increase as the sensitive becomes more consciously aware of them.

The felt-sense can be viewed as a visceral and instinctual bridge between different feeling states, which directly informs the intuitive. If you'd like to learn more about the felt-sense as it relates to this kind of awareness, authenticity, and healing, it has been written about by psychologist Anodea Judith (author of *Eastern Body, Western Mind*) and Peter Levine (author of *Waking the Tiger*).

The Visual Sense

The visual sense is a heightened awareness of visual stimuli. It helps shape how your brain interprets the things you see. It is one of the most fascinating kinds of intuition. Information, largely delivered through images, influences the intuitive through spatial awareness, subtle visual cues, and pattern recognition. Like having a vivid imagination or experiencing a lucid dream, the intuitive brings something of himself or herself to the experience. Sensitive-intuitives for whom the visual sense is magnified may also receive messages in their mind's eye during meditation or when working with their imagination, perceiving images, colors, and vibrant scenery. These images inform intuitives about their environment.

Legendary film director Martin Scorsese considers this kind of inner vision an actual language.[21] A sensitive individual may or may not have an overall visual sensory intelligence that interprets meaning from images. Scorsese calls this intelligence *visual literacy*. Scorsese, a gifted sensitive-visionary, believes visual literacy is as important as verbal literacy, due to the increased demand on society to process information through images: "For the younger people, born into this world, it is crucial that they get guided and learn the differences between art and pure commerce." This kind of intuition may be associated with visual-spatial learning, thinking in pictures rather than words. Some visual learners rely more upon the right hemispheric intuitive functions of the brain. Relying on the right hemisphere, which is preferential for spatial awareness, facial recognition, visual imagery, and music interpretation, heightens a sensitive's visual acuity. As stated earlier both hemispheres are usually involved in multisensory processing, although individuals who are sensitive may rely more on unique sensory pathways, which can be considered generally as right hemispheric action.

Some theorists suggest that the sensitive-intuitive has a highly functioning faculty called the mind's eye, where they perceive and detect information. We can all learn to call upon the mind's eye through meditation. Sensitive-intuitive people have an automatic ability to perceive through this mental-visual function. An early adopter of this idea was Thomas West. In his 1991 book *In the Mind's Eye*, he suggests that students and employees in the future will require strong visual skills. He said we would need "ready recognition of larger patterns, intuition, a sense of proportion, imaginative vision, the original and unexpected approach, and the apt connection between apparently unrelated things."[22] It seems we are already there.

In educational settings, the gift for visual-spatial learning may be overlooked. Linda Kreger Silverman, Ph.D., author of the groundbreaking book *Upside-Down Brilliance,* explains how she first discovered the visual sense while working with children with learning differences, such as dyslexia. "The first child I observed with unusual visual-spatial abilities was profoundly gifted (above 175 IQ). So I assumed that visual-spatial learners were profoundly gifted. Then, I discovered that children who fit the characteristics of giftedness but did not test in the gifted range due to hidden learning disabilities, were usually visual-spatial learners."[23]

The Aural Sense

The aural sense, which is associated with auditory perception (hearing), is the ability to perceive sound waves by sensing vibrations with the ear that are generated by changes in the pressure of the surrounding medium (usually air, possibly water or another substance). The brain interprets the vibrations. For a highly sensitive person for whom the aural sense is vibrant, it also crosses over into the realm of inner experience where meaning is assigned. Physicist Albert Einstein, who said "imagination is more important than knowledge," often perceived mathematical solutions through musical vibrations.[24] A profoundly innovative thinker, Einstein's scientific sensibility was highly intuitive.

One of the less-celebrated facets of Einstein's life was the influence music had on his creativity, learning, moods, temperament, and thinking processes. He played the violin and reportedly might have chosen to be a musician had he not gone into the field of mathematics. He said, "I live my daydreams in music. I see my life in terms of music."[25] We can witness melodic influences embedded within his theories, which are balanced, elegant, harmonious, unified, and infused with simplicity. He made advances in our understanding of the mathematics of physics, light, matter, energy, time, and gravity. Music perceived through his heightened aural sense helped him relax, focus, and tap into his creativity. When sensitive-intuitives relax and use music to enhance states of deeper calm using the aural sense, it helps release stress. Einstein surely felt this inner calm through his deep connection to music.

A sensitive-intuitive with a gift for musical composition is Cuban composer Aldo López-Gavilán. In an interview on *Performance Today* about his composition *Emporium* he said, "I heard the score clearly in my head, but when I began to play, it was very difficult."[26] Hearing the music, melody, or vibration may not always translate to the other senses being able to match what was so profoundly heard, felt, and perceived. Sensitive-intuitives have the distinct ability to process the depth of this aural function. Sensitives who use this sense may hear multiple levels of music, like a good composer who can tease out all the different sections of the band, chorus, or instrumentals.

At Johns Hopkins University, a study was done which involved music and aural learning. Aural learning in this capacity was studied by the way the brain naturally encoded musical concepts. The type of encoding studied focused specifically on self-censoring, internalizing musical sounds, and improvisation while creating a new composition. Researchers studied jazz musicians who improvised on their instruments in an MRI machine. While the musicians created musical ideas using their aural sense, the process of conceiving and executing a musical idea was more fluid and spontaneous (a form of aural intuition). During this process the medial prefrontal cortex was stimulated, an area of the brain linked with self-expression and activities that convey individuality. Since jazz music doesn't rely upon words to convey meaning, the more the musicians relied on their purely aural sense, the more creative their musical ideas became.

Lucid Dreaming

Lucid dreaming occurs through visual and somatic awareness. It is the distinct feeling of being awake or conscious while dreaming. Lucid dreaming happens during the REM cycle of sleep and has been used effectively to treat nightmares, help increase motor movements in physical therapy, and improve sports performance. Sometimes the lucid dreamer consciously directs dream content to receive intuitive answers to real-life problems. I call this process *lucid dream-intuition*. Lucid dream-intuition has been explored mainly as an esoteric concept in the past by highly visual dreamers documenting mystical phenomena, such as shaman Carlos Castaneda, dream teacher Robert Moss, and spiritual medium Jane Roberts.

Tibetan Buddhism has a form of esoteric healing called *dream yoga*, where the depths of lucid dreaming correspond to four levels of higher awareness using the *dream body* or *vision body*. The four levels are *awareness* (recognizing that we are dreaming), *transformation* (learning how to interpret fear), *multiplying* (receiving radiant light from a universal stream of energy), and *unification* (uniting with light from the universal). The goal of achieving these states is to become awake while dreaming. Buddha, through his enlightenment, became spiritually awake. During Buddha's journey to enlightenment (or awakening process) spiritually and philosophically, he taught that we may be the most spiritually awake in deep dreamless sleep and most asleep in so-called waking reality. Therefore, seeking enlightenment in waking life, we can use our dreams to "wake up" or become fully conscious within dream states because dreams are one type of illusion. Lucid dreaming is considered the launching pad for exploring deep inner space intuitively where we can understand the machinations of our own mind. Theoretically in dream yoga, lucid dreaming is considered a *nocturnal meditation* that mirrors waking meditation, when we practice mindfulness and learn our fears. We can also use it to empower ourselves. When you are a lucid dreamer and you become aware within your dreams, you can learn through developed states of consciousness: you do not need to fear your own mind.

Modern science has begun to study how intuition is related to various brainwave states, including alpha, theta, and beta sleep states. Alpha is used in watching television or during reading, when the attention is focused on something while there is also a light relaxation. Delta is the deepest state of relaxation and occurs during REM sleep. These sleep states are interconnected with the different processing levels of the mind (conscious, unconscious).

Studies show that lucid dreaming during REM can be used to understand the underpinnings of altered states of consciousness, such as psychosis and nightmares. Conversely the beneficial attributes have been described by lucid dream researchers as "being able to reason clearly, to remember the conditions of waking life, and to act voluntarily within the dream."[27] Lucid dream intuition is a fluid intelligence that guides a dreamer into unresolved mental or emotional content that they need to address for healing. Dream intuition also helps solve problems by using colorful messages that a dreamer relates to through personal symbols the dreamer emotionally associates with.

Clinically psychotherapists like Lauren Garrett have posited that the intensity of lucid dream content may have "a significant impact on the waking state nervous system" through the existence of a somatic awareness called the dream body. In her research she draws upon clinical researchers Ogden, Minton, and Pain,[28] who connected a proprioceptive dream body, a somatic or physical intelligence, to both waking and dream neural networks. During a traumatic experience, the somatic dream body connects to both hypo- and hyper-aroused nervous system states. As we know intuitive-empaths have an advanced perception of the felt-sense or somatic awareness. This ability may be used in dreams as an intuitive intelligence. It may communicate feeling states of the body through dream content so we may consciously understand signals of physical distress or emotional upsets. Dream yoga would propose that when these states are consciously realized by the intuitive-dreamer, they can be transformed in waking life.

REM is one of the deepest kinds of sleep and researchers have connected REM with different forms of intuitive lucid dream awareness, such as out-of-body experiences, telepathy, psychic thought, and precognition. These different modes of intuitive dreaming may be connected to our five separate types of brainwave (or neuronal) activity while we are falling asleep and remaining asleep. They are alpha, beta, delta, gamma, and theta brainwaves. Each has a distinct purpose and help us by releasing different neurotransmitters to activate specific sleep states. Neurologically, during dreaming, these various frequencies help humans to rest, repair, and balance mental functioning. Good sleep hygiene, habits, and practices that increase restful sleep cycles help the dreamer cope with complex stressors from daily life and increase intuition. There is even a rebound effect: if we miss a night of sleep, the brain resets the sleep schedule to make up for this lost sleep time. This compensatory effect helps restore functions through proper sleep, even when healing our emotions. If our brainwave activity gets maxed out, we will suffer from too much (or too little) energy in our brain and we feel less intuitive.

Our brain waves work as an overall balancing function to help us synthesize the day's events. Some research has shown a possible link between mindfulness, meditation, and lucid dreaming. In 2015, researchers studied *meta-awareness*, the ability to be aware with focused attention on one's individual thought patterns, during the day and night, including the relationship between mindfulness and lucid dreaming.[29] Their results showed that the frequency of lucid dreams was found to be related to achieving higher states of mind to enhance positive moods and mindfulness while awake. This relationship was only present in those participants who reported a familiarity and practice of regular meditation.

Dream intuition typically occurs as an extension of waking intuition, except it happens when we are at rest too. The research studies mentioned may be precursors to understanding this delicate effect. If we have a natural ability and fluidity of our thought process during the daytime, it makes sense that we would use more efficient states of cognitive function while at rest. If, like this last study showed, mindfulness is one avenue for achieving such states, we may be able to increase lucid dreaming and intuition when we practice mindful awareness. Often this is felt as a stroke of genius during the dream. We wake up with an "Aha!" and quickly jot down notes about it (if we are diligent).

The tricky part about dream intuition is that it is highly connected to the context of the dream, and as we all know, when we wake up, we immediately feel the amnesia effect of waking consciousness. If intuitive dream insights are not recorded immediately, the clarity may get lost in the fleeing dream consciousness.

ANNALISE'S STORY

Ever since I was a child, I could remember dreams with great detail. My parents started to notice a weird pattern. Sometimes I would dream of a family member getting sick or passing away. They didn't make a big deal about it, and I was a serious kid, so they took me seriously versus chalking it up to childhood embellishment. I felt this ability randomly throughout my life. One time I woke up and remembered that I saw a woman who said her name was Anna. I saw her big as life in my dream. She told me to contact her son and tell him she would see him soon. While I do work in the celebrity world, I had no idea who this woman was or what she was talking about. Tragically I found out several days later who Anna Nicole Smith was after her son Daniel passed away in the Bahamas.

Internal Knowing

Also known as *intuitive cognition* or *anomalous cognition*, internal knowing is the outcome of a full range of sensory modes that are separate from reasoning or rationality. The collective senses are working through a higher-order process considered sensory intelligence. This is a lightning-fast consciousness that perceives, analyzes, and judges so we may act.

You could say that internal knowing is metasensory awareness. If *metathinking* is "thoughts about thoughts," *metasensing* is perceiving sensory information at a higher level of awareness. These metasenses are more impersonal than our routine processing of sensory information and considered beyond the self, sometimes even spiritual. In some theosophical circles such as Waldorf School education and anthroposophy designed by Dr. Rudolf Steiner, intuitive thinking is considered a spiritual path. Steiner believed the metasenses developed so we may experience the primordial reality, cosmic field, nonlocal consciousness, or the expanded reality. This access to universal consciousness shapes humankind when sensitive-intuitives perceive the universal intelligence and interpret the meaning. Anthroposophical schools teach intuition as a peaked form of metacognition, which is possible to achieve but is susceptible to cognitive distortion. Cognitive distortion comes through dissonance, or opposing mental forces (such as judgment, analysis, and criticism). This distortion filters inward toward the analytic mind, which translates abstract information into symbols and other representations.

Intuitive thought has been used in spiritual models to describe nonlinear reality. For example, Helena Blavatsky was a forerunner of using intuition to contact the cosmic plane and receive universal insights. Her work was highly controversial and the intuitive methods she used were well documented. She used intuition to receive higher universal knowledge through what she called a "spiritual body." Intuition can be explained without the spiritual undertones as thoughts and feelings that bend time and space. Examples include psychic ability like clairvoyance and telepathy. These perceptions are not integrated or processed by our typical rational thought process. They are pure cognition. They come from outside the normal range of the time and space continuum, revealing some fact or truth that was formerly unknown.

Due to our preference for logical, linear, and rational thought, humanity may have lost some of its purely instinctive, intuitive perception. Intuitive thought is independent thinking. It does not rely upon words and logic for realization. If intuitive thought is rooted in the spiritual sensory experience, we can attribute it as having individual meaning for the seeker. Intuitive cognitions may arrive through mental pictures, imaginative musing, creative inspiration, and strengthening of will.

Famous sensitive-intuitives include Albert Einstein, Carl Jung, Charles Schwab, Frida Kahlo, Forest Whitaker, George Washington Carver, Jada Pinkett Smith, Keanu Reeves, Marie Curie, Nikola Tesla, Richard Branson, Caroline Myss, and Tom Cruise.

CHAPTER 4

SENSITIVE VISION

He goes into his brain and then you just see he is in another world. He still does that. Now I just leave him be because I know he is designing a new rocket or something.[1]

— MAYE MUSK, ELON MUSK'S MOTHER

Sensitive-visionaries are magical innovators who use their sensory intelligence to imagine and create a new reality. Whether they are developing new technology or dreaming of a better world, these remarkable individuals are the futurists who bring solutions into the light for the benefit of humankind. Through their expansive inner sight, they see possibilities that have not yet materialized. Their imaginative pursuits carry them into inner worlds where they see how they can develop modern solutions to societal problems. When they marry patience, commitment, and leadership with their visionary qualities, they turn imagination into opportunity. The sensitive-visionary intelligence is clearly identifiable through examples of scientists from past centuries, such as Leonardo da Vinci and Michael Faraday, and from our current century, like Elon Musk, the creator of PayPal, Tesla, and SpaceX.

Some sensitive people might share a feeling of separateness or otherness. For the sensitive-visionary, this is a distinctive sign.

Visionaries are highly innovative, and they enjoy novel experiences. They are willing to spend much of their time immersed in their specific areas of interest. These interests, while exciting to them, may bewilder others. Whether the innovation is a fascination with film editing, mathematics and string theory, or performance art, visionaries have in common this sense of total immersion into their passions.

As we have discussed, visual acuity relies upon the sensitivity and interpretative function of specific areas of the brain. The highly attuned visual sense of visionaries keeps them emotionally invested in doing things that involve visual problem solving. If you are a visionary, you may feel drawn to fields where you can put your acute spatial awareness to work, among them the fields of architecture, home construction, city planning, engineering, videography, cinematography, interior design, film theory, photography, stage design, computer software coding, and graphic design.

One of the unique problems that visionaries face is that they are making mental leaps forward in time as they envision future solutions to real-world problems. While this gift sets them apart in a positive light, it can also be difficult for them to communicate when their contemporaries do not understand their inner worlds, their fascination with creation, or their innovative thinking. An example of this is Elon Musk's early childhood. He was taunted ruthlessly by other children for his differences, particularly his inventive creativity.[2] According to several biographies, when he was a small boy, he had been unable to fight back against several local school bullies. At 15 he studied martial arts and learned to hold his ground.[3] The decade between grade school and high school is an awfully long period for a child to have to defend his right to think creatively. Because they are dreamers by nature, the futurists of our society are often so far ahead of the curve that they are viewed as odd and get picked on in childhood—even if these same traits earn them recognition and praise in adulthood. Most visionaries are painfully aware of the difference in their perspective and will retreat inward where they can rely on their own storehouse of knowledge and imagination for safety and comfort.

Visionaries have an inherently productive nature, which is driven by a solutions-oriented style of creativity. They anticipate future events and can perceive opportunities for societal advancement by providing new creations our society needs. These futurists' advancements are often read about in science fiction before they become reality. Take for example Michio Kaku's future vision of a time when scientists push the boundaries of physics by opening a "gateway or portal to another universe" using artificial intelligence. To create this portal into a parallel universe he imagines the physics would require "fabulous amounts of energy."

Kaku created a theoretical computer-generated model of an atom smasher half a billion miles long to envision how travel to a parallel universe might be possible. He constructed a visual example of his atom smasher around an asteroid belt of our solar system. In his construction, Kaku used twin beams of particles in opposite directions to activate his portal by directing them at imaginary base stations. In Kaku's example he uses the enormous energetic potential around the earth's magnetic and electric fields to bend the beams' particles. Through explosive force they rip open a hole in time and space. His excitement is palpable as he explains this action: "Accelerated beams are gradually bent into an elegant orbit around the sun by a succession of bases." To stabilize the small rip or hole Kaku created in space-time, he further explains, "We need negative matter to create a wormhole. We are going to inject tiny molecular robots where I will have already programmed these robots with all the information necessary to seek out habitable planets and to construct a new me on the other side." It sounds like reading science fiction out of a Philip K. Dick novel. Although as Kaku describes re-creating a copy of himself on the other side of his parallel universe stargate, he has already envisioned and theoretically created our one-way ticket "through the rabbit hole." Eventually science will use such theoretical models created by visionaries like Michio Kaku.

Novelists weave the possibilities of future societies into their narratives, highlighting current-day issues by magnifying them for readers to explore philosophically. I would hazard a guess that authors Madeleine L'Engle, Isaac Asimov, and Suzanne Collins were and are sensitive-visionaries. They were blessed with the gift to perceive societal threats clearly and their writings reflect a strong desire to bring their out-of-the-box style of thinking to the process of finding solutions for them.

The dangers of being a visionary are being prone to anxiety and spaciness, trance states, distraction, ungroundedness, or highly divergent thinking (to the point of becoming delusional or paranoid in the extreme). When visionaries are not supported in their dreams, visions, and aspirations, their sensitivity will trigger feelings of frustration, melancholy, anger, impatience, and loneliness.

They see life so utterly differently than most of the population in a contrast between their imagined reality and what life is like. If their heightened visual acuity is paired with aesthetic sensitivity, they can create beauty and precision. This intelligence literally transforms problem solving through *visual perfection*. The vast difference between their idea of perfection and life's blemishes creates deep discord in the subconscious, or inner conflict. If this is the case, visionaries will feel a deep need for human connection and belonging. This is the remedy for visually disconnecting from the external world. Like everybody else, their perseverance is necessary to forge reality from their dreams. However, due to their sensitivity, they can get maxed out from the intensity of the mental and visual sensations they experience. If they are not careful, such sensations can lead to cognitive overwhelm. When this happens their emotions run dangerously high. If they are unable to disconnect, to use their gifts for entertainment and escapism, their frustration becomes an emotional pressure cooker. It is essential for sensitive-visionaries to develop skills to calm their central nervous systems so they may regroup and accurately discern between taxed emotions and too much sensory input.

Sensitive-visionaries can learn to use their visual focus to relax. Meditation and movement modalities can relieve mental tension. As a result their depth of processing can expand and they discern or "see," "feel," and "hear" more of reality.

JANE'S STORY

Whenever Jane lost her car keys, which was often, she would call her husband, Martin. He always found them by searching what he called his "mind map." Jane learned from Martin's mother that he was a wily, creative kid. He was given ample time in childhood to roam the woods behind their house, solving mysteries. Unencumbered by any kind of restriction, he reportedly used his imagination to investigate cases he saw on TV. In his spare time, he loved organizing his vintage sports memorabilia. When I met Jane, she told me of Martin's remarkable "superpower." He could easily find lost items like her wallet, earrings, or a bill pile by mentally searching through their house. He could also recall specific details of someone's face, memorize combinations of numbers, and give directions easily. When I finally met Martin, we discussed how he discovered his visual giftedness.

I don't really like to talk about my early years because they were rough. I spaced out in class and my second-grade teacher told my mom I spent a lot of time "looking out the window." I feel some shame about that. When they came to announce students for the gifted program and I didn't get called I remember feeling awful, like, why didn't I make the cut? In high school I found a math niche. The elegant maths like physics blew my mind. Computers fascinated me! I could spend hours in the lab learning code. When a subject catches me, I don't burn out when my interest is high. Physics is beautiful and engrossing. Finding Jane's car keys . . . Yeah, that gets kind of annoying. What's easy for me seems incredibly difficult for her.

I think a lot of people who have cool visual spatial stuff going on don't even realize it. I started to notice it when I was in college, people around me needed my sense of direction. It's funny now when I think about it. If we were going out to a new place and a friend would have too many beers, he would ask me to drive him home because I could remember where he lived. Word got out and I became DD [designated driver] for most of the kids in my dorm. It can be a little monotonous when people figure this out about you because they rely on you for all kinds of menial, tedious stuff.

VISUAL-SPATIAL INTELLIGENCE

Visionaries are gifted with visual-spatial intelligence. It processes their environment holistically in images. They have easy access to the mind's eye. The visual mental skills associated with this intelligence are the ability to mentally manipulate two-dimensional and three-dimensional objects or figures in space. They can identify and analyze geometric and visual space through high-functioning depth perception. Maintenance of body image, visual recognition of aspects of musical stimuli, and comprehension of expression have all been linked with visual-spatial skills located predominantly in the right hemisphere.

Developmental psychologist Howard Gardner defined the theory of multiple intelligence. In his theory of eight distinct intelligences, he brought acceptance and prominence to visual-spatial intelligence. It was first described by Gardner as "a human computational capacity that provides the ability or mental skill to solve spatial problems of navigation, visualization of objects from different angles and space, faces or scenes recognition, or to notice fine details."[4]

There are two important concepts in visual-spatial intelligence. First is the concept of physically seeing with our eyes and then the brain's interpretation of these visual perceptions (interpreted through visual cortex in the occipital lobe). Second is the projection of the mind's eye, which has been described as a mental screen or visual-spatial processor used to holographically project reality within the mental field.

An intelligence provides the ability to solve problems or create solutions that are valued in a culture. Spatial intelligence is a visually based neural-mapping system that is activated by internal and external visual stimulation. Your visual intelligence reveals itself practically as an eye for detail, being highly aware of your surroundings, or in a photographic memory. As a sensitive-visionary you will always be stimulated by the visual interactions between your tendencies to perceive novel or unique solutions and the opportunities to learn something new.

THE MIND'S EYE

In college I learned there were photoreceptors called rods and cones in the retina of the eye. These specialized receptors help the retina turn energy into neural impulses in an action called *transduction*. Generally, the iris via the pupil controls the amount of light that enters the eye. The lens (behind the pupil) focuses that light so you can stare directly at an object or image. Your retina has several layers. The top three are involved with vision. Within the third layer we find the photosensitive cells of rods and cones. Light travels down the first two layers before your rods and cones sense it. This is pretty standard Anatomy 101 stuff. What I didn't learn about rods and cones until I was much older was that they also connect to the fascinating *parietal eye.*

The parietal eye is known in medical anatomy as a third eye. It is located in the pineal gland. This is the same gland that Descartes studied when he observed reflexes that "bounced off" of it and influenced behavior (physical movement). The parietal eye is photoreceptive as well, though it doesn't physically see images or objects in our visual field like our regular eyes. It has been described as the eye that doesn't see. It is still considered a photosensory organ and part of the epithalamus present in many animal species.

The parietal eye helps regulate circadian rhythms. It also triggers hormone production for thermoregulation, including reproduction. In humans it uses different biochemical detection methods to perceive light. It also has an interior lining that forms a rudimentary system that includes a retina and lens. The most exciting fact I learned about the parietal eye, besides the rods and cones, is that it also connects to the visual cortex. The visual cortex is responsible for conscious processing of visual stimuli.

The brain's *parietal lobe* integrates the sensory information from all sensory receptors in the somatosensory cortex, including the visual cortex. As we have discussed, the somatosensory cortex is the main manager of sensory information from all sensory pathways. It interprets multisensory information and processes it. In one study done with Buddhist monks who practice meditation, mindfulness, and meditative movement, they were able to reduce stimulation from the external environment. It was determined in the study that these practices allow the monks to shut down their parietal lobe to improve and enhance inner focus with the mind's eye.[5] Neurologically, the impetus for reducing parietal lobe activation in Buddhist monks and studying the interior function of the meditator's mind's eye was to understand transcendent experiences.

Individuals like linguistic algorithm developer Clif High, popular podcaster Joe Rogan, and ethnobotanist Terence McKenna have an alternative, subjective understanding of the interior mental functions of the mind's eye. They have described using psychedelics like ayahuasca's "spirit molecule" (Dimethyltryptamine or DMT) to induce hallucinogenic states. Collectively these individuals describe using a nonordinary visionary consciousness and seeing with their mind's eye another world that was more real than real, but is not here in a material existence sense. Through the hallucinogenic effects of DMT, the visual aspects of "tripping" have been described as loss of ego, experiencing a shared reality called hyperspace, knowing the nature of the universe, and traveling through a holographic field (quantum holography). While I don't condone drug use, it is important to learn from individuals who have undergone these experimental trance states. I realize this all sounds mystical. Yet within the mysticism lies strikingly similar experiences that may advance our understanding of ecstatic visionary perception. DMT hallucinogens appear to use a visionary faculty that may offer insight into states of consciousness that involve visual aspects of perception using the mind's eye.

By crossing the threshold of these deep ecstatic states, maybe the parietal eye senses in a different way. Like Dr. Nolan's study on exceptional intuition, sensitive-visionaries could have an advanced function of the visual cortex to see more in the visual spectrum through a rare type of quantum holography. Or visionaries might have highly attuned visual senses that detect and interpret patterns of energetic information. This visual sensory information likely feeds into their neocortex during expanded states of consciousness.

LUCID DREAMS

Recognizing the signs, signals, and subtle traits of inner vision as a form of sensory awareness can be challenging. One of the first identifiers is the vivid lucid dreams visionaries tend to have. Visionaries can wake from a dream and feel like the lines between real life and the dream world dissolve. They may also have difficulty differentiating between the real world and their fantasies. As we learned from the chapter on intuition, lucid dreaming is a function of visual sensory and somatic awareness. Lucid dreaming has been written about from many perspectives, including as a healing mechanism (dream analysis) and through dream yoga (Tibetan Buddhism). Dreams have been used clinically to reduce nightmares in sleep disorders such as night terrors.[6] Remarkably, they have even been used to increase patients physical mobility while undergoing physical therapy when they were taught specific visualizations while lucid dreaming.

Once visionaries have realized they have the gift (or working capacity, if you prefer) to draw upon their imagination to accomplish things, they may use their active imagination to develop an escape route from a harsh outer reality or as a refuge from stress. Dreams often provide the testing grounds to explore their imaginative thinking and healing process. Healthy detachment from reality helps free visionaries from the constraints of physical reality. In the dream state, they can freely explore and test their creative ideas without criticism. Because the dream world uses thought processing that does not rely on verbal communication, it is a faster mode of creative processing. Sometimes visionaries who are experts in their field use their fertile dreams to make discoveries.

THE BENZENE RING

August Kekulé was a German chemist who has been credited with founding modern organic chemistry. There is a famous story about Kekulé's dream that led to the discovery of benzene. Benzene is a carbon-based compound that can link itself to other long chains of carbon molecules. According to Kekulé, during a speech at an 1890 symposium, he was dozing in front of a fire in Ghent, Belgium. He was a professor of chemistry at the time. While dreaming he envisioned a snake biting its tail. He called it "a self-devouring snake." There have been many historical and psychological interpretations of Kekulé's dream, but the essence of all of them fall along the lines of personal symbolism. The way in which Kekulé perceived the snake as devouring its own tail was a foreshadowing symbol of the underlying unity in nature. This representational action led him to discover the long chains of the carbon molecules in the ring that can connect to others.

VISIONARY TRANSCENDENT EXPERIENCES

Transcendent spiritual experiences are closely linked with visual acuity. Many prophets and religious leaders have described visions that illuminate their path or warn them of future events. From Old Testament figures such as Moses, Daniel, Joseph, and Ezekiel, to Carl Jung, whose depth psychology focused on dream interpretation and the shadow side of consciousness; the civil rights leader Martin Luther King, Jr.; and medical intuitive and writer Caroline

Myss, the visionaries I can identify have a knack for foretelling catastrophic events, sensing past lives, and visiting spiritual planes that exist beyond the physical world.

As a longtime dreamer and visual problem solver, I can relate to the expansive state where dreams offer spiritual insight. They transport us to another landscape that is uniquely familiar to the dreamer and also feels like a different world entirely.

Many of my friends and colleagues have shared privately how their dreams inform them about their life's purpose, or a specific mission they feel they are on in this lifetime. Several of them have suggested they literally traveled to a different world in their dreams (parallel universes, different planets, multiverse) that felt like a home they left behind to do work here on Earth. I can share one of my own dreams that depicts this type of content quite clearly.

TAYLOR HIGSON BOSE

My dream started in the auditorium of an academic conference. The audience was in a frenzy awaiting the release of the new science. The collegiate space reminded me of the halls and classrooms I had frequented when I was back in school, at once old world and futuristic. The audience members had small computers to communicate with the session's moderator. I was watching and reading several of the commentators' dialogues describing the introduction of a scientist who would be releasing the information to the public. I recognized the name: Taylor Higson Bose. I knew we had worked together. I typed in my response to the moderator that I knew this scientist personally and had worked with him on different projects. Someone immediately blocked me. I tried typing in the story of our collaboration. Censors removed my entries, leaving only general information about the science.

Suddenly a public relations specialist cut off the chat. She made an announcement that Taylor Higson Bose was at the live televised conference. He came out on the auditorium stage and everyone applauded. The excitement was tangible. Bose described some of his science. He relayed to the live crowd and television audience that he would help introduce the science funded by the government and then return to the private sector, where he would continue working on further advancements. I was aghast. After listening to his speech, I realized I already knew this science and was disappointed he didn't disclose more. In the dream I knew I could use telepathy, so I scanned the apartment I thought he would be staying at while he was in town. There was no sign of his luggage or personal items. Feeling disappointment at knowing he wouldn't be there after the broadcast, I left the auditorium and found myself in the university commissary's kitchen. Telepathically I lifted a ladle from the pot rack overhead. I heard people talking behind me and saw Taylor surrounded by onlookers. He was happy to see me. He warned me about sharing information about the work we did together. The people behind him began to point and whisper, "She's the one he wrote about." Then I realized I was the subject of the study they had released.

I understood his reasons for creating this public perception of distance between us and knew we were still friends despite the politics around the government study. He left the building and I connected to him telepathically asking about the new science. He revealed more of what was studied and I questioned the information release. Before I woke up, he shared a joke about my style of dreaming. He said, "Well, I know how to get your attention." Surprised by his candor and curious as to what he was talking about, I asked what he meant. He replied, "I give you a problem to solve, throw in a little bit of intrigue, and insult you to get your attention." Within the dream I laughed and felt joy, happiness, and relief. Then I woke up...

This dream went into great detail about fields of human development, DNA, learning, energetic influences, and how to tap into human potential. When I woke up from the lucid dream, I was exhilarated and wrote down the complete dialogue between Taylor Higson Bose and myself. I felt like I'd had my own little Einstein moment and was filled with promise at what my dream content explored. It was multidimensional and involved working with highly sensitive people, children, and education. As I told the dream to my husband out loud, I realized Taylor Higson Bose phonetically sounded like the elementary particle Higgs boson, also known as the God particle.

PAST LIFE

Another powerful example of the phenomenon of "seeing" in the mind's eye is the phenomenon of past lives. Here is an example of a young boy whose parents described his "before-life memory" to me during a coaching session. When he was old enough to describe it, the boy had told his parents how he had died in a previous lifetime as a German soldier in World War II. He explained seeing himself dying on the battlefield from a grenade explosion and quickly traveling to an afterlife. He described this colorful world in detail to his mother:

> Our son told us that before he was born, he lived in a primitive hut on the outskirts of a small settlement. The huts had sticks on the outside and the whole thing was cone shaped. On the inside there were two mats to sleep on, located on either side of the room. There was a campfire in the middle. A chimney was a hole in the roof. He said it let the smoke go out. The way he described it to us it sounded like it resembled an Aztec temple, though it was a bit more futuristic because it was made of metal. The walls were made mostly with black metal that had big rivers of energy flowing down them in streams or lines.[7]

In a subsequent conversation when he was a preteen, he was able to remember other details and describe them in his own words. The young man remembered his time living with a group people in the settlement near God. Of his memory of coming back to Earth in his current lifetime, he said:

> I remember that God called me. He said it was time to go, and I went to the temple. Inside there was a box. It was carved out with golden corners, and they were embossed with patterns.

There was a holographic scanner that showed me pictures in the air of my choices for a mother. I saw my options for mothers and remember clearly choosing the most beautiful one. I chose to go. I remember getting younger until I was just a baby.[8]

Although the boy had a clear photographic memory of his before life, he logically doubted this memory of his between-life experiences. This doubt arose as he was describing it to me. His parents had observed his artwork up until then, which continually, almost obsessively, portrayed crashing tanks, airplanes from the World War II era, and Nazi symbols. It appeared to me that his traumatic memories and visions were still active in his conscious mind. His parents reported this had become a very tense issue for them during his first years in school while he socialized with other children. His play was intently focused on war games, acting out battle strategy, and German historical facts. This preoccupation was sometimes misunderstood by other children. While my advice to his parents revolved around helping him direct his passions into pursuits that supported his inner vision, sometimes these mental dreamlike intrusions can be disruptive. I will talk more about healing methods for visionaries who experience past-life memories, and mystical and religious experiences in the last chapter, Soul Medicine and Transcendence.

To external observers, visionaries might seem spaced-out or oblivious to their surroundings. Their tendency to use altered states can be difficult for friends and partners as visionaries are literally "checked out" at those times. Sensitive-visionaries must learn to recognize themselves as such and then get grounded and take action. They would thoroughly enjoy learning to create opportunities for themselves and diminish social problems. Once they have recognized their gift, visionaries can learn the tricks, tools, and life skills of self-inquiry and reflection, which will help them navigate the mundane world of conventionality and find valuable context for their gifts.

The sensitive-visionary often perceives the world from novel angles. Their gift for spatial awareness enables them to turn objects and scenes over in their minds and explore their dimensions. So often because of their spatial recognition and original thinking they can design, envision, and imagine exciting new possibilities. They are natural-born architects, creative directors, engineers, and designers. Famous sensitive-visionaries include Andrew Wyeth, Alice Walker, César Chávez, Jorge Luis Borges, Frank Lloyd Wright, Madeleine L'Engle, Martin Luther King, Jr., Pablo Picasso, Steven Spielberg, and Walter Murch.

CHAPTER 5

SENSITIVE EXPRESSION

All the world's a stage, and all the men and women merely players; they have their exits and their entrances, and one man in his time plays many parts.[1]

— WILLIAM SHAKESPEARE

Sensitive-expressives harmonize or attune their inner self to their environment through their sensibility for *artistic fusion*. Artistic fusion is the synthesis, or process of combing two or more distinct aesthetic influences, into a whole. For expressives this means they feel deeply aware or in tune with nature, other people, and environments, and they naturally translate *aesthetic meaning*. Using their heightened awareness of beauty, a specific type of aesthetic sensitivity, they use complex emotional and aesthetic sensing to respond to the dynamics between the intensity they feel, beauty they see, and interplay of living life. Expressives have a gift for communicating what takes place within this dynamic fusion of self, nature, and with others through eloquent expression. What makes the sensitivity-expressive so unique is that *they share what they synthesize*.

Whether it is done through verbal means, like writing and singing, or nonverbal means, like dancing or sculpting, expressives harness the power of their imagination through artistic creation. Sensitive-expressives have a creative genius for evoking feelings in others by putting their own feelings into words and physical form. There is one thing that binds all their thoughts, ideas, emotions, and dreams together: the need for a physical outlet. They must express themselves routinely or else they may feel stifled, lethargic, and ill.

Expressive people always aim to infuse meaning into their creations. They use their minds and spirits to find inner meaning through contacting their muse and bringing its message to the world. The muse brings insights about the mysteries of the human experience. Sensitive-expressives can sense the meaning of language and symbols presented through art. Their artistry is their vehicle for influencing others, including society. When expressives depict the problems of our age, they do so with aplomb. Their creations can be transformative. Their challenge, however, is that they have such a deep desire for meaning that they are often left feeling unfulfilled or dissatisfied with life. Due to this inherent drive to find meaning through art, sensitive-expressives make incredible actors, art historians, art teachers, choreographers, costume designers, communications professionals, dancers, graphic designers, interior designers, filmmakers, linguistic experts, literary reviewers, musicians, painters, performance artists, potters, screenwriters, and writers.

The stereotype of the starving artist would suit many expressives. They tend to become frustrated by societal norms. This frustration drives artists to form colonies of likeminded people, places where they can have freedom of expression and live outside restrictive constraints. Their own creativity is challenging enough without "straights" judging them.

Creativity is a powerful driving force that burns from within their skin and bones. When it is infused with the instincts and wisdom of their hearts, this type of creativity lights up those who encounter it. It is no coincidence that music is often described as soulful, that books can touch the heart, or that paintings can transcend our reality with vivid imagery. Sensitive-expressives have the gift of pulling us into their world so we may perceive life's meaning through their eyes. Their art is the mirror through which we peer at ourselves.

If an expressive is walking along a picturesque beach alone and sees one shell that feels out of place, they would likely ask themselves why. They may suffer emotional imbalances due to experiencing too much pain and heartache. Feelings of loss underlie their despair. This sense of loss may build up to the point that they decide that they don't fit in and never will. Ongoing grief is a burden they often cannot avoid carrying.

In terms of expressive artists such as musicians, we need to look no further than the iconic masters Bob Dylan, Jimi Hendrix, Kurt Cobain, Janis Joplin, John Lennon, Marvin Gaye, Miles Davis, Nina Simone, Paul McCartney, and Ella Fitzgerald. Sensitivity allowed these creative artists to harness their inner life. Their songs transformed our reality. Since both hearing and vocals evoke powerful emotions, the creation of music can be a full-bodied revelatory experience when it is made by expressives. Many artists say they transcend normal reality when in the process of musical creation. Musical magic is a combination of being in touch with the artists inner nature, the outer nature, and the divine alchemy—leading to the creation of life itself.

Sensitivity can be used like a tapestry by artists who feel the subtle vibrations of a thought, an emotion, or an attitude. Once they are attuned, they may choose to follow a thread with words, beats, and measure. The process of individuation in each artistic endeavor reveals an artist's translation through their own beautiful language of life, meaning, and purpose.

The composition process is beyond words, of course, but musicians have attempted to describe it. Carlos Santana, who is a staunchly poetic advocate for music and its place in healing our society, has said, "Ever since I was a child, I was always very attracted to melodies. Whether I hear Jeff Beck, or a choir, an ocean, or the wind there is always a melody in there."[2]

Expressive filmmakers are visual storytelling masters. They see stories in their inner vision and then use creative language and images to reveal them to us, to draw us into a story. In his 1891 essay "The Decay of Lying," Irish poet and playwright Oscar Wilde writes: "Life imitates art far more than art imitates life."[3] My interpretation of this line is that he was proposing a new philosophy on the use of artistic expression. Wilde likely saw that life imitating art could serve a healing function through the individuals who dare to strive for true creative artistic expression. Interpreted as an outlet for emotion, art provides a container (no matter which of the various mediums is being explored) for our collective human pain and suffering. It gives us an opportunity for cathartic release. For sensitive-expressives acting, storytelling, and filmmaking are powerful avenues for creating conversations with opposing viewpoints for audiences to explore societal narratives.

EXPRESSIVE ART

Expressive art is the practice of using imagery, music, storytelling, dance, drama, poetry, writing, movement, dreamwork, and visual arts in an integrated way to foster human growth, learning, and healing. In expressive art theory, art that reflects life is not merely an imitative instinct. Expressive art creates a mirror for humanity's self-conscious desire. It provides an outlet for true self-expression. Art drives human self-actualization. If dreams can be viewed, like Jung proposed, as a healing mechanism for transforming images within the collective unconscious, art can provide a similar transformative healing action. The two are not too far apart. Dreamers and artists are similar. They are quintessential creators of different unknown realities where anything is possible. Lori Fox, one of my colleagues, who is also an artist, has called this distinctive healing method, using a visionary function in an elevated spiritual dimension, *transpersonal cinema*.

If the expressive arts can provide outlets for humanity's emotional expression, then sensitive-expressives are the masterful artists born to perceive the wide range of human emotions needing release. Art is one of the highest forms of self-actualization through fulfillment of an artist's talent. Its manifestation helps us realize harmful cultural forces at work such as psychological tension, stereotypes, and the collective intrapsychic energies that need to be purged. One of my favorite artists, Marc Chagall, once said, "Art seems to me to be a state of soul more than anything else." When art serves a social healing function, artists use their art form to actualize and heal humanity's inner conflicts.

Modern storytellers and filmmakers create stories that impact the way we feel and react to life. As I have touched on in other chapters, it is important for us to discern the differences between art as a force for healing and art as exploitative. Life may have always had exploitative or manipulative aspects. However, technological advancements bombard us with more manipulation than ever before. Sensitive-expressives and artists drive through these widespread systems with their own style of expressive art. If today's societies are more inclined to submit to power and control, it will be the artist's job to subvert it and reveal a true cultural identity through the power of their stories.

When expressives are feeling strong and resilient, they can nourish themselves with their creativity and passion; expression is their revitalizing source. Sensitive-expressives can also develop other skills to enhance their gifts of communication, such as deep, reflective, and empathic listening. They feel better and more purposeful if they can learn how to tap into and feel their own healing through self-expression.

Expressive art therapy using art, drama, dance, music, and play can be a great asset to a highly sensitive being who needs help to release pent-up or stifled creative energy. Holding negative memories of trauma or repressing unwanted thoughts can suppress their creative nature. Expressives must create freely and be true to their authentic selves. If they want to be of service, expressives can help others find meaning and significance. This drive might be inherent, born into the sensitive-expressive.

Joseph Campbell touched on this concept in his work on cultural archetypes. He believed all artists had a similar drive guiding them inward. He likened it to an energetic cord pulling them within, where they could explore the subterranean levels of their own creative imagination. Campbell labeled this inner terrain the mythos. It is through this inner world that artists often describe an enlightening contact with their muse. The muse has a historical origin. In Greek mythology the muses included nine sisters who held powers to inspire (or withhold) creative thought. Sensitive-expressive artists travel beyond the ordinary into the realms of the muses and find a creative spark. It might be called a creative lamp of illumination. This light guides them into other worlds that are explored through all their senses. Expressives have the ability to perceive these depths through their heightened awareness and then describe with an articulate brilliance what they come upon. Often they find a new discovery and bring it forth into our world. Joseph Campbell called this specific action of discovery the hero's journey.

In mythic tales when the artist undergoes the hero's journey, they come back revivified and healed. In the case of the performing artist, such as an actor, audience members witness this deep exploration of the self (an archeology of the soul) in connection with the muse.

The world needs sensitive-expressives now because of their ability to restore and balance their own health through the energy of creativity. This gift makes the world a brighter, more caring, and safer place for dealing with the often overwhelming and traumatic experience of being human. Expressive artists give us the confidence to explore our own inner depths because they have made the journey. They reveal to us what was encountered there. Through the great artists of our civilization, we courageously face tragedy, grief, loss, and the comedy of life together as one.

GARY'S STORY

My first scene with Robert Duvall would be in the parlor of the old mansion on a plantation established in the early 1800s. It would be the second setup on the shooting schedule of the first day. The crew of Horton Foote's film Convicts *drove in a caravan to shoot the first day of principal photography. The set was a 30-minute drive in trucks and minivans, past the worn French doors, the interweaving ironworks of New Orleans, tangled metal facades laced into elegant spiderwebs, the graveyards lined with elevated sarcophaguses—in case the levies broke. We passed one parish after another, descended a long bridge to open farmland; wrecked truck bodies from the 1930s, dilapidated barns, goats over misty high grass with cocks crowing morning alert. Cows grazed where time had stopped in the tranquility of local color by a rusted feed tiller. I was about to do a scene in a film with Duvall, something I could hear inside my thoughts over and over again.*

I sat on the porch in an old wooden rocker, working on the sensory drunk required to play this alcoholic, wealthy fop in a top hat. I reviewed my scene and thought about the following scene later that day, when I was supposed to fall off a horse while sodden and drunk. I was to do the stunt myself. As I rocked the chair back and forth, I tried to envision the convicts who worked the farmland in drab gray outfits, the stripes along the legs adding an air of penal formality. I looked out into the rows of yet-to be-grown crops. The sun dawned red and hit the porch as an actor dressed as a convict sat down beside me in the other oak rocker with a coffee cup. James Earl Jones is one big man. "I hope I'm not disturbing you. I can see you are getting into form," he said with perfect CNN depth and clarity.

This was my first conversation with one of the greatest theater actors of our time. James Earl's versatility as an actor is known through a lifetime of recognizable performances. The Tony Award winner was also known on the screen as Mufasa the wise in The Lion King, *Terence Mann in* Field of Dreams, *and Darth Vader in* Star Wars. *He gave me the rich tone of one actor to another, allowing me to work on my character and speak to him as if I were into the fourth snort off my silver flask. I smiled slightly from my sensory drunk and spoke from a faulty Southern accent that I still did not trust. "Sah, you ahh James Ea'l Jones." We laughed. (As an actor I was where I had always dreamed I would be in the best possible sense of that dream.)*

I dropped the accent, the sensory drunk, and told him that in 1975, as a young soap actor, I'd seen his father, Robert Earl Jones, in Death of a Salesman, *starring with and directed by George C. Scott. It was at Circle in the Square, and I had a clear image of his father on stage with Scott. James gazed out onto the rows of seed beds and said in his magnificent baritone, "Ahh . . . Yes."*

I did not expect that response. I had touched some kind of inner pain in him, and we had not yet had two minutes of our first conversation. I became speechless. I did not know what to do. I also did not know I was about to assimilate one of the most salient lessons on the theater and life that I would ever learn. It was not just dealing with "the show must go on," but a deeper insight into the code of life itself; a vision of kneeling before the alter of honor, respect for others, thankful for the gift of basic information by example. It was a lesson of courage and clarity from the mountaintop, the kind that informs and grows the rows of lettuce, beans, and the cotton grown by the farmer. For me it was the music of a simple concept that sustained this actor in his darkest hours of a dangerous profession. "The show must go on" was no longer some meme from the mid-1800s vaudeville venue. Without looking away from the farmland, James told the story of George C. Scott and Robert Earl Jones.

During the run of Death of a Salesman, *he had gotten a call from George inviting him to see the play that night and go backstage after curtain. James did as instructed; saw the play, went backstage. Scott opened the door in full makeup, a white bathrobe, and invited James in to sit. He asked him if he'd like a drink. James thanked him but did not really drink. He said that Scott then sat down, thanked him for coming, that he did not want James to hear about it secondhand, which was the reason for the invite. "George looked at me sadly and said, 'I have to let your father go from the production. He's not up to the task.' George then broke down and sobbed in front of me," he said.*

"I told him I understood, that it was not about any one actor but that the show was all that mattered. It's about the piece—not the actor. I told him that I would speak to my father if George felt too uncomfortable to tell him. But George said it was his responsibility and he had to tell him tonight."

James then went on to say that both actors walked to Robert's dressing room. They sadly informed the 76-year-old actor of his dismissal, and it thereby ended this great man's lifelong acting career running back to the first years of the 20th century. James Earl Jones said his father sat quietly and took it like a pro, also stating that the play was the thing and that he understood. Then they all cried. Three great men of the American stage, in an unforgiving profession whose job it was to ease, enlighten, care for, and entertain the masses. All three cried collectively for the love of the show, its continuation, and the respect they had for those they serve—the audience. The next night Death of a Salesman *did go on—but without Robert Earl Jones. That collective strength of those three men of courage burnished an image into my being for life.*

In Chapter 1, I used Daniel Day-Lewis as a specific example of the sensitive-expressive because his profound personal experience of a sensory anomaly was well documented. Many actors feel this profound depth of their life experience. As you can read through Gary Swanson's preparation while working on the set of *Convicts*, he used his form of acting training to create his character using his own senses, experience, and emotions. His language and expression put us right there with him on set. The eloquence, pace, and language he uses unleashes our imagination. We are there on the porch. We hear and feel the tone of James Earl Jones's sadness that day. We don't need to analyze or interpret the situation. As an actor and artist, Gary has the innate talent to create the environment and let us see, hear, and feel as he does.

In terms of Daniel Day-Lewis's vision, I followed the story as it unfolded. While he may have backtracked years later to minimize the acuity of his visual experience, we can be sure that he was sensitive enough to experience something extraordinary. A visual anomaly that looks real, feels real, and behaves as if it's real can be not only spooky; it's life-changing. It can make us question our identity at a core level.

Defining what that specific experience is has become a kind of hot potato in professional circles. In his time Jung would have called witnessing an image of a deceased loved one a *transpersonal experience* because it transcended the boundaries of normal conscious processing (visually). Day-Lewis's ghost was an internal image brought to life on stage. An image that appeared to move about, speak, and behave as if it was very real in the external environment. Some people would label it a hallucination. But another type of image, called a *hypnagogic image*, can help us understand the difference between a hallucination and other kinds of visual sensory anomalies. *Hypnopompic hallucinations* are visual, tactile, or auditory sensory events that appear in images. They feel utterly real and interactive during transitional states from wakefulness (hypnopompic) to sleep (hypnagogic). Sometimes just before someone falls asleep, an image suddenly appears in the mind's eye that often feels alive. It is called a hallucination because only the perceiver can see, hear, and feel the image. Open-minded contemporary psychologists would probably call it a *spiritually transformative experience* (STE). This term emphasizes how the perceiver felt about the experience more than what the experience was. STEs are defined by the presence of an expanded reality and the augmentation of the senses. Anytime this happens it can cause people to perceive themselves and the world differently. It expands an individual's identity, altering values and perceptions. Usually there is a greater appreciation for the purpose of life.

Sometimes when expressive artists experience a STE and then return to our shared reality, they find that people doubt their story. When this happens sensitives are left absolutely alone to consider the meaning of their expanded view of reality. They must comprehend their enhanced sensory awareness without the loving support of their community. The desire to connect with their community can cause expressives to hide what is happening to them. They might change their view of their experience or put more distance around it by watering down the actual mental and physical aspects of their visions. Fear of being labeled crazy may be the most prevalent reason they doubt their experiences. We typically define seeing something that others don't as delusional, schizophrenic, or hallucinatory. There is a stigma associated with gifted dramatists, musicians, and performers that promotes negation of the sensitive-self. In the extreme, society draws comparisons to vulnerable patients in psychiatric hospitals or artists who have died from substance abuse.

Throughout history many expressive geniuses have described experiencing anomalous phenomena while working in a creative mode. The association between artistic thought and insanity has been established. But this is more of a cliché that only occurs in rare cases. Maybe if we would all embrace a little "healthy madness" occasionally, perhaps by skirting the boundaries of what is socially acceptable, we could reach for genius and inspiration without fear. As Jimi Hendrix once said, "You have to go on and be crazy. Craziness is like heaven."

Famous creatives who struggled with mental health issues, such as clinical depression, bipolar disorder, mood swings, and hallucinations, include Sylvia Plath, Vincent van Gogh, Georgia O'Keeffe, and Ludwig van Beethoven. Sensitive-expressives are right to fear their own magnificent inner natures. Creative artists have one of the highest rates of depression as compared to other professions that have unpredictable long hours, little control, or increased stress such as teachers, accountants, and salespeople. If you asked most artists, they would likely tell you that being artistic wasn't a choice—they live to create.

Maybe the need to create is universal because nature is a huge, expansive, and creative force. Artists feel this natural presence within life in their own special way. They are not divorced from nature's influence within them. For one human, such as an artist, to harness this majesty, she would surely feel overcome frequently. It is just too massive an energy to hold on to for very long.

Some creative artists are masters at transmuting this intense energy. They endow it with personal meaning and serve as conduits for the rest of humanity to witness beauty being unleashed through the human spirit. This is the reason why artists often feel wonder about the human experience. They are capable of being in direct contact with the healing spirit of nature and bringing its forces of energy into a new creative light.

The truly creative mind in any field is no more than this: A human creature born abnormally, inhumanly sensitive. To him . . . a touch is a blow, a sound is a noise, a misfortune is a tragedy, a joy is an ecstasy, a friend is a lover, a lover is a god, and failure is death. Add to this cruelly delicate organism the overpowering necessity to create, create, create— so that without the creating of music or poetry or books or buildings or something of meaning, his very breath is cut off from him. He must create, must pour out creation. By some strange, unknown, inward urgency he is not really alive unless he is creating.

— PEARL S. BUCK

LEE STRASBERG: MASTER
ACTING COACH AND TEACHER

In one of his classes, acting coach Lee Strasberg once said—and I'm paraphrasing—that sensitive people should not be actors. He taught that actors must *learn to be sensitive* by honing their instruments (their bodies and souls). But Strasberg indicated it was difficult for sensitive people to become actors. He attributed it to their more delicate nature.[4] He considered sensitivity an inherent "actor problem" that could hold actors back from authentically expressing their inner lives. It just would become too painful to act. Acclaimed actor Marlon Brando (*On the Waterfront, The Godfather*) may have agreed with Strasberg, who was connected with him at the Group Theater. Brando reportedly said, as a word of advice to younger actors, "The more sensitive you are, the more certain you are to be brutalized, develop scabs. Never evolve. Never allow yourself to feel anything, because you always feel too much."[5] It's a tough attitude toward performance. Perhaps developing a thick skin enabled him to survive his craft.

Despite the criticism about creative people being overly sensitive, it is possible for sensitive-expressives to thrive in cold and callous settings, including the entertainment industry, which is known for its uncaring commercialism and exploitation of artists for profit. History has shown this is possible. Modern examples of creatives who are also sensitive include Denzel Washington, Jessica Chastain, Ryan Gosling, John Leguizamo, Viola Davis, Will Smith, J. J. Abrams, Ellen DeGeneres, and Tiffany Haddish. These are prime examples of sensitive-expressives who use their talents to great effect, bringing laughter, tears, and joy to all they reach.

GENA'S STORY

I was an abnormally quiet child. I couldn't communicate. I took everything in, except I didn't verbally express myself like other kids. My mom brought me to a speech therapist, because despite the fact that I tested normally by all the doctors' and schools' standards, I wouldn't talk. They called it mutism *and labeled me "special ed." Thank God for my artistic mother. Mom fought for me and steered me toward art as an outlet. By the time I was in middle school, I was communicating better, although I still struggled as a wallflower. During a high school drama camp, the acting coach noticed I wouldn't take my shoes off and stayed away from the other kids most of the time. It became a big deal since we were asked to explore our grounding and feel the grass, sand, and dirt without shoes. I hadn't realized how self-conscious I was. I feared touch. As Coach pressured me to confront my fear, I started experiencing serious mental health symptoms that were obvious ticks (OCD), and my ability to communicate shut down again. The camp counselors suggested I take a break and receive some counseling—my issues were more than they could help with. Using art therapy I was able to push through my fear of touch and recognize how my anxious mind was trying to protect my body. I was compensating for extreme social anxiety issues. After four months of intense art therapy, I was able to process my fear and returned to drama camp a year later. As I finished the final showcase, I found a unique edge I had: comedy! One of the acting teachers pulled me aside after my final project and recommended that I continue developing this talent. I prepared for a long time. When I did a comedy routine a local comedy club (in New York City), all the acting students came to watch and cheer me on. I felt a huge moment of triumph! From the comedy gig, I got picked up by a famous late-night talk show host and I write scripts now.*

Sensitive-expressives are always confronting the biggest existential question: "What is the meaning of life?" Due to their willingness to delve into these mysteries, they provide us with the songs, images, and stories conceived from their own vantage points that give us answers, and move, educate, and uplift us. They make us laugh and open our hearts. Their art helps us expand outside of our day-to-day realities and touch the radiance of our common human condition—art becomes salve for the collective soul.

Next we'll delve into the Mind-Body Method, a structured plan you can follow to identify how your sensitivity may be challenging. Through the second half of this book, I describe unique coping mechanisms I have found that sensitive people can develop as sensory defenses for extreme sensitivity. Then I discuss the healing modalities you can use for self-care.

Part II

THE MIND-BODY METHOD

CHAPTER 6

SENSORY SELF-DEFENSE

Shyness is invariably a suppression of something.
It's almost a fear of what you're capable of.[1]

— RHYS IFANS

Sensitivity develops in response to both positive and negative environments.[2] It has been argued by researchers that sensory processing sensitivity helps mediate intense early-life experiences. When viewed beneficially, sensitivity is considered an attribute that enhances flexibility, which increases reactivity. Sensitives are more readily responsive within an environment, and we have the ability to focus ourselves with an engrossing concentration.[3] Sensitive people who have had early-life experiences that are traumatic tend to be more negatively affected by their subtle sensory processing due to the overwhelming power and intensity of their emotions. This type of sensory defense mechanism connects with *emotional reactivity*. Extensive studies have shown that while sensory processing sensitivity is not a clinical disorder, the disrupting effects of emotional reactivity clearly co-occur with anxiety and depression.[4]

Faster sensory discernment affects cognitive ability as sensory information travels through different neural substrates. Then it activates emotional reactivity that affects somatic (physical) and interoceptive (internal) awareness. By understanding global sensory processing in the brain, difficulty with sensory integration can be understood through unique styles of sensory defense. Sensory defense is the mind and body's way of alleviating extreme sensations as they flood inward into one's awareness.

When the somatosensory cortex perceives sensory information through the five senses, it translates this information through a highly sensitive person's unique mechanisms (discriminative sensory functions) of sensory processing. The sensory processing system's neural networks create cortical representations and translate them into auditory, somatic, and visual information. Due to the complex inner workings of the somatosensory cortex and its influence on these cortical representations, sensory modulation predicts the efficiency of sensory integration. When a sensitive individual perceives floods of sensory information from environmental stimuli (bright lights, loud noises, or emotions from others), they may have sensory processing difficulties.[5] Sensory modulation helps regulate and scale responses to the environment. When effective sensory integration fails, through unique physiological reactions[6] and brain activity,[7] more pain is felt physically, emotionally, and mentally.

In this section of the book, I lay out a four-week Mind-Body Method to help you identify your unique sensory processing style. Using the MBM helps you to maximize your gift rather than using old cognitive patterns to perceive reality. For sensitives, what appears trivial might spark an internal emotional chain reaction that leads to a shutdown. Let's step away from using any kind of judgment when learning how you might be compensating for heightened sensory awareness. At its base level, sensory defense is only a coping mechanism to combat the intensity from sensory overload—it has nothing to do with how strong or capable you are. The first target of the MBM is to identify *warning sensations*. Intense sensations are not emotions, although they are usually confused for such by sensitives because of their highly tuned nervous systems. The next step in the method works to ameliorate long-term patterns held in the mind and body by releasing stored tension (such as abdominal, neck, and back pain).

Identifying past patterns of heightened emotional reactivity as it relates to processing sensory information is game-changing. The end result is feeling more balance and freedom in daily life. We may not be able to rid ourselves completely of annoying symptoms of sensitivity. We can become excellent sensors for what triggers them. From the time people gifted with heightened sensory abilities are small children, we are highly aware. The struggle we face, as sensitives, is not in achieving a higher form of consciousness. What we grapple with most is the balancing act of being highly aware and participating fully in the world without feeling a need to shut down or wanting to anesthetize ourselves to avoid pain and people. These issues stem from fear—of loneliness, pain, rejection, and shame, and of having a breakdown because we cannot cope. Consider this mental, physical, and spiritual balancing act as being twofold. We feel unresolved pain in mind and body from past trauma and overwhelm, while we continually confront new sensory information flowing inward.

When this combination escalates and we aren't taking the time for routine, self-healing hypersensitivity develops. Hypersensitivity is extreme emotional fragility. There are two different theories about hypersensitivity. One theory suggests that hypersensitivity is completely separate from sensory processing sensitivity. The other suggests they are connected. As you'll see from my explanations of the sensory systems and their connection to sensory intelligence, I believe they are connected. Theoretically they must be because they involve the senses.

Our senses are the bridge between our sensory awareness and sensory intelligence. Sensory awareness is the attention to sensory stimuli as it filters inward from our five senses. Sensory intelligence processes this input into meaningful information. The important distinction between awareness, or the perception of the sensations received from the environment, and intelligence is this: sensory intelligence creates feelings of vulnerability or fear. Our sensory pathways are purely physiological and do not generate fear of the environment. Our sensory intelligence does. Fear stems from this intelligence's interpretation of present experience as it compares to past experiences through *sense memory*. How else can we describe the impact a beautiful song makes on us, or the kinds of food we are drawn to, or the people who enchant us? These impressions and the feelings imbued within them form sense memories. Sense memory refers to the recall of physical sensations surrounding emotional events. Except in instances of true life-threatening fear, which is a survival instinct, sensory intelligence filters and sorts the information received on a routine basis through sensory impressions based on past experience. Then this intelligence influences how sensory stimulus impacts the central nervous system by adapting and updating the mind and body's responses based on current models of reality.

Sense memory may be related to anxiety and increased fear responses. A study on sensory processing sensitivity and mindfulness-based techniques found people high in sensory processing sensitivity[8] who also experienced anxiety were more positively impacted by a mindfulness exercise when they focused on the *acceptance of receiving stimuli* and changing the HSP's judgments about it. The most beneficial mindfulness task noted by the researchers was a "leaf on a stream" exercise in which individuals imagined an action of placing each thought or image that comes into awareness on a leaf and watching it float down a stream. Individuals high in sensory processing sensitivity were able to reduce distraction and avoidance during the leaf mindfulness task when they disengaged from applying direct meaning, thoughts, or feelings to a task. The implications from this mindfulness study shed light on how HSPs might apply importance to sensory information, which causes anxiety when they imagine past or future issues associated with certain types of stimuli.

Sensory intelligence can be trained like a muscle to help us become strong, confident, and expansive with our awareness rather than experiencing vulnerability. In order to forge that strong link between awareness and using sensory intelligence, we must heal old wounds. We do this by taking responsibility for the protection of our delicate senses. In the MBM we achieve our potential by healing the past, recognizing triggers in the moment, and building trust in our sensory intelligence. When you follow these steps, you can tap into your sensory intelligence more often. Sensitivity gives you the benefit of leading-edge conscious thought so you can excel with your gifts.

To lessen the burden on our nervous systems, we need to soothe our senses regularly. It is our responsibility to do so; although there are people who can lend us support, nobody else can soothe our senses for us. It is literally an inside job because sensory overload, or feeling maxed out, is a wholly personal experience. I developed the MBM to assist highly sensitive people in building trust in their sensory intelligence and healing from the wounds of past experiences. A big aspect of the MBM is identifying signs of sensory overstimulation that cause routine distress and then providing the right sensory therapy. You can begin by learning how to identify the environmental cues, including difficult people, that lead to sensory overstimulation.

If you are highly sensitive—an empath, an intuitive, a visionary, or an expressive, or someone who possesses a combination of all four gifts of sensitivity—then you may be delighted to know your heightened ability to perceive is going to help you manage your ability to receive. It's a beautiful paradox. What ails you is also the cure for what ails you!

Highly sensitive people are under too much stress already, and it's taking a toll on their health. Several doctors I've interviewed who are familiar with the issues of gifted sensitive people have told me that we sensitives are disproportionately represented among the people they treat. A therapist friend of mine once said, 20 percent of the population; 70 percent in the doctor's office. This figure isn't real, although it shows that sensitives are already aware they seek medical advice, attention, and help for sensory issues in high numbers.

From personal experience these visits may bring a handful of suggestions and helpful advice (or medication). What they do not address are the causal factors for our illnesses. This is because sensory awareness is not a clinical term, nor is it taught in most medical schools. While modern medicine works on the diagnoses of symptoms through biochemical, pathological, and mental health (which can directly relate to sensory issues), you won't hear the words *sensory awareness* in a doctor's office. Sensory awareness encompasses the senses and the sensory pathways. Sensory intelligence is consciousness connected to thinking and cognition, including the body (known as felt-sense). Developing our awareness of how the entire chain of events unfolds when we are stimulated by our senses is the strongest indicator of whether we will ultimately find emotional balance and experience optimum physical health and healing. Sensory therapies are the holistic methods that help us experience more personal freedom rather than feeling bothersome symptoms from sensitivity. The most common issues treated by medical doctors due to sensory overwhelm are anxiety, problems with attention, depression, and abdominal pain.

CENTRAL NERVOUS SYSTEM AND SENSITIVE STATES

People who have experienced a traumatizing event or multiple complex traumas (PTSD) are more sensitive to their surroundings. After suffering a shock or trauma, a survivor's somatic awareness becomes highly activated, which increases sensitized states in the body. A sensitive person uses hyperawareness or hypersensitivity to detect information from the environment that might be useful for finding safety. The flipside of being incredibly alert or using hypersensitivity is that it brings on other unhealthy states like anxiety, panic, and paranoia. These are signs that the CNS is working overtime and the mind and body are still "on guard."

There has been a lot of research done on trauma and the hormones involved in sensitized states. We know that stress hormones like cortisol and adrenaline are released in the body when a situation is perceived as dangerous. Cortisol mobilizes energy stored in the muscles, increases heart rate, and elevates blood pressure. At the same time, some higher cortical functions shut down (like the language centers) to preserve energy and prepare the body for immediate action. An injection of energy floods the body and blood draws outward into the muscles to prepare for running to safety or fighting for survival. The body's survival mode of high alert has been aptly called *sensitization*. When we are sensitized, it is difficult to refocus our sensory awareness on anything but our intense thoughts and feelings in the moment because survival energy tells us we must deal with an immediate threat. Sensitization heightens all the senses when the nervous system is highly engaged. These stress hormones must be released to calm down and reset the CNS. The hypothalamic–pituitary–adrenal axis (HPA) regulates the fear response. The HPA has been directly linked to PTSD by monitoring levels of circulating cortisol during resting states. From evidence of heightened HPA response in chronic PTSD, we know the HPA endocrine system functions in two ways: it increases activation when exposed to a stressor, and contributes to PTSD when there has been insufficient cessation of the fear response (such as reimagining the incident, or reprocessing).[9]

It's a catch-22. We sensitives already have a lowered threshold for perceiving sensory information from our environment, so we feel even more intense and vulnerable when under acute stress. Sensitive people are also more consciously aware, so our CNS is already primed, or conditioned for a more exaggerated response to sensory stimuli. The cascade of sensory responses from the CNS is a direct result of a sensitive's ability to regulate and attune with their environment through their heightened awareness.

MEDICAL STUDIES ON PAIN AND SENSITIVITY

I have already mentioned the important results from the 2015 Italian study on pain and trauma that suggest that individuals who experience recurrent ESP phenomena reported higher levels of past trauma. The authors of the study propose that consciousness provides a regulatory function during emotionally and physically painful traumatic events through dissociation. Sensitivity might also be an influence. There have been some studies done on hypersensitivity and pain responses that reflect different types of coping mechanisms that help sensitives moderate painful experience.

In psychology and personality theories, sensitivities like emotional awareness of physical sensations through interception have not been fully adopted into mainstream medical science. In the latest SPS research, scientists have theorized stronger activation of brain regions with specialized emotional processing functions, such as the anterior insular cortex (AIC) are involved in heightened sensory awareness. This may be an interconnected emotional facet of sensory processing sensitivity since the cingulate cortex connects bodily sensibility with emotion, various types of cognition, and movement. AIC areas that are specialized for emotional processing are involved with other important areas of the brain than handle feelings and sensations, such as the limbic system's amygdala and hypothalamus. These systems contribute to larger regulation of the autonomic and endocrine responses, pain perception, and muscular movement.

Two important studies on sensory processing sensitivity have revealed a unique relationship between emotional factors and increased health issues specific to the HSP personality. The first examined health complaints using the HSPS and found sensitives had greater perceived stress and more frequent symptoms of illness.[10] In this study sensory processing sensitivity was a more powerful predictor of health than self-perceived stress for self-reported measures of health. The researchers proposed two hypotheticals for this phenomenon: that heightened sensitivity increases general physiological arousal leading to more chronic stress, or, alternatively, that HSPs may be more consciously aware and paying mindful attention to minor physiological sensations.

In a 2016 study,[11] researchers found by examining the different factors of the HSPS and health complaints the traits of ease of excitation and low sensory threshold (LST) were positively associated with more mental and physical distress. Within these results they also found that the personality trait of neuroticism contributed more than sensory processing sensitivity as a predictive factor of illness. So understanding how the relationships between sensory processing sensitivity, temperament (for example, introversion or neuroticism), perceived stress, and illness interconnect is essential for addressing the cause of a HSP's reactions to pain sensitivity.

To understand how sensitive our nervous system is and how consciousness and sensitivity may serve as a regulating function, let's look closely at the sensory system.

THE SENSORY SYSTEM

Sensory neurons are nerve cells responsible for converting stimuli in the environment into internal electrical impulses that carry information to the brain and body—impulses flow in both directions. In a reflex arc, these messengers are responsible for a neuronal cascade that creates potential for taking fast action. An automatic reflex bypasses the brain so that the body may respond quicker. Almost immediate reaction follows a nerve pathway through the spinal cord to the appropriate body part.

For example, when sensory stimuli are encountered (like light, heat, or noise), the information from sensory stimuli (like sound, brightness, and quality of vibration) immediately travels through sensory neurons. They flow directly into the spinal column. This information then interchanges through a connection called an *interneuron*. Interneurons are awesome! They are the unsung heroes of sensitivity. As its name suggests, an interneuron is a neuron that transmits impulses between other neurons. Sensory information continues as an impulse through a sensory neuron, where it transmits a message to the motor neuron and triggers muscle contractions.

A *reflex arc* is an anatomy term that explains the biological and physical control of the reflexes. In humans most sensory neurons do not connect directly into the brain; they synapse in the spinal cord instead. This fascinating fact helps us understand how these spinal synapses create faster reflexive speed. These reflexive actions happen due to the activation of spinal motor neurons. Don't worry, dear sensitive reader, the brain does eventually receive this sensory input while the reflex is being carried out. That is how we know we can take some control over our sensory intelligence's interpretation of the sensory information that streams inward through our awareness. We know that the brain does take care of the subsequent analysis (or interpretation) of the signals taking place after reflexive action. I don't want to belabor my point on how incredible our inborn reflexes are. For sensitivity's sake, there are two types of reflex arcs: autonomic and somatic. Autonomic reflexes affect internal organs and the spinal cord. Somatic reflexes affect the muscles and are managed by the brain and spinal cord. The systems involved in somatic reflexes are somatic receptors in the skin, muscles, and tendons. Afferent nerves and efferent nerves are the pathways that carry information to and from the somatic receptors. When sensory information is too intense, overwhelming, or floods inward, we naturally withdraw from it as an instinctive reflex to prevent pain, internal stress, damage, and overwhelm. When we start connecting these dots, we realize the sensitive-empath may have an innate ability to feel these somatic reflexes in their body and in others.

SENSORY DEFENSE

When our vulnerability is triggered through sensory stimulation or sensitized states, we develop coping mechanisms or sensory self-defense to regulate feelings of distress. Our body reveals or reflects the type of defense we use depending on the situation. The classic defenses against sensory triggers and sensory overwhelm are *withdrawal/retreat, shutdown, resistance, internalization,* and *hy-*

pervigilance. Let's take a look at each in turn before we begin our discussion of how to soothe the senses as part of an ongoing regimen of self-care. Equipped with wisdom and understanding, we can prepare ourselves by identifying our protection mechanisms born from sensitivity.

Withdrawal/Retreat

If you have ever seen a newborn held in its mother's arms, cooing and engaged, especially with a fixed and focused stare on its mother's face, and then quickly avert its eyes due to a sudden loud noise, you have witnessed this kind of simple reflex in response to sensory overstimulation. It is known as the *startle response*. From the time we are infants, we learn how to withdraw from too much sensory stimulation.

Mothers of children who have sensory processing issues will often say they knew something was wrong when their child wasn't easily held or fed or wouldn't look them in the eye at a certain phase of early life development.

There is a large range of behaviors attributed to sensory overwhelm. Withdrawal is one of the first learned responses born from a natural reflex. As infants we use withdrawal because we are otherwise helpless, unable to do more than turn our heads, shut our eyes, and send our focus inward to search for the dark quiet expanse where we came from in utero. There are some human development theorists that believe even in the womb, a place which has been considered an inviolable sanctuary, we can suffer trauma before we are born, making us more sensitive after birth. A study using eye-tracking technology published in *Nature* has garnered attention for assessing eye gazing as a measure of human development. Researchers discovered when and how long a baby looks at other people's eyes in the first few months after birth is one of the earliest predictors of whether a child will develop sensory-processing issues such as autism.[12]

Other than extreme cases of avoiding all human contact, occasional withdrawal is not a bad thing. It is simply a natural defense mechanism we learn to avoid overstimulation of the nervous system. This kind of stimulation includes picking up sensory information that makes us cringe, gag, or feel discomfort. For example, loud sounds (voices at top volume, sirens blaring, harsh music), intense bright lights, aversive tactile sensations (gritty paper, nails on the chalkboard, pantlegs rubbing together), and violent imagery (horror movies, violence on TV) are all commonly considered toxic by sensitive people because they disrupt the normal flow of our sensations and override our normal sensory defenses. There are more specific tactile examples of cringeworthy sensation, such as peeling open a roll of aluminum foil, piercing through plastic wrap, or holding or touching Styrofoam containers. The taste of fluoride can trigger a gag reflex. Sensory triggers run the gamut and depend entirely on the person. While one individual may be able to go to the dentist and have a cavity repaired without novocaine, others will avoid going to the dentist for years due to fear of the sensations they will experience in a one-hour examination and tooth cleaning.

Withdrawal can be problematic if it occurs when anticipating something will likely happen in a certain environment. Avoidance behavior is so closely linked to anxiety that they may seem interchangeable. When a negative feeling or situation (like a sudden noise, bright lights, or people who feel suffocating to be around) brings an intense sensation, it prompts us to withdraw from it. We then try to avoid similar episodes in the future.

Recently I was at a youth basketball tournament. Players ranged in age from 6 to 12. The gym was filled with coaches, teams, referees, parents, and grandparents making it a highly chaotic albeit well-organized event. As my family sat on the sidelines watching our youngest daughter play, a young boy next to us was lying on his side, winter jacket draped over his entire head, so all we could see were both his legs sticking out. His little legs propelled his whole body in a circular clocklike motion in a frenetic panic. While the fans cheered loudly, players automatically threw the ball or ran about the court, I watched with sadness as this young fellow forced his body into violent circles on the ground. The circular motion was his attempt to balance his vestibular system, through a tactile defense, to drown out the loud noise and proximity of being around too many people.

In her book *Emergence,* Temple Grandin goes into tactile sensory defense and vestibular balance with explicit detail. *Emergence* is a moving depiction and intimate view into this type of sensory overwhelm. At the gym the young boy needed his guardian to take him out into the hallway to reset his sensory system. A break from the entire scene would have helped him cope with this perfect sensory storm. Clearly he was maxed out by the lights, noise, movement, and people in the environment. His behavior was a cry for help. In childhood, without an observant adult who recognizes these reflexive coping mechanisms, sensitive children are *forced to conform to the environment.* This endurance of sensory overwhelm informs our sensory intelligence. Internally, once the stimulation dies down, our sensory intelligences says, "I'm not safe here. Prepare for danger." When we don't receive the proper training in childhood to learn how to reset and stabilize our own sensory systems from overwhelm, we continue to fight through these situations with our automatic sensory defenses. Even into adulthood we are influenced by how we must conform to social norms. But the point is we shouldn't have to grit our teeth and bear such harsh circumstances. Subjecting ourselves to such a painful assault on our senses feels like white-knuckling behind the steering wheel in a head-on collision. We brace ourselves in a situation perceived as dangerous. Our nervous system takes the brunt of these energetic forces.

We can learn our threshold for sensory stimulation and teach our sensory intelligence a new outcome. We do this by taking conscious action, soothing our senses, and teaching our sensory intelligence we are okay, we are safe. If you ever find yourself in the type of situation where you feel yourself clenching your teeth, balling up your fists tightly, bracing yourself by crossing your arms and legs, covering your ears, or even bolting from a conversation, these are physical symptoms of the nervous system ramping up. The body attempts to withdraw. Tightening or clenching the musculature is a physical response to stop bothersome sensations from streaming further inward. When tightening, bracing, or clenching grows into a long-term pattern, different muscle groups develop a certain type of muscular *body armor*

Having identified your triggers, you can work gradually through different events or circumstances to find the right sensory threshold you can tolerate. The key is to practice incrementally, slowly, and to build trust in your ability to handle your surroundings along the way. In adult life there are certain situations we cannot always avoid, such as workplace meetings. If you know you will be stressed by an event, plan specific ways to manage the stress ahead of time. Giving yourself a breather in the bathroom or by stepping outdoors might be enough. Don't force yourself to succumb to an onslaught of sensory overwhelm if you can prepare for it. Reducing stressful sensory input gives you more control over the situation.

There are some things we can take control over, such as environmental influences, and others we can't. We all have a normal withdrawal reflex built into our physiology through the central nervous system that we can't control. It is a basic spinal reflex intended to protect the body from harmful and damaging stimuli. In medicine and anatomy, it is called the *polysynaptic reflex*, and it responds to the stimulation of sensory information through both the sensory and motor neurons.

There are two different kinds of these reflexes: monosynaptic and polysynaptic. The *monosynaptic reflex* is when a sensory neuron synapses, meaning a nerve impulse is transmitted directly to a motor neuron, resulting in an automatic reflex. The polysynaptic reflex is when there are more than two synapses that connect a given sensory neuron that is firing to a motor neuron. This reflex is the body's response to pain. Withdrawal is influenced by physiological reflexes embedded in our physiology. But we also have mental mechanisms that cause us to avoid things we withdraw from reflexively, which are learned reactions that operate through the mind-body connection and our sensory intelligence. All these influences affect our behavior and shape our somatic and sensory awareness. We can learn how to calm our nerves by using sensory intelligence to help us gently heal.

Shutdown

Shutting down is not a clinical term; therefore, you won't see this phenomenon written about in the annals of clinical psychology. Even so, we inherently know what it is. It is a total lack of engagement with the environment, a partner, friends, family members, or life. Shutting down is a dangerous suppression of survival energy, a turning inward into a frozen state of denial. It is a complete lack of emotional processing. Psychologically nothing is happening. There is no growth, movement, or exploration of the immediate surroundings or emotions in an individual's life when they are shut down. You might say that this behavior is the ultimate form of withdrawal, albeit cognitively induced instead of reflexive.

Once again we are looking at a survival or defense mechanism. The condition of shutdown is like an energetic wall or screen where we hide or project our emotions. We dam up emotions that are too dangerous to feel. This approach keeps us safe—we hope. Shutting down may occur either due to a chronic state of overwhelm that becomes unmanageable, or an acutely stressful experience that brings it on suddenly as a response to severe and sudden pain. In this latter instance, you would recognize it as a state of shock.

Survivors of trauma have often described shutting down as a feeling of numbing, depersonalization, escapism, and hopelessness. If a shutdown relates to an addiction to a substance (for example, alcohol or opioids), it is likely one aspect of a long-term pattern of self-anesthetizing done to reduce seeing, hearing, and feeling too much in a dangerous environment. Alcoholics and drug users are often people who have learned to cope by using substances to lessen their residual pain from childhood. Substance users will tend to feel helpless to create positive change in their lives. Sadly this is the outcome of learned behavior and is a coping strategy for medicating severe or chronic depression and anxiety. In addiction, if heightened sensitivity is likely connected to trauma, then a sensitive person may have relied on substances in the past. When this underlying connection is understood, it is life-transforming learning that these substances were used to cope with sensory overwhelm. Knowing this truth does not solve addiction. It sheds some light on how and why sensitivity influenced trauma and this pattern of anesthetizing the self. It can be understood as a contributing factor. By paying attention to sensory triggers in the present moment, we can observe how sensory intelligence interprets the environmental causes behind them. We become more informed. By learning how sensitivity has shaped addiction, we can create change, forging new patterns to release the painful emotions held in to keep a sensitive safe.

We most frequently confront the adverse effects of an emotional shutdown in our intimate personal relationships. One person in a relationship may be warm, expressive, and inviting, while the other is emotionally cut off, isolated, or shut down. The shut-down person demonstrates a lack of feeling. This numbing of sensory input helps the sensitive partner manage fear-evoking situations, such as rejection, humiliation, or repressed anger. It is hell on the relationship. I remember working with one individual who told me, "I would rather have anger or rage from my partner than be iced out cold." The loving partner of a HSP, especially someone with a history of trauma, needs to be made aware of possible triggers and understand to approach gently.

When shutdown is a pattern used routinely in a relationship, the sensory systems connect with coping mechanisms from emotional hypersensitivity. Sensory triggers cause a defensive pattern when a sensitive has learned "no matter what I say or do I will be blamed" or "there's no use trying." The dynamic between two individuals, the sensitive and the person they are in relationship with, will likely predict how a sensitive person can heal their emotional hypersensitivity. There are many ways of coping with emotional pain in relationships such as compartmentalization, detachment, or rationalization. Stepping back from a confrontation, sensitives can witness their internal dialogue, which may have been largely unconscious. An internal voice (a form of sensory intelligence) judges or predicts the outcome of a personal interaction with someone they love. It calculates emotional risk.

Take for example an instance in which a client of mine had been clean and sober for more than 10 years. He was also a practicing Buddhist and relied on this spiritual philosophy for feeding his emotional and spiritual life. While on a book tour in New York, he found himself drawn out into the night life after his book signings and readings. Contrary to his normally ascetic lifestyle, he started relying on alcohol and going out late at night. After a night of disconcerting excess, he called me for an urgent meeting, and we met to discuss his concerns.

First he explained his wife didn't know he had started drinking again. They had made a pact between them that they would stop drinking socially. It was not for spiritual reasons or that they felt addicted to substances; they felt they had matured through their younger years of partying, and they mutually felt they didn't need it. He described their social life and it didn't rely upon alcohol. After listening to him detail an argument he had with his wife of 20 years, I learned that he was experiencing shame and anger because he lost his ability to deal with his emotions during their fight. "It came over me so suddenly, and I couldn't handle it. I'm ashamed of how I treated her." As a very successful artist, he normally had plenty of money for his family. He had already gone into semiretirement and he wasn't making much money. The argument started because his wife had decided to start a new business, and it hadn't been successful. Faced with a new reality of not having enough money and watching their savings dwindle to nothing, he felt helpless to do anything about it. Rather than discuss his concerns about her spending habits while his concern grew, he described emotionally shutting off (and not communicating with his wife) due to panic. He ended up hurting himself and her with a rage he felt he couldn't control. After letting out his emotional distress, he realized he was compartmentalizing his emotions, and this led to relying on drinking to avoid his anger.

One way to identify hypersensitivity and emotional shutdown is to use the internal voice of sensory intelligence to reveal the hidden thought processes. I call this exercise the Silent Partner because sensory intelligence has a way of calculating outcomes based on past overstimulation, emotional reactions, and memories that may have increased sensitivity. Sensitive-empaths, the feelers who are gifted with emotional intelligence, may be the most vulnerable to emotional rejection. No matter what the cause, emotional rejection will affect their optimism and outlook on life.

At the extreme, if we are caught in a pattern of behavior like stonewalling—which is not a conscious attempt to hurt a partner, but an emotional or physical withdrawal because we are psychologically overwhelmed[13]—then we can draw out this former emotional overwhelm by listening intently to the internal voice. Shutdown has the distinct characteristic of lack of communication due to fear. I invite you to listen to the Silent Partner through a writing exercise.

THE SILENT PARTNER

Conflict avoidance is literally a fear of fear. It is our anticipation of events because of an influence from the past. The extreme dislike of confrontation is a residual effect of being raised by a controlling or coercive parent. When a sensitive wants to avoid conflict, shutting down is an escape route from the perceived difficulty of the other partner *potentially* trying to control their emotions, behavior, or actions. It is also an attempt to calm the nervous system, or self-soothe, during anticipation of a stressful event or situation. Refusal to engage in conversation, broaching certain topics, or emotional avoidance are just ways to handle the struggle to cope with emotional flooding from the memories of past conflict and the feelings associated with them. We can use the sensing technique of the Silent Partner, a writing technique used to process emotional sense memory safely to help us zero in on these causes and change our response to them.

When we feel overwhelmed by past emotional memory that we were unable to feel or process at the time, we must consciously identify these emotions and work through them in the present. Emotional shutdown has the power to influence our relationships in very harmful ways, so it benefits us as sensitive partners to realize when hypersensitivity is activated and learn new ways to approach our significant other with emotional safety. We can soften our edges by being gentle with ourselves first. When hypersensitivity is born out of traumatic emotional memory, we can pinpoint when and where we came to this vulnerable place.

You'll need a piece of paper and pen. It helps to use paper and pen because it connects us viscerally to our materials so we can feel our hands put emotion to paper. We observe, track, and watch our narrative unfold without being controlled or manipulated. This takes the form of witnessing what happened, like a good therapist. Once you have your materials ready, write at the top of the paper, "How did I get here?" Close your eyes for a moment and find the area that feels just in front of your physical eyes with your mind's eye. Glue your attention to this space. Let your awareness flow into the present moment.

Take two gentle cleansing breaths. Once you feel grounded ask yourself: *What is the core of my issue?* Whether it is communication with a partner, or recent conflict, or an inability to see what has led to feelings of dissatisfaction with the current situation, let your internal voice guide you. Don't filter or censor yourself. Let the internal voice roll and write down the exact communication you receive. Please don't judge, condemn, or issue any kind of edicts to the internal voice, or deny energetic information that appears through your visual field. Pay attention and listen to the quality of the voice if you hear it. Is it angry or sad? Are there any intrusions into the internal voice like images or sensory impressions (colors, shapes, or associations)? Use your mindful awareness to pay careful attention to the quality of your voice. There is no right or wrong way to actively listen, and by creating this safe container for artistic outlet, you learn how to diagnose your sensory processing style. For example, do you feel any pressure or temperature changes in your body? Does the voice sound like someone you know, like a parent or a sibling? Do images appear like a movie or story? Is there a train of thought that develops into a story?

Once you write a full narrative, allow yourself to ease into it slowly. You may realize a memory or image is related to the internal voice. Draw this memory with symbols, or through descriptions of what comes up emotionally (feelings, gut sensations) while recording your thought process. Memories are stored visually, so you may experience a flash of intuitive information in your mind's eye. Write this down as well. A pictured story will take shape. Realize this is your sensory intelligence informing you about your unique processing style. Usually there is a primary sense mechanism like visual acuity that we rely on. If you are gifted with visual acuity, you'll see very clearly in your mind's eye what takes shape. If you are gifted with the aural sense of hearing, your internal narrative will speak directly to you. If the felt-sense is your predominant sensory channel, then you will feel sensations within your body that guide you to understand your thoughts. These aren't mutually exclusive, and you can be strong in several sensory styles.

If you have been avoiding someone in your environment because their behavior is connected to a sensory memory, be kind to yourself in uncovering the reason why. Understand it has been created through a defense mechanism that aims to protect you. If your narrative describes some pain from your past, realize that any inaction is due to emotional risk. This is not a personal flaw. You can observe your inner life without strict judgment about it and learn how to let go. The Silent Partner divulges your true emotional state through reprocessing. In mind-body medicine this type of exercise relies on the deep connection between biological and autobiographical content. This information reveals itself clearly through somatic experience that was once activated during a stage of heightened mental and physical stress.

Remember, being shut out can be one of the most painful experiences our loved ones endure in their relationship with us. To a sensitive individual, particularly a sensitive-empath, being emotionally iced out can viscerally feel like an emotional loss so great it can hardly be dealt with. A sensitive-intuitive may perceive its hidden meaning as manipulation or game playing. This is anathema to sensitive individuals who see interconnections woven so tightly through the fabric of life that they perceive such manipulations as a slight on themselves and others. Sensitive-expressives must feel what they encounter and synthesize meaning in order to validate themselves and feel whole. If they feel shut out in any way from authentic communication, this will resonate as being cut off, disconnected, or excluded. Sensitive-visionaries need human connection to feel grounded and restored through emotional contact.

Everybody is sensitive to some degree. At its heart, for every human being, shutting down is a form of suppressing your own emotional life to avoid overwhelm. When we delay processing of sensory input because it is associated with intense negative emotion, the intense emotions and sensations are held in the body.

RESISTANCE

Resistance is a push-and-pull feeling that runs counter to openness, a cooperative attitude, and teamwork. It flows between a willingness or wish to engage in life and a hard pulling back against it. The physical feeling experienced by a resistant person can be described as off-balance. It feels like you are on a teeter-totter that is flipping between the hope of action taking or making a change, and a counterforce of older, more familiar patterns and the status quo. Often the behavior of those who are caught in resistance is confused with passive aggression. Passive aggression is resistance or avoidance of the demands or request of others. For the sensitive this type of resistant behavior is motivated by different impulses driven by sensory intelligence. Resistance is a sign of fear ignited in the face of change. It can also be defined as counterwill.

Counterwill can be confusing to the one who is experiencing it, as all outward signs and conscious intent point toward growth and change (such as making a promise to quit drinking, smoking, or eating too much) followed by a quick propelling backward. It engenders a one-step-forward-two-steps-backward approach to life.

Sensitive individuals feel resistance when their sensory intelligence warns them they are in danger from something unknown. If a new situation is encountered, there is a lack of sensory information to inform sensory intelligence how to protect the self and anxiety may rear up. We see this in the health coaching field when sensitive individuals who are ready for a change seek out a health coach or personal trainer, feeling solid and resolute. The sensitive has made the initial decision and is ready to make a change. We can all relate to this. Every year we get fired up around New Year's to cross off those goals on our list. Maybe it's weight loss or gaining strength in our body. We want to achieve a certain outcome. Sensitive people usually feel an additional dash of guilt if they haven't stridently been able to cross off their goals because they are typically über-conscientious about their health (remember that doctor's office statistic).

If a sensitive person takes extra steps and engages with a health coach to help them execute their goals, the coach believes their client is ready to engage with them at a high level. Whether it is immediately afterward or midway through the coaching process, the sensitive client will hit a very real wall and reject the ideas, suggestions, and advice of their coach. They will refuse to believe their coach can help them, creating every kind of challenging opposition. A sensitive will revert to an old behavior and habit and get stuck in a palpable funk. Friends or family may remain supportive; normally they will chalk this behavior up to stubbornness, a bad attitude, or laziness. Outside observers don't realize what is really going on inside the HSP. When a sensitive person is confronted with something unknown, or perceived as negative, that harkens back to another painful life experience when they suffered the labels, wrong attitudes, or shame of a coach, teacher, or parent in their lives, they feel the associative discomfort of that original experience (in their emotional memory). It's a domino effect within the sensitive, even if they aren't consciously aware of their emotional triggers. Usually it is a sense memory of failure that arises, even if subconsciously, and drives the client into a state of resistance to protect the fragile sensitive-self. The subconscious is the level of our mental processing that forms habits. This is where the habitual aspects of coping from sensitivity become challenging.

INTERNALIZATION

For sensitive people who have persevered through a great deal of suffering in early life, internalization is the "hidden" aspect to healing. Internalization is when we assign a personal meaning to our external experiences, such as life events or specific kinds of circumstances. We bring them inward to define our sense of self. It can also be explained as the use of external attitudes, ethics, ideals, values, and morals, including the opinions of others, to shape own personal identity. Together these concepts could be thought of as the *hidden self.*

Internalization is a silent phenomenon, as an attitude or characteristic we project on ourselves. They become internally fused with the self by a wordless process through images, thoughts, and beliefs. This may at times be obvious, as when someone openly says, "You're stupid, lazy, arrogant, or dumb," and we agree. For sensitives who are very attentive, perfectionistic, and self-motivated, it may be their receptive proneness to paying attention to specific information that validates an internal bias. These informational attributes can be drawn from anywhere. Most come from our relationships. Simply, interactions with others shape our internal ideas about ourselves. When we decide that someone else's comments, feelings, and attitudes about us are true, *we make them real* by inheriting the qualities we believe are being directed at us and then we use them to create our identity.

If sensitive people live in negative and challenging households, they may be more susceptible to picking up on the cues in the environment than the rest of the population. They will internalize the negative aspects of life. If they feel the emotional pain of others, sensitives may take the blame for it. Internalization of this negativity impacts self-esteem and can create an unhealthy emotional behavioral logic. It also leads to anxiety. Emotional behavioral logic sounds like this: "I will stand out if I rebel," or "They'll like me if I put in extra effort."

Anxiety from sensitivity can lead to distraction, and distraction can lead to negative internalization. Distraction in this context means *attentional escape.* Sensitives use different states of attention to escape feelings of boredom, discomfort, or negativity. In his book *Scattered Minds,* physician Gabor Maté describes how internalization is expressed through anxiety when it comes to attentional issues. "ADD has much to do with pain, present in every one of the adults and children who have come to me for assessment. The deep emotional hurt they carry is telegraphed by the downcast, averted eyes, the rapid, discontinuous speech, the tense body postures, the tapping feet and fidgety hands and by the nervous, self-deprecating humor."[14]

We know that sensitives who are easily stimulated and unable to identify their feelings experience higher levels of anxiety than those who can name and identify their emotions. Anxiety is a condition marked by unsettled reactions (such as intense thoughts and emotions) to perceived harm. When sensory overstimulation causes anxiety, this connects to sensitivity as an acute capacity for feeling/perceiving; it is linked with strong imagining or vivid imagery, increased bodily sensation, and hyperfocusing on uncertainty. What is imagined and being perceived mentally (in other words, seen, heard, and felt) becomes very real to the highly sensitive individual, even if it doesn't accurately reflect what is genuinely happening environmentally. Sensitives who are anxious excel at visualizing and imagining threats. If negative issues arise in their environment, a sensitive who experiences anxiety mentally plans for any eventuality. This requires an immense amount of mental effort and energy.

On the bright side, sensitives who have hypersensitivity to their own internal thoughts and feelings states may be ultra tuned in to their interoception (internal body states). This is a good thing as they can accurately sense and feel their own needs, emotional energy, and correct feeling states once properly identified. On the downside, if a sensitive experienced negativity from their environment and they projected it inwardly on their own feelings, this hidden internalization function is involved with attempts to manage uncertainty, also called anxiety or worry.

WORRY

This type of anxious sensitivity becomes an underlying problem when our nervous system translates *acuity of feeling* into ceaseless fear over what might happen next—essentially, worrying or fretting about the future. Let's break down what happens during this translation of feeling worry so we understand the processes involved. A sensitive person may have felt overstimulated (alert, cautious, edgy) and combined the physical overwhelm with an internal value (doubt, insecure, distrust). Since sensitives can feel more somatically (feel sensations on the body more intensely) they will imagine the reasons behind them. This is a sensory processing issue. The sensations-versus-emotions piece creates a new cycle of worry.

The worry cycle has several components to it: a physiological reactivity, an affective or subjective feeling state, and an inability to assess internal resources, and routine behaviors. The physiological reactivity or hyperactivation of the sympathetic nervous system is felt by elevated heart rate, increase in blood pressure, and shallow breathing. A sensitive will have a unique type of an affective (emotional) response coupled with the body's physical activation that translates as feeling tension, nervousness, and agitation. Usually cognitively there is an overestimation of risk and underestimation of available resources (catastrophic results, intolerance, negative self-talk). There are also behavioral patterns like double-checking and avoidance. The worry cycle is embodied with the mind and body as it becomes a sensitive's plan for managing stressful situations.

If you experience worry often, there are highly effective sensory exercises you can use to lessen this cycle, especially if from moment to moment you feel overpowered by your thoughts about your feelings. Worrying over them triggers your anxiety even more. If you are super attuned to your feelings in your body, when your awareness of how you are feeling is topmost in your mind, it may also make you super conscious of the stress and tension within your body. Many sensitives have this high discrimination or sharp awareness of feeling states and thoughts about them. I look at this higher discrimination as *a good thing*. You are not alone: many of the new studies on this kind of sensitivity show people with higher discrimination (using interoception) are also incredibly creative and have an increased capacity to use hyperfocus as a strength to complete difficult and complex tasks.

Your mind and body are connected through the perception of your physical sensations, evoked emotions, and the corresponding anxiety as it occurs. Try to think of it like this: while cognitively processing input from your senses, you will literally become aware of this mind-body phenomenon at work. That is a lot to take in. Sensitives have the capacity to receive all this energetic information. Anxiety functions as an outlet for it.

If you have sensory processing sensitivity and you also experience ease of excitation, you will likely have sensory processing issues like anxiety. Eventually, without conscious awareness of the feelings associated with your sensitivity, you may have difficulty self-regulating. Said another way, you might have difficulty integrating overwhelming or overpowering information when intense sensory sensations trigger anxiety. Your body naturally holds this buildup of anxiety as stored tension because it doesn't have anywhere else to go. Sensitive individuals may overrespond (hypersensitivity) or under-respond (hyposensitivity) to this tension.

One of the best ways to treat this sensory overwhelm is to break up old patterns of anxiety with different types of sensory healing, like mantras (repetitive sounds), guided imagery, and relaxation exercises. Breaking the anxiety cycle begins with relaxation even if it feels extremely difficult to stay focused at first. Using concentration with somatic awareness and visual imaging can calm the mind and body. By using attentional awareness and staying present with physical tension you can use sound healing or positive imagery to modify and release worry. This healing process begins with a thoughtful appraisal of situational awareness. By recognizing intense triggering sensations like loud, sudden noises (a shriek of laughter) in conjunction with mindfully monitoring the mind and body's immediate stress response, we build the capacity to tap our internal resources more to cope with overstimulation. We can calm the nervous system using the exact same sensory channels to heal. For example, once we identify that we have an anxiety reaction, we can learn how sudden this reaction comes on. You could consider this your anxiety-cycle reaction time. Once you know how fast and what kind of sensory stimulation triggers anxiety, you can interrupt the pattern and establish new coping styles. Using mindfulness and increasing conscious awareness, you create positive outcomes by accessing your internal resources. Some examples of inner resources are self-compassion, acceptance that all emotions are welcome, and reinforcing your boundaries.

One 2013 study used mindfulness-based stress reduction (MBSR) to help patients diagnosed with generalized anxiety disorder (GAD) cultivate their awareness and attention to the present moment with less judgment by using images of facial expressions. GAD patients had higher amygdala activation (which is involved in emotional processing) when viewing neutral facial expressions. MBSR was used as a therapeutic intervention to help participants in the study become aware of their powerful emotions and then learn how to be more comfortable with arousing emotional experiences. In their results they reported, "Functional connectivity between the amygdala and PFC regions [prefrontal cortex] increased significantly from pre- to post-intervention. These changes following mindfulness correlate with improvements in anxiety symptoms."[15]

The increased connectivity between the amygdala and pre-frontal cortex is important for several reasons. Since the PFC area is located in the frontal lobe, it helps with important executive functions like concentration, focus, and attention. The amygdala and PFC are intricately connected and together they help us learn new concepts and then store them in our memory. If intense social anxiety is present, we could see how anxiety will disrupt focus, the ability to remember what has been learned, or it may affect performance measures like testing at school or work productivity.

We'll assess the underlying factors that have contributed to your anxiety reaction in the first place. Then, using narrowed and focused attention combined with breathing and calm relaxation, you'll immediately reduce anxiety. Several techniques are discussed in the sensory therapies section in the next chapter.

START TO BREAK THE WORRY CYCLE
USING SOUND AND VIBRATION

Sensory processing issues like feeling anxiety as a response to sudden, intense sensations and emotions can be transformed using sound. If you have built a defense strategy like internalization as a means for dealing with worry, you can drive through it by using sound vibrations to break up these old thought patterns. Internalization is considered an emotional-behavioral personal logic that is an internal way of processing our thoughts about intense feelings. Therefore giving internalization a voice through vocal expression can heal it. Using new sounds, unique styles of language, body movement, and vocalization in response to overwhelming sensation gives anxiety a visceral and physical expression. When the body traps anxious energy, energetic movement can release it. It doesn't matter what is expressed, meaning the words or language used; there is a healing effect or physiological change when we give anxiety a good outlet. We need to teach the body it is a safe place to experience powerful emotions through enhanced safety connected with self-awareness.

Once again this depends on you, the sensitive individual. What sounds are most effective for you to reduce anxiety? In one Italian study, researchers discovered repetition of the ancient languages of Sanskrit vocalizing mantra and Latin prayers saying the rosary both deactivated the fight-or-flight response, slowed heart rate, and engaged the parasympathetic nervous system, or "rest and digest" mode.[16] These therapeutic benefits of calming and soothing the mind and body through deactivation of the nervous system have also been studied using music. When sound waves produce a calming effect on thought, such as when listening to music, they may be more effective than prescription drugs for reducing anxiety.[17] Physiologically, listening to music reduces the stress hormone cortisol. The powerful effects of music also influence the immune system by increasing the body's production of special antibodies and natural killer cells, the cells that attack invading viruses and boost the immune system's effectiveness.

For those sensitive individuals who have LST and a high AES, in having greater awareness of beauty, listening to beautiful music is a harmonic sensory approach that is therapeutically beneficial to reduce anxiety and reveal internalization. This is why Lee Strasberg's method is so effective for performance artists like actors or sensitive-expressives. Most sensitive-expressives and sensitive visionaries have high AES. As such they are more responsive to therapeutic approaches that forge this connection of sensory awareness, mind, body, and aesthetic healing, like hearing peaceful harmonic sounds within music. Tranquil and positive music helps connect to the parasympathetic nervous system so we may feel safer from anxiety due to heightened awareness.

Expressive art therapy for sensory overwhelm uses artistic creation for integrating sensory stimulation. Artistic outlets include sound, play, and expressive creative acts like drama (acting), painting, playing music, and writing. One of the main reasons expressive art therapy is highly effective for treatment of sensory overwhelm is that it helps identify the initial traumatic connection that exists between negative internalization and sensory processing. When sensory triggers from trauma are left untreated, they are stored in memories. Physiological effects that continue to impact the mind and body from sensory triggers are increased heart rate, elevated blood pressure, and the release of stress hormones. Sensory triggers can be identified through sense memories. Sense memories are the sensory impressions and physical sensations related to an intense emotional experience stored as a memory, Emotional memories are both positive and negative. If the emotional experience was negative, we see the downside of a sensory trigger as it limits a sensitive's quality of life. Sensory triggers force us into patterns of perceived safety. Feeling an unconscious sensory trigger leads us to use reactive coping mechanisms while managing intense emotions. These initial coping means are not always effective. If trauma has survived through this silent internalization process, a loss of language results. Finding the hidden internalization and expressing what couldn't be communicated when an original trauma occurred leads to catharsis. *Expressive* here means to communicate what is happening through a visual energetic memory language that is encoded on the mind-body.

Gone untreated, memories of traumatic events have the power to influence the now. For example, if your sensitivity rises during a period of anxiety, it is because your mind wants to prepare your body for an onslaught of threats. At such a time you may experience comprehension paralysis and a loss of words. Your language centers may shut down while your brain resorts to imagery. Our only communication channel left is visual, so we imagine ways we have learned to cope with stress.

Since your perception, thoughts, and motivations are unique to you, making art is a good way to reveal hidden beliefs that are underlying your anxiety. Any art form that includes writing a personal narrative, dramatic technique, movement, singing, or vocal expression can help disrupt the emotional residue in your mind-body that stems from original traumatic influences. Making art is a positive way to creatively dialogue with yourself. Modern medicine would not necessarily find hidden internalization from anxiety, but artistic methods do. If you can identify your anxiety pattern early enough, then your chosen art form becomes a lifeline for freeing difficult emotions with expressive catharsis.

Without proper identification of anxiety, you may believe you are the only one with a problem. If you haven't developed the coping skills you need to feel comfortable reaching out to commiserate with your sensitive peers on specific difficulties you share, you are missing out on a source of support. A lack of external outlets like peer support may lead to more internalization. So be on the lookout for groups, special people, and opportunities (areas of interest, passions) that can help build your resiliency as a sensitive individual. It's okay to reach out for help. We are social creatures and isolation within the sensitive-self leads to a fixed image that can be difficult to change.

HYPERVIGILANCE

Hypervigilance is the arousal state wherein a sensitive person constantly scans his or her environment for danger. It is closely related to trauma and has been well studied in the context of PTSD and secondary traumatic stress (STS), as well as in the context of prevention of revictimization by therapists and doctors who seek to employ trauma-informed practices. Hypervigilance is a state of excitation that occurs when the attention is drawn outward into the environment. The mind-body of the highly sensitive individual activates survival energy to search for threats. It is another side of the classic response fight-or-flight response.

While most of the time hypervigilance occurs only in extreme situations, such as life-threatening events, for sensitive individuals it may become an ordinary response. It does not require such extremes to activate hypervigilance. Any stimulation that floods the sensitive person can trigger worry, agitation, fidgeting, irritability, or rapid mood cycling. More symptoms of hypervigilance include lack of focus (distraction), difficulty sleeping, digestive upset, hair-trigger startle reflexes, and paranoia.

MARGIE'S STORY

My whole life I have suffered from asthma. During the past two summers in California, dealing with the raging fires has been severe and taxed my poor lungs. While people walked around in my neighborhood complete with masks and hoods over their heads and faces like it was a zombie apocalypse, I shut my windows tighter, hoping to filter out the smoke. It didn't work. Smoke still found its way in and I felt my energy drain. My body was so exhausted I had to take sick days off from work. My lungs were so sensitized they would enflame with the slightest hint of smoke. When I moved to Washington six months ago, I hoped to find a better living situation away from the suffocating smoke. I thought the moisture of the Pacific Northwest would be more cooling. I had high hopes when I found a nice place north of Seattle. It looked perfect, so I took the plunge and bought a condo.

As summer hit my next-door neighbors started having pit fires in their backyard. Apparently they also liked smoking their own meat in a meat smoker too. Here we go again. I sent the residents (who it turned out were also HOA presidents) a heads-up note about my asthma and asked them very politely to stop. The wife was on Facebook and wrote posts about how much she loved sitting on the back porch connecting to the fire. Every night! She and her husband were both health and wellness coaches! It was not only an insult looking at their photos, my lungs started burning just as they had during the California fires.

I had deliberated for at least a month over how to write back to my neighbors asking them to knock it off. I researched the local fire marshal, fire laws, and what recourse I had to defend myself legally. What actions could I take? As you rightly pointed out, this procrastination had a lot more to do with my own beliefs than confronting them.

The exercises we did were helpful. The first question: "What is my fear?"

As I thought about this, I dug down into my hesitation to contact them again and found I can't stick up for myself.

When you asked me about where I felt this sensation in my body, I immediately felt a prickly sensation in my heart and lungs. I had never made that connection before of the burning feeling in my lungs that might have been related to my asthma. The rating scale was helpful too: "How strong is it?" By resting my attention on the feelings in my chest, I actually felt a 6 or 7 in pain. When I explored this further with the question "What feeling is associated with it?" I immediately felt some clarity: anxiety!

Of course it was anxiety. Why had I not been able to see this before? When we walked this back and found the connection, I felt empowered. My own health was seriously at risk, yet I was procrastinating because I felt bad for the wife who would have to lose her connection to her nightly fires (something she obviously enjoys). Why was I willing to spare my own health and safety for someone else's feelings? I never want to be the bad guy. I am sure this has something to do with my beliefs and inner feelings from childhood. The movement exercise we did helped me recognize how this mental conflict was causing my physical symptoms. The bilateral stimulation really moved the anxiety through. This is a deep connection I am not going to forget.

MIND-BODY METHOD, A SYSTEM FOR SENSORY HEALING

Conscious awareness of our coping mechanisms from sensory overwhelm is the backbone of the MBM. Since you are so highly aware, let your heightened awareness identify your own unique sensory processing style. Then you can transform your experience using what you know. For example, are you a visual processor? Do you feel intense sensations in a specific place on your body? When you encounter a new situation what happens internally through your perception of mind and body? All humans tend to either approach or avoid new situations. There has been an eons-long debate about whether the senses are passive or active. I believe they are both and the beauty of the method is in its simplicity. If you follow the steps laid out ahead, the exercises reveal through sensory and energetic means where your gifts really shine. It is not rocket science. This journey of discovery is fun when you realize how your sensory gifts give you an edge.

I have broken the course down into several weeks, making it easy to follow. You'll want to take each step one by one and process the information carefully. No need to rush through, as it takes time and patience to process what you learn through the steps. Since it takes time to process all your realizations, time is also needed for integration of these new concepts.

Working in health care has taught me many things about sensitivity. I'd have to say the best tidbit I've ascertained is that we cannot heal what we don't consciously understand. In terms of sensory processing, that means what we can't sense—hear, see, feel, taste, touch, or smell. That's why sensitivity can be so troublesome for doctors to treat. If we go into our doctors' offices describing mysterious symptoms, they'll do their best. There isn't a prescription for feeling rushes of heat in the extremities, sensations of pins and needles on the skin, or vibrations ringing in our ears. Making matters more complex, every sensitive's nervous system is unique. What we can depend on is the body. It never lies and has incredible curative ability. We must locate the source of our pain or discomfort to help the body heal.

The design for this method didn't just come from wanting to reduce painful reactions from sensitivity and healing illness (although I believed it could). I knew sensitivity had the power to shift quality of life by experiencing ecstatic states like joy, bliss, and deep spiritual connection. Since sensitivity has the distinct advantage of taking us to deeper depths and higher heights, I wanted to learn how I could go to these depths without the jarring experience of anxiety. What I uncovered through my own personal work became the method. I believed if I developed a plan that was straightforward enough, other sensitives might want to use it too.

Sensitivity has a bad reputation because of all the issues related to it. It is well known for its crippling effects like shyness and neuroticism. Yes, there are a whole host of reactions that can and will cause illness if we choose to avoid our mind and body. Once we become consciously aware of how our sensitivity works, we can also choose to relieve our pain and enjoy the fun aspects too. Remarkably, one of the most overlooked aspects of sensitivity is that it can lead us to our happiness. When we know where our sensory threshold is, where pleasure turns to pain, we can turn inward toward our heart's true desires, like being in love. That is what sensory therapies are: a form of routine deep self-love. When we give ourselves love, we feel more cared for and it heals us.

I once watched a great teacher, Katey Inman of Anchorage Yoga, tell a student sternly, "Don't ever apologize for being you." Yes, we can make mistakes and apologize for those. There is a big difference. We can ask forgiveness if we screw up. We should *never apologize for being sensitive*. Sensitivity is part of you. It's one of the attributes that makes you so special, so don't let the world's judgment about it influence you. If you let an impersonal world dictate who you are, it'll get you wrong every time. Sensitivity is your blessing, manifested in the gifts.

Week One: Determine Your Sensory Threshold

As we have learned, there are mental-physical approaches to soothing the senses, including energetic. We need to know what sensory systems are working overtime to provide the right sensory therapies that promote healing. Detecting your sensory threshold is crucial for prevention of illness, so we start with identifying sensory triggers from your environment. Since your senses constantly perceive stimuli through your eyes, ears, mouth, nose, and body, you'll need to take a week and learn how your sensory awareness and somatic awareness already impact you. You know you can rely on your sensory impulses to inform you because they work non-stop as cellular messengers delivering important sensory information through your nervous system.

The first week you'll stay attentional and present to sensory overwhelm. Do an inventory of the most common feelings you experience. Start with the main types of emotions connected with physical arousal: *annoyance, apprehension, distraction, disapproval,* and *aggressiveness.* There are different layers of these main emotions. You can list several different layers if these have been stirred up from sensory overwhelm. If annoyance escalates to more arousal, you will feel anger, then rage. With disapproval you may feel arousal as defensiveness, sadness, and grief. When apprehension escalates it feels like anxiety. You may feel positive emotions too. It is okay to list a whole myriad of sensations that are present because they are important bits of information that will inform how affected your nervous system is. Positive emotions that also stir arousal are: *optimism, love, awe, interest,* and *surprise.*

The crux between sensory overwhelm and rebalancing the nervous system is sensory threshold. Sensory threshold is the homeostasis between perceived sensation, processing sensory information as it streams inward, and the amplification of feeling. How effectively has your perception shaped your ability to process sensations that amplify your feelings? When a sensory threshold is met, if sensory stimulation continues, an impersonal world draws inward and arouses the emotions, possibly hypersensitivity.

Get a piece of paper and make two columns. Title one side as *sensations.* Title the second column as *emotions.* For example, if you feel aggravated, irritated, highly emotional, distracted, and eventually stressed, list those feelings in the emotion column. In the first column, list any sensations such as buzzing, cold, pressure, tightness, and numbness. This simple task helps you identify a baseline level of sensations and emotions you will track over the next week to watch for sensory overstimulation. If sensory over-stimulation goes unchecked, it has influenced a mental and phys-ical feedback loop that may have had an impact on the formation of illness such as anxiety, chronic fatigue, and depression.

Week Two: Protect the Senses

We must protect our sense organs, learn the difference between sensations and emotions, and nurture our senses. Learning how much wiggle room a sensitive person has before a complete over-whelm breakdown depends on emotional balance, life stability, unique sensory threshold, and the environment. Before we feel overwhelmed, there is a very palpable sensation escalation. Sensa-tions are not emotions. Sensitive people have a higher emotional reactivity to sensation, so we get confused by what we see, hear, and feel, and by our physical and emotional reactions to what we perceive. We routinely feel aggravated, antsy, distracted, irri-tated, pressured, and critical before we feel the total accumulation of external toxicity flooding inward. By determining through sit-uational awareness where we need to reduce sensory input we can achieve a healthy balance of strength and resilience versus feeling fragile and exhausted.

This description of unexplainable sensations by a 40-year-old highly sensitive mom of two shows us how emotion can be inter-woven through the physical experience. It is a classic example of how the CNS translates sensory information: "Okay, here's a strange one: When my feelings are hurt by someone I really love, even if I intellectually feel it's not a big deal, I get pain in my palms, especially my left wrist, veins, and palm ache really badly. It has been like this my whole life. Am I the only one?"

Keep track of subtle cues in your body. Noticing these sub-tle signs that are always present in our body is our greatest asset to discerning our sensory style. If we get more familiar with our body, it can help us retool old patterns from sensory overwhelm, even traumatic memories. My client Daniel called it, "regrooving."

The body helps pick up warning sensations from the environment through perception of bodily states. We might want to distract ourselves from the discomfort of these warning sensations. The signals are there, nonetheless. It is up to us to pay attention, take control, and find balance during this escalation. If we don't know what our sensory overwhelm is connected to, we do a body scan first to catalog more detailed sensory information.

Body Scan

An easy way to determine how you process sensory information is to do a body scan with somatic awareness. This body scan develops your attention to subtle bodily sensations. It helps teach the difference between the sensation perceived and the emotion it causes. It will also directly inform you what style of sensory processor you are. Research has shown that doing a mindful body scan can reduce stress and decrease aches and pains by identifying sensory information associated with the body. Body scans can assist us by improving the relationship we have with any discomfort we may feel in our body.

Once again grab a large piece of paper. Also have crayons, colored markers, or felt pens ready. When you have your materials handy, start the body scan by stilling your body. You can sit in a chair or lie down on the ground. Quiet the mind by finding a restful position. Once you settle in, close your eyes and use focused attention or an inward gaze to notice where your conscious mindful attention resides. If you feel distracted by outside noises, just guide your focused attention back inward. Take a moment to notice your eyes. While your attention focuses inward breathe easily and let your brows soften and the muscles around your eyes release. You might sense the corners of the eyes are lifted; allow the small muscles to drop with heaviness, letting go of any tension. Let them ease. Using your inner gaze, pull away from the eye region with your soft awareness, noticing any sensation, colors, or feelings from the top of your head. Don't rush the process; glue your attention to your sensory awareness and let any information you sense stream inward, noticing what you pick up. Slowly begin to move downward from the top of the head down, paying close attention to your jaw. If you feel any sensation notice what it looks and feels like to you. When you're ready let your attention flow into the neck muscles. This is usually a highly energetic area with lots of nerve endings. Use your senses to feel this area at the nape and base. Take an extra moment here to scan through it.

Sense the aliveness and energy in your neck, then move to the front of your face and jaw again, letting your breath move into any tense spaces along the jawline. Allow these muscles in the lower jaw around your mouth to release as you gently breathe in. You might open your mouth slightly and allow your tongue to go slack. Let out a nice, strong "ahhhhhh" as you continue scanning your lower jaw. Let the tongue rest easily in your mouth. Moving awareness away from the mouth, gradually sense the space underneath your mouth, under the jaw, and into the front of your neck. Help your awareness remain still and focused by breathing in and out. The breath guides you. Observe the smooth contours of your face and neck. Notice any sensations from the inside out. Continue moving lower into your shoulders. Feel the movement of any sensation. What is alive and active in the shoulders?

Gradually, slowly breathing along through this transition, feel the muscles of the neck and shoulders soften and release as you continue to scan. What do you notice? Is there any tingling or vibration? If so, allow energy to melt these sensations as you observe their presence. As you move down the length of your arms, let your chest relax and notice your breath become even more calm. It relaxes your chest muscles. Paying close attention to the energy as it flows and moves down your arms, what sensations do you feel along the way?

Continue to scan down the chest. Breathe gently and feel the belly release as you pay attention to the breath. The chest opens and with each relaxing breath you allow your awareness to sense and receive any important information your body wants to convey. This is the heart-center where you live and breathe. Allow the time and special attention to stay here, and feel your life moving within your breath. It supports and holds you.

When you're ready feel the energy of your body move downward and deeper with focused awareness. Your breath travels down into your belly and naturally allows your chest to open up and expand. Your shoulders relax a little as your chest and belly open. You are supported by your strong spine and rib cage. Stay here and take a nice rest, feeling your breath, slow and deep.

When you feel ready, your awareness moves lower and focuses on the pelvis. Breathing in you can extend the sense of calm and relaxation into your lower body. Feel this transition as energy moves slowly, waking up the muscles. Your attention focuses in on the shift to even more relaxation. Imagine what light or sensation might be present here as you scan your pelvis. Breathe into any light or sensation you find and allow it to guide you. Breathe in again and touch this part of your body. What rises up to meet your touch? Feel any heaviness here, and breathe into it to creating even more. As this heaviness rests deeper into the muscles, relaxing them further, your attention moves down along your legs. Pay attention to the colors that move or rise up. If there are sensations like tingling, stay mindful as you rest your awareness around them. Stay present with what you see and feel. Breathing slowly and steadily, you feel your leg muscles let go and a deep calm comes over them. As you guide your energy into your ankles, this calm from your legs flows and follows downward into your ankles. You feel them release and relax. As your awareness moves along, it finds your feet. Feel the energy of your feet. Allow peace and calm to find your toes. You might stretch them out and then allow them to relax further.

Body Scan Results

The body scan uses conscious mindful awareness to receive sense impressions from the body. While it does take time to complete a body scan, it is one of the best ways to stay informed and present to what is active through somatic awareness. Draw an outline of a body on your paper. With the colored pens and pencils, catalog the sensations you received during your body scan. If you noticed bright colors, use the corresponding color in that body area and shade in what you saw and felt the color was. If the experience was more of a felt-sense, draw or use words to describe what you felt—energized, vibrant, tense, soft, overactive, tired, or exhausted. Use your own words of what was felt to describe the sensations you received.

The more you learn how your sensory awareness translates sensations with the body, the easier it becomes to track sensations and reduce sensory input by paying attention to warning sensations. Many sensitives have described these warning sensations as unusual symptoms of the nervous system as tingling, burning, itching, numbing, gut pain, skin crawling, paresthesia (pins and needles), and restlessness. These are all common warning signs that the nervous system is working overtime, handling too much sensory information. Our sensory awareness is our first line of defense in prevention of symptom onset. Illness is only an advanced progression of sensory imbalance that has moved so far internally it has begun to affect the internal organs and their systems (circulatory, respiratory, digestive, neurological).

Sensitive people often ignore their body outside of the symptoms they experience because dealing with sensations full-time feels exhausting. This denies access to mindful awareness of warning sensations when they are present. Bodily avoidance and emotional avoidance are evidence that we are neglecting our ability to use the body and emotions to guide us into healthy action. Completing a body scan is an easy, neutral step to help us identify sensation.

It does take work to heal sensitivity, but using mind-body-oriented therapies, we can find more peace and joy in life. The best way to nurture and sooth our sensitive-self is with sensory therapies that correspond to each individual sense by providing the appropriate form of healing. For instance, when we see a child purposely put their hands over their ears, we might think nothing of it. Except this signal indicates the first warning sensations. Covering the ears is an attempt to dampen painful sound. It may just register as a mild annoyance for other people in the vicinity. For a sensitive loud sounds are intense and painful. Similarly, visual overstimulation can result in distraction, floater images, pulsing in the eyelids, tension headaches, and stress in different areas of the head, neck, and face. If we have been eating a diet that irritates our super-sensitive digestive tract, we'll feel abdominal pain as nausea, inflammation, or stomach upset.

Week Three: Assess Five Types of Mental Tension

Lee Strasberg defined five areas of mental tension in his method. These correspond to areas of muscular tension in the head and neck, where they affect awareness and mental processing. He theorized that mental tension was stored in muscles found in the mouth, such as the tongue and the lips, the jaw, the temples, between the eyes, and at the back of the neck.

While Strasberg never directly addressed sensitivity in his teaching, mental tension is clearly connected to sensitivity. I have found the techniques Strasberg created to help actors develop somatic and sensory awareness so they could process sensory information highly effective for sensitives too.

Strasberg's sensory work to evoke an internal reality and cure tension is exciting. He encouraged actors to use their bodies as vehicles for the portrayal of reality under imaginary circumstances (as in performance). The body was fertile ground for altering habitual ways of responding to their environmental circumstances. The sensory exercises were designed to break through old unconscious muscular habits. Nowadays we are familiar with the signs of mental stress like anxiety, distraction, irritability, memory, and concentration problems. Strasberg was way ahead of the curve. He diagnosed the types of mental stress as they correspond to muscular tension in the face, jaw, and temples.

How is this relevant to you in your everyday life? Well, you can learn to use specific sensory exercises to help you release the mental tension affecting your feelings. By relaxing the musculature of the face, nerves, and stored tension, and connecting these to sensory overwhelm, you can increase your awareness of how your mind and body react in different emotional and situational contexts. When sensitive individuals become aware of the sensations that trigger their defenses, they can heal themselves. Routinely.

Lee Strasberg believed sensory work needed to be done in conjunction with movement to release hidden forces in the musculature. Before he would guide students through a process to release tension trapped in their bodies, they were required to address their mental tension. In developing the MBM, I followed the same idea, because it works. Mental stress must be addressed first. Until you address mental stress, you won't be able to relax and receive the physical healing benefits of the sensory therapies.

DENNY'S STORY

My fiancée had warned me many times about meeting her family. She pushed the visit off more than once. I started to develop a complex worrying it was me meeting them, not them meeting me that she was afraid of. There are too many clichés that touch on that point I know I don't need to emphasize it. We drove the four hours north to get to her childhood home in Virginia. On the way I was surprised how green and gorgeous it was. This part of the country looked like it was plucked out of The Hobbit. I started thinking maybe she was exaggerating how bad this trip was gonna be.

When we arrived at the country estate, I started to sense extreme tension between my fiancée and the small group of people on the porch who were getting up to come greet us in the driveway. I shook it off as nerves and gave a strong handshake to her dad and uncles. Everyone relaxed a little and we went into the house where the family had prepared a potluck to celebrate our wedding.

The first thing that struck me were the animal heads. Deer, bears, and fish were preserved on the wall with what looked like sick, paralyzed stares. It was bizarre. I already knew her relatives were old-school, as she had told me about her upbringing. She was a vegan like me and we were both extremely conscious of inhuman practices in the food industry. We were like-minded when it came to non-cruelty. I always kept the "live and let live" philosophy close to mind and didn't get engaged in arguments about my politics. I thought I would be okay. I didn't realize huge steaks were being served. I felt this physical illness; nausea overtook my stomach. The thick slabs of meat were over-the-top. I excused myself as politely as I could and went out to walk on the back deck to clear my head. It was instinct. I needed to refill my nostrils with fresh air and get away from the stench of grilled meat. As I walked on the far side of their porch, I felt my neck seize up and I just fell down. Dizziness set in, then a black curtain came down over my eyes. My fiancée came out and helped me sit up. Eventually I heard whispers and some laughing from inside the house. When I got up and was finally able to walk, my neck felt like it was in a vise. After we discussed what happened, I realized my migraine headaches were rooted in social situations from the tension I was holding in my upper neck and shoulders. It makes a lot of sense. I have dealt with TMJ my whole life and have already start working on releasing the stress I have been holding in my jaw and face.

Release Mental Stress with Focused Relaxation

I used the golden light breath technique to release mental stress. You can find this audio file online too (go to the Resources section on page 283). I will guide you through it here. You can read these instructions into a recording device and then listen to them. While you can find the deeper relaxation meditations on my website, I always encourage you to record meditations yourself. The more you listen to your own voice subconsciously, the more you'll relax and break old patterns you want to change. Truly self-healing.

Okay, we're ready to begin. Find a restful position that is easy to hold for a while. You'll want something supportive like a couch, bed, or even a chair with a headrest. It is best to have your head in a supported position because we're delving into mental stress and stored tension. If your head is supported, you'll have less work to do and can relax even more.

Attune to your body by closing your eyes and turning your gaze inward. Focus your awareness and feel the presence of your life energy. Find this aliveness through a stilled focus within your visual field. Sense where your body begins. This may be just in front of your eyes as we start. Find this attention or awareness and stay attuned and present with it. As your inner gaze fixes just in front your eyes, my voice will guide you. My voice goes with you as you move your gaze to the muscles just to the sides of your eyes. Take a big deep breath in. As you do my voice guides you deeper into the small muscles around your eyes. As you breathe out, you imagine a golden light surrounding you like a halo of golden energy. This golden light is warm and smooth and peaceful. On your next breath, you feel the golden light move inward as you inhale. It travels to your eyes, and then gradually flows like soft golden rivulets into the muscles outside your eyes. As you breathe the golden light in, it moves into these muscles and you feel some tension release. As you breathe in, you feel the golden light rest upon your eye muscles, and you let go of more tension. You hear the sound of my voice guiding the golden light. Now you feel it travel outward to your temples. As you breathe in, golden light drifts deeper into the muscles of your face and you feel more relaxed. The tension of your face releases. Thoughts release and dissipate as the golden light travels deeper into the now heavy muscles of your face. Between your temples golden light moves inward to between your eyebrows. As you breathe in, listening to the sound of my voice, this muscle between the eyes softens. The golden light rests here and you feel your jaw muscles go slack and release.

Breathing in and listening to the sound of my voice, feel the golden light travel down your jaw. The temples release even more as you breathe out. The golden light flows like liquid, easily finding space to move. Breathing more deeply now, your relaxation doubles. You feel the energy in your lips and mouth smooth and release. As you listen to the sound of my voice, the calm energy finds your tongue and it feels heavy resting in your mouth. Breathing in, your jaw muscles feel heavy too; rest on this heaviness. Breathing out, the golden light travels back out of your mouth and you feel the muscles around your lips are heavier, softer. You feel this calm traveling into the back of your neck. Breathing out and hearing the smooth, slow sound of my voice, you release any pressure. The back of your head feels warm and heavy. The weight of this heavy warmth relaxes your mind. You feel calm and peaceful. Breathing in and out, slow and smooth, an inner calm travels down your neck into your shoulders.

As we stay here together, your breath takes over. It supports the release of your neck muscles. Slow and easy you feel your neck supported by your breath so you can rest easy. Golden light softens these muscles even more. As you breathe in and out, paying attention to the golden light, your relaxation deepens. You focus your attention on steady relaxing breath, paying attention to the smooth easy rhythm. Feel your chest expand as the golden light heals the neck. Your relaxation allows this healing.

There are more relaxation exercises, such as guided meditation, using mantra, and sensory exercises for healing mental stress, online. The good news is that you have many systems of holistic health care to choose from. My favorite system for easing mental stress is the ancient art of Ayurveda.

Ayurveda Respects the Senses

Ayurveda is one of the oldest healing traditions in the world, and originated in India. I have drawn deeply upon Ayurvedic medicine in the method because it contains several pillars that lay the foundation for routine sensory health care. As I learned this fascinating system of medicine, the one pillar that stood out the most was *respect for the senses*. Respect for the senses is one of the major Ayurvedic teachings for achieving health and wellness.

In Ayurvedic philosophy the senses are understood to be delicate pathways of perception for the mind and body. They are described as gateways used for discerning the life-giving qualities of the world around us, such as beauty, bliss, harmony, serenity, and peace. When we neglect the importance of our sensory pathways of perception and experience difficult energetic forces like discordant noises, unfavorable tastes, or emotional imbalance, we become vulnerable mentally and physically. Ayurvedic thought holds that we must use our senses appropriately so we may discern what is needed for a balanced life. The lifestyle choices we make, from the foods we ingest to our daily habits, are best made when we use our senses as divining rods of health.

I'm oversimplifying here because Ayurveda is a wide system of teachings based on ancient Vedic texts. But according to Ayurveda, illness occurs when there is an imbalance in the relationship between the self and external influences. Repeated abuse of the senses confuses and damages them. In addition to disrespecting the senses (*asatmendriyartha samyoga*), the two other main forms of imbalance that create illness are making neglectful choices (*prajnaparadha*) and living out of rhythm (*parinama*).

Here is how Ayurveda has influenced my own system. The main goal in the MBM is identifying and reducing sensory input, healing sensory overwhelm, and living in harmony. By respecting

and protecting your senses, you achieve healthy sensory awareness and advanced sensory intelligence. You also learn how to
make careful choices based on your type of sensory processing. In
Ayurveda living rhythmically means designing routines (proper
nutrition, sleeping, and sensory therapies) that coincide with
the seasons of the year. It also means respecting the seasons of
your own life including childhood, adolescence, adulthood, par-
enthood, and elderhood. According to Ayurveda and my own
method, managing our thoughts and emotions through these seasons of life by protecting and healing our senses regularly, we can
access higher states of consciousness and experience trust in our
own gifts. When we are balanced and living in harmony aligned
deeply with our own nature, we can strive for transcendence. One
of the most important health aspects from Ayurveda that I also
draw upon is eating right for your constitution.

By reducing our exposure to harsh and intense sensory stimuli
and reducing neglectful choices, we promote mental, emotional,
and physical healing. Then we can reduce the automatic defense
mechanisms that overwork or tax our touchy nervous system. By
replacing defense mechanisms with sensory therapies, we soothe
our senses with deep self-care. For clarity, neglectful choices
involve suppressing the body's natural urges, such as hunger and
fatigue; entertaining harmful thoughts; hanging around with the
wrong people; and failing to meditate or exercise. You'll need to
look at your current habits to find where you might be vulnerable
physically (your nutrition, diet, and movement), socially (the people you associate with), and environmentally (your home, location, and family influences). Living out of rhythm means resisting
the natural flow and change in life. Embracing change is both a
physical and a spiritual concept as it is a path of wisdom and the
awakening of self-mastery.[18]

In Ayurvedic perspective sensory damage can also harm our
consciousness. Not being aware of how maxed-out the senses are
can lead to taking on too much stress. We can discern this stress
through life choices. If our choices are neglectful of our senses,
they lead to harmful thought processes, and living in a state where

we are unconscious of the body. When we aren't being truly conscious of our sensory threshold, we ignore, push on, and give up
on our internal healing mechanisms. Viewed in this light, making
decisions from an unconscious place will harm your mind, body,
and spirit over time.

Here are some examples we can draw from and see how real
life can quickly force us into neglectful choices. Our world is loud
and chaotic. Advances in communication, the 24-hour news cycle,
and increased violent imagery displayed in our media command
our attention. Our senses are flooded with meaningless information. Loud music and constant beeping, humming, and ringtones
stimulate our ears. Spicy food and fatty, sweet, and chemical-laden
food stimulate our taste buds. They can also distract us from a
chaotic environment due to their intense and delightful flavors.
Visual stimulation comes from constant screen time on phones,
computers, and television. Tactile stimulation comes from overex-
posure to harmful fabrics, chemicals, or other products that touch
the skin. Emotional stimulation varies but includes communication with mentally and emotionally unstable people, environments that feel suffocating, or toxic relationships.

Our sensory influences are complex. They are observable
when we begin to clear the mind of these influences and pay
attention to what we are focused on. It is time for each of us to
learn how to heal the senses and reduce sensory stress so we may
come into balance.

The process starts with a simple assessment: *Are you maxed
out?* In the first week, I asked you to assess your baseline level of
sensory awareness, or sensations and emotions you are currently
experiencing. If the emotions column lists many complex feelings
in the highest arousal zone (rage, grief, or vigilance), you are most
likely experiencing sensory overload. From your body scan, you
will have identified the primary way you receive sensory information through visual or auditory senses, or the felt-sense. These
sensory communication channels also correspond to different
styles of sensory self-defense. From the descriptions of the coping
mechanisms (sensory defenses), you can identify the current style

being used to offset sensory distress. Then you observe how these are helping or hurting your own healing. From all the information you have gathered, you will know which sensory stimulation has been the most toxic for you. Now we learn how to apply sensory therapies for healing sensory overwhelm.

Week Four: Assess Sensory Overwhelm from the Substances You Gravitate Toward

Mental, emotional, physical, and spiritual sensitivities can be healed according to their root cause. The reasons and complexities of these sensitivities can be interwoven allergies. The integrative health model, particularly in nutritional science, terms allergies as *sensitivities*. When someone learns they have an allergy or sensitivity to something, they avoid whatever the cause is to prevent symptoms such as hives, rashes, breakouts, or, in severe cases, anaphylactic shock. Research on these kinds of sensitivities is extensive, well rounded, and includes categories such as food, chemicals, and manufactured products like rubber. Yet if the individual with an allergy does not know he is vulnerable (sensitive) to a certain food, chemical, or product (take the nightshade family, which includes tomatoes, potatoes, eggplants, and peppers, as an example), his body might be dangerously affected.

Nightshades are fruits and vegetables that belong to a family of plants known as *solanaceae*. The fruits, vegetables, and other plants in this family are common. There are over 2,000 of them. People with sensitivity to nightshades can't digest them. If they are unaware of their food sensitivity, they will experience painful occurrences of inflammation of the joints, diarrhea, gas, bloating, nausea, and headaches. As we know from gastrointestinal sensitivity explained in the empathy chapter, these can bring on other emotionally sensitized states like anxiousness and moodiness. An extremely popular nightshade that is often overlooked in terms of quelling these states from sensitivity is tobacco.

While we know that tobacco has been linked with cancer, this plant has a long history of medicinal usage. It came into popularity by European colonizers who described it as a "wonder drug." Sensitive people who smoke may be using tobacco to relax and relieve anxiety and stress. If this is the case and they have a sensitivity to the nightshade family, not only are they physically vulnerable to the fruits and vegetables, they are also vulnerable by inhaling the dangerous smoke from *Nicotiana tabacum*. This is an extremely bad combination that can result in chronic inflammation, arthritis, digestive upsets, lung issues, and mental impairment. As a sensory health coach, I always look at the root cause of why a coping mechanism started in the first place.

When sensitive people are overwhelmed, they will usually feel some relief by using alcohol, drugs, and food to suppress overpowering sensations. While I understand these mechanisms to reduce pain, they teach us to rely on our instincts and internal resources less. These substances do have some positive effects on physical and mental pain relief. I believe the cost of their usage outweighs the benefits. While we may receive pain relief, the coinciding harm that is being done is not worth it in the long run. Self-medication for sensitives is dangerous because we are already powerfully affected by relatively mild substances. The short-term fix to reduce pain from overstimulation will eventually lead to a breakdown because we are not consciously tapping into our inner resources. By assessing overstimulation in our natural state, without using substances, we can dampen sensory stimulation in the environment and provide healthy coping mechanisms.

Coffee is a similar, if not more controversial example, due to its popularity. Sensitive coffee drinkers around the world are shivering inside as they read this at the drastic thought of having to give up their favorite breakfast drink. I sympathize, and I don't want to be a buzzkill. There are too many studies that say it is good for our health as a reason to justify drinking it, or, conversely, that it is toxic. Interestingly it may not be the coffee bean that has harmful effects on a sensitive individual. It might be the unregulated pesticide used as an agricultural additive. Coffee is a stimulant. It has already been correlated with increased sensitivity. Caffeine exacerbates overstimulation because of its alkaloid ingredients. The overall ruling is still out on this beautiful plant and its incredible bean. With the information provided, sensitive people need to honestly look at the effects of coffee. Does it overstimulate you or not?

It is an easy problem to solve. While you assess your sensations and emotions during your first week of cataloging potential for overwhelm, taper off caffeine gradually. During the first day, cut back from two cups a day (or whatever your standard coffee consumption is), and taper back one half cup each day. Follow and track your emotions, moods, and sense of resilience during this one-week period, and you will know. Are you having any problems with attention and lack of focus without it? Using the tapering method gauges the influence caffeine has on mental outlook, feeling states, and overall wellness. Despite the usual withdrawal symptoms of caffeine, there will be other more glaring signs like ongoing headaches, possible tremors, and tearfulness (fluctuations in mood). Many sensitive people have reported feeling buzzed when drinking one cup of strong coffee. The effects will vary. While coffee may be considered relatively harmless, it can be a highly stimulating drug to the sensitive person.

Coffee and cigarettes are the most common forms of substances used to cope with sensitivity. There are others that are equally popular like beer, cannabis, wine, and food (sweet and salty flavors in particular).

Search for Triggers

Overwhelm is directly impacted by sensory triggers. Often when we are searching for sensitivity triggers, we must face the cruel reality that we have to give up some of our vices like coffee or nicotine, which cause ongoing stimulation of our nervous system. This may be true for you. Try not to avoid or displace any responsibility for your choices.

We don't always know how or why we started using substances to cope with life. If we look hard enough, we can identify the why. Using these assessments provides a clear picture to stop, look, and listen carefully to the sensory issues involved. Assessing mental and physical symptoms brings the true reality into focus. Be honest with yourself and determine your own reasons for using substances to dampen discomfort.

In order to identify the causal factors behind sensory triggers, you must observe your feeling states while in different contexts. Fertile ground for these new discoveries is often our own family. Keep a notebook or diary handy. Pay attention to the social context you find yourself in most often. The best testing grounds are work, home, and visiting your in-laws if you have them. Observe and track the sensations you feel. While you track sensations, step back from the emotionality of the feelings you observe and write them down. Keep this journal consistent for a few weeks. The only way to accurately assess current coping mechanisms from sensory triggers is by tracking your movement through life and documenting how you think, feel, and respond to situations. Pay attention to your dreams too, as they often reflect and draw attention to waking-life issues.

You can't create any real or lasting change unless you honestly assess your life conditions. I liken this to paying top dollar for a good therapeutic massage. You take the time needed from your busy schedule, excitedly whisk yourself away, and fully submerge in the delightful healing hands of your massage practitioner. While you let go of your worries and cares with each thoughtful touch of your massage therapist, you feel more stable and at peace. As you connect to your strength inside, you walk out of their office, head held high, moving confidently back out into the bright lights of the world. This serene, lovely feeling may even last until you get into your car and through the drive home. If you come home and suddenly find yourself immediately startled by a loud, chaotic, and frenetic household, you can bet most of the healing effects from your massage evaporate.

That doesn't mean you can't find the right mind-body therapy needed or build a more regular routine to reduce sensory stimulation. Just keep in mind that your home has the power to influence your health moment to moment because you spend a lot of time and energy there. You would be wise to build daily practices into your home so these practices become habits in a sacred healing space.

First we must correctly diagnose what is happening. Even if coping mechanisms stem from old wounds, they contain a structure with information on how we have chosen to escape and evade unpleasant thoughts, feelings, and perceptions. Maybe we started drinking socially to cope with the pressure of social situations. Or we might have started smoking to relieve anxiety, not consciously realizing we were anxious. Whatever our reasons, the hard work is admitting we are hurting ourselves.

I am often told by sensitives they resent their body because of the attention paid to it. One of the saddest things I come across is an attitude of hating the body. Let's change this perspective together. When we carry a belief that we are cursed by our sensitivities, it doesn't allow room for growth, change, or finding new ways of loving oneself (which can be really pleasing for a sensitive!).

Self-Care

As a sensitive person what you use to soothe your senses is mind-body therapy. This is a form of routine self-care. In the next chapter, I discuss the different types of therapies you can use as self-care treatment that will heal your physical senses. You can pick and choose the sensory therapies you like best for your self-care routine. They all use proper breathing, relaxation, and sensory healing to promote calm so your central nervous system will relax. This general calm produces a healing effect on the nervous system. Your senses are the delivery method. By embracing an integrative health-care strategy, you can address multiple facets of yourself (mind, body, spirit) in order to create overall constitutional balance and harmony. Your mind affects your body's health. Your body's health affects your mental clarity and moods. The goal of mind-body therapies is to reduce stress and reduce reliance on defensive coping mechanisms.

Western medicine considers Ayurveda and other mind-body medicine therapies as *alternative medicine* or *complementary medicine*. Use those terms in your search when you are looking for a care provider. We have already discussed Ayurveda's perspective on the problem of disrespecting the sensory channels and living with imbalance. By using alternative medicine to target symptoms that Western physicians may not be able to treat or diagnose as a prevention strategy, you can restore your overall wellness. If sensory triggers are the first warning sign of a nervous system working overtime, then sensory therapies that include a mind-body approach are the first defense to gently repair the nervous system.

The nervous system is our main barometer for evaluating the specific state of our mind-body. When the complete sensory system shifts into heightened alert mode, real physiological changes take place. During accidents, unexpected events, and danger, the CNS helps us act quickly before thinking. When the threat passes, the CNS kicks us out of alert mode and normal functioning resumes. During this fear-triggered process, most of our bodily reactions are out of our conscious control. Suddenly, our instincts take over. Physiological changes send blood rushing to the muscles in our extremities (our legs and arms) to prepare us for combat; our pupils dilate to flood light into our retinas, improving our eyesight; our gastric juices decrease (and our mouths dry out) to retain moisture for enhanced blood flow and perspiration, and to heighten the sense of smell.

If you notice any of these signs happening in your body, it's time for an assessment. As a recap your first step is to *document sensations and emotions*. Remember there are subtle differences between them. Sensations are stimuli streaming inward from your environment. Emotions are how these sensations make you feel. If you have trouble diagnosing these differences, *do a body scan* and determine your sensory processing style. The third step is to *release mental tension* (record and then listen to the guided meditation included). Then, with focused relaxation, *identify your sensory triggers*. I gave a few examples like food allergies, alcohol, caffeine, and their effects to give insight on how to track your triggers. If your assessments show you are currently fighting off overwhelm (increased complexity of emotions, feeling you have lack of resources to deal with them, gastrointestinal upsets, anxiety, or depression), identify what sensory self-defense mechanisms your body uses to fend off more sensory overwhelm.

Armed with this new information, you can determine whether your sensory self-defense mechanisms are in crisis mode. If you are in immediate crisis, start to move through it step by step by monitoring your breath. Take for example this next situation, which actually happened to my editor. She was at a book-signing party and a crowd of people were pressing around her—this was a particularly triggering stimulus. The lighting was bright and loud music was playing. People's voices were being raised, and the room was hot. She started to panic and held in her breath, searching for an exit. You get the picture.

In such a moment, tune into your breath. Is it held in or free-flowing? These two breathing modes indicate whether you are in crisis mode or not. Are you holding your breath or breathing with calm slow inhalation? This is the one surefire rule to determine a state of physical or mental crisis. An intensely guarded body will never regulate the breath.

By monitoring your breath, you can identify the right therapeutic approach for your needs. If the body is the mediator of past experiences through emotional memory, the breath is the starting block for retraining the mind-body's conditioned response to overwhelm. This is where we connect Strasberg's work on identifying mental tension with my own. Focus on breathing as a relaxation technique magnifies where we hold mental stress in the face, neck, temples, between the eyes, or back of the neck. Working with the breath also increases somatic awareness as we draw attention inward and observe our inner perception of breath as it connects to our physicality. Focusing on the breath draws us out of sensory overwhelm by using attentional awareness through the breath's control. Regulation of breath normalizes our physiological processes.

Proper, focused breath has been shown to stop a panic attack in its tracks. During periods of high anxiety and panic, using different breathing rhythms can shift the body out of a fight-or-flight reaction and induce a parasympathic response. This is also known commonly as "rest and digest" mode. The parasympathic nervous system is part of the involuntary nervous system responsible for system relaxation, slowing heart rate, promoting digestion, and balancing hormonal activity. The parasympathetic nervous system, together with the sympathetic nervous system, make up our autonomic nervous system.

When you begin your breathing practice, observe whether there is shallow breathing combined with jaw tightness. Drawing attention to this physical response opens a train of thought connected to stored physical tension. Pay close attention to this physical tension as it will inform you about emotions. If you feel a flood of information of any kind (through pressure, clenching, tearfulness), open up your mouth wide and let several sounds out. These sounds can be nonsensical or gibberish, "ooh" and "aah." This will break up any old patterns and allow you to relax and receive the healing effects of your chosen sensory therapy. We'll learn even more about specific breathing techniques in the next chapter.

CHAPTER 7

SOOTHING YOUR SENSES AND POWERFUL EMOTIONS

Once the mind is crystal clear, we begin to perceive the objects of the world the way they are; our perception is no longer distorted.

— YOGA SUTRA[1]

After you have done a full body scan, assessed your sensory processing style, and determined your sensory defense mechanisms, you can begin sensory therapies to heal your sensory overwhelm. As we have discussed, it is best to start with mental relaxation and stress relief through the breath. Breath work can include visualization, mantra, and intentions for healing. These combinations calm and soothe the senses at the same time. It's a win-win. Now let's learn some different kinds of breath techniques we can use for self-healing.

PRANAYAMA TECHNIQUES

4-7-8 Conscious Breathing (for Relaxation)

To observe where you hold mental stress, use the 4-7-8 breathing technique, known as *relaxing breath*. It comes from the yogic tradition, specifically the fourth limb *pranayama*, for achieving a state of mental and physical relaxation. Pranayama are breathing techniques used to guide the fluidity of the breath. Relaxation through breath helps control mental agitation, distractions, and fleeting emotional states affecting the mind. Breathing tunes our attentional mind to our self-awareness. It helps us control energetic agitations and brings stillness and mental clarity. Pranayama breaks down into two words: *ayama*, to extend, and *prana*, life force. Breath helps direct the life force. By drawing from pranayama breathing techniques, we are using the movement of prana through the breath to achieve an energetic state of calm, relaxation, and safety with the self. Our mouth, nose, lungs, and diaphragm are all engaged in pranayama, so it works on multiple sensory organs and systems.

Begin the 4-7-8 breath by placing the tip of your tongue behind your upper front teeth. Imagine your tongue as a butterfly alighting on a small branch. Be gentle. The tongue placement is not a hard or forced motion. Maintain this soft tongue position through the entire breathing series. 4-7-8 begins with an inhale through the nose. Deeply inhale through the nose for a count of four and hold your breath for a count of seven. Then blow air out forcefully through the mouth for eight seconds. Once you have tried this for a few rounds, on the final exhale you can purse your lips. Imagine your lips pursed around a straw and blow the air out through your mouth like you are blowing into a balloon. You can also audibly make a sound as you blow out on the last breath. For anxiety or physically energetic agitation, use this breathing technique daily. When you first begin, use twice daily. Don't go beyond more than four breath cycles, or rounds of breath, at one time. This can be overstimulating to the mind and our purpose here is to track, observe, and relax by observing the breath. Once you become more familiar with diaphragmatic breath, start extending the breath cycle by slowing down as you breathe. When you are more advanced with 4-7-8, stop at eight total continued breath cycles.

Purpose: Conscious breath is used as a breathing method to reduce anxiety. It can be done in an emergency to stop a panic attack. The benefits are profound and help us maintain focused regulation of the breath. This breath resets the nervous system, reduces blood pressure, and enhances mental focus.

5-5-5-5 Conscious Breathing (to Reduce Anxiety)

The 5-5-5-5 breath is another anxiety-reducing rhythm. I call it the *breath box* technique. Sitting in a relaxing position, use your inner vision and imagine a box. The breath will work like the 4-7-8 breath technique. It begins with an inhale for five seconds. You hold the breath in for five seconds and then exhale for five seconds. After the exhale hold the breath for another five seconds. The breaths will alternate with a breath in, a sustained hold for five seconds, and then a breath out for five seconds, and then a sustained hold for another five seconds. Use the visual box as a sensory tool in your mind's eye to stay on pace and guide the breath—an image to vividly mark each five-second interval around each side of the box.

Purpose: Yogis will often incorporate music, mantras, or other relaxation tools for meditation to increase mindfulness along with the breath. In the beginning it is okay to be a little tentative and not incorporate too many sensory inputs as we are trying to reduce sensory stimulation. When you have mastered the 5-5-5-5 practice, try visualizing different calming and cooling colors on the box. The benefits are sustained fixed attention on regulation of the breath. It helps with calming the nervous system, and can regulate heart rhythm, increase lung capacity, and lower blood pressure.

Viloma Breath (Alternate Nostril Breathing)

Viloma breathing balances the right and left hemispheres of the cerebrum, which makes it effective for regulating anxiety. A practice from hatha yoga, the root syllables *vil* (*negation* or *against*) and *loma* (*hair*) together translate as meaning *against the flow*.

This alternation of breath in the physical form represents the cycling of sun and moon. Nostrils (energy sensory channels) are physical representations of balancing ourselves within the earth and cosmos. Viloma pranayama breath inhalation and exhalation is not continuous—rather, you pause and hold the breath in between.

Viloma pramayama can be a difficult rhythm at first since it is an interruption of our normal breathing process. It can be done sitting up or lying down. If sitting up face your palms up in your lap and rest in a relaxing position. If lying down assume a face-up position flat on the ground or floor, supported with a bolster under your knees, or use of a yoga mat (or towel or blanket). Rest your arms near your sides with your palms facing upward.

As you keep your body still, close your eyes and quietly observe the soft drawing in and expelling of your breath.

Take a few normal breaths, filling your lungs completely and exhaling air from the lungs completely.

After a few rounds of breathing, interrupt your inhalation as follows. Inhale for three seconds, pause, and hold your breath for three seconds. Exhale.

Repeat. Continue to do this for three seconds, inhaling completely and exhaling completely between the pauses.

Purpose: This exercise will help build the feeling of confidence to regulate the body, increasing your awareness of your biological

and physiological processes. This type of breath work also elimi-
nates shallow breathing, cessation (holding of breath), and irregular breathing. This technique helps with many biophysical
processes, and reported benefits include relieving anxiety, regulating breathing, improving circulation, lowering heart rate, lowering blood pressure, improving digestion, relieving tension from
PMS, and balancing energetic forces (or prana) within the body.

Bhastrika

As you become more confident with your breath work, you can
advance into *bhastrika*, also known as *bellows breath*. It is also a
pranayama breathing technique in which breath is forcibly drawn
in and out as if you are a bellows stoking a fire. Bhastrika pranayama is considered one of the most important breath exercises in
pranayama. It can be difficult as bhastrika pranayama exhalation
sets the force, pace, and rhythm, not inhalation. The mind will try
to reverse this syncopation. Both the exhalation and inhalation
are forceful, creating a highly energetic pace that builds energy
in the system. Considered warming, the physical body awakens
through the intense breath. Look for a pranayama teacher or yoga
instructor in your area when you are ready to try bhastrika.

Tying a consistent breathing practice with attentional sensory
awareness can be practiced easily and it is a highly effective alternative health-care technique. Sensitive people will discover their
unique breath patterns through routine practice and consistent
awareness. Becoming more flexible by stretching and holding the
breath is a constant action with energetic benefits that restore sensory balance.

Purpose: Sensitive people who breathe properly experience
less anxiety, repair their immune systems, and calm their digestive systems. Breath work is a valuable resource that requires no
doctors, treatments, or medical knowledge to reduce sensory
overwhelm.

SOOTHING THE FIVE PHYSICAL SENSES

Healing Touch

When I was working in the mental health field, I learned about a nurse by the name of Dolores Krieger. A prominent healer and a professor emerita of nursing science at New York University, Krieger brought the benefits of therapeutic touch into the mainstream of medical practice in hospitals. Therapeutic touch is a hands-on approach to patient care with the purpose of reducing the physical tension that results from difficult hospital treatments. It promotes healing, reduces pain and anxiety, and helps balance energy in the body, all of which alleviate the recipient's distress.

The instinct for touch is born in us for proper attachment, comfort, and soothing. *Touching* is a great reference book on the therapeutic value of touch by Ashley Montagu. Montagu found that premature babies thrive when they are placed on their mom's chest after birth. This form of natural loving touch, called *kangaroo care*, shows us that if infants are not touched and held often in infancy, they will literally die. Throughout our evolution as a species—like our closest genetic living relative, the chimpanzee, that is known for its shared fur-grooming rituals—we likely lived within a communal setting and spent a great deal of time making social contact. That includes social interaction by staying close, foraging for food together, and touching. Like chimpanzees we probably used touch for many purposes, such as communication of emotions or affection, repairing wounds, and regular grooming. Babies do not thrive without being touched. And frankly neither do we adults. Healing touch has been used for thousands of years by ancient cultures in the forms of acupuncture, massage, pranic healing, and traditional medicine. Regardless of which method is being used for healing, touch affects sensitivity as it impacts our skin, our largest sensory organ. In research touch is considered a discriminative sensory input. Mechanosensitive skin receptors offer affective (emotional) input by the way they innervate the skin and send sensory information to the brain.[2]

Skin is our protective sheathing that insulates us from the outside world. Several layers of the epidermis contain large networks of nerve endings. The receptor cells in these nerves translate sensory information into electrical signals that travel through the nerve fibers of the spinal cord to the brain. Here they are interpreted as different types of sensations: heat, cold, pressure, pain, and vibration. Anything that touches the skin causes a sensation. Once this sensation is received, touch receptors rapidly adapt, respond, and send sensory information. Touch receptors perceive sensation. These receptors don't regulate any stimuli that touches the skin. Therapeutic touch is beneficial because it provides a soft, fluid, and soothing form of contact. Calming, restorative, and gentle touch have a direct impact on neurotransmitters and our emotional health.

As a highly sensitive person, you need to receive the positive benefits of loving touch, if not by someone else, like an adept lover or a massage therapist, then by you yourself. It is okay to take matters into your own hands and learn to do self-healing massage.

Beneficial chemicals are released into the bloodstream during an experience of loving touch—through either massage or application of positive pressure. These chemicals enhance circulation, improve immune function, and restore healing sleep. Several studies have shown that one of the biggest benefits of receiving a massage are its neurohormonal effects. *Neurohormones* are chemical messengers secreted by cells in the brain. They include dopamine, epinephrine, oxytocin, and serotonin. When the skin is touched in a soothing manner, the nervous system releases more beneficial neurohormones, improving mood and increasing positive feelings.

Different kinds of massage can be therapeutic. Start simply with gentle massages such as cranial sacral, reflexology, aromatherapy, and hot stone. Watch out for more vigorous forms, however, as these can be too intense. Swedish or deep tissue massage, trigger point therapy, and Rolfing are examples of bodywork that go deep into the tissue.

If you are reluctant to seek massages from outside professionals, ask an Ayurvedic practitioner how to do *abhyanga*, a soothing hot-oil treatment done with dosha-specific oils. Doshas are the elemental attributes of fire and water (pitta), ether and air (vata), earth and water (kapha). They will tailor your specific abhyanga oil for your specific sensory needs. Abyhanga massage therapists can also help you discern if you need therapeutic oils that energize, cool, or lighten the senses. Generally oils such as coconut, sesame, almond, mango, and olive are best for the skin due to their nourishing qualities. They become dosha-specific when oils are infused with flowers, plants, or herbs associated with specific elements (like fire, water, air, earth, and ether) or concocted to address certain symptoms.

Depending on how you feel, you also could choose to enliven and stimulate the skin and your senses by using energy- and mood-enhancing essential oils, such as orange, lemon, or bergamot, mixed with carrier oils, such as avocado, grapeseed, safflower, sunflower, or hemp. If you are feeling highly agitated, stressed out, or ungrounded, use heavier oils, such as sesame or almond. If you are irritated or feel overexertion or exhaustion, use calming and cooling carrier oils, such as coconut or olive. Combining aromatherapy and massage can help heal skin aggravation and ease problematic sensations while also delighting and calming the olfactory sense.

To perform abhyanga massage on your own head and neck, pour a quarter-size amount of oil into your palm. Rub both hands together, warming the oil, and then work it into the scalp, easing in the oil in with the tips of your fingers. Keep your hand motions gentle and use circular strokes, massaging your entire scalp. It feels a lot like a gentle shampoo. Next work the oil in circular motions into your face, starting at the forehead and around your temples. Work downward from your temples and give some nice attention to your ears, being very intentional with your finger strokes. Rub the whole ear, including the stiff outer edges. Work down your neck, making sure to provide loving strokes to the front of the neck. Replenish the oil as needed. Transition to the front of the collar bone, moving from side to side. Then with soft strokes, transition to the back of the neck. Before you transition again, make sure to rub the back of the neck directly on the top of your spine up and down. Once you feel some muscular tension release, transition by rubbing the oil into the tops of your shoulders.

A light massage of the shoulders helps release tension in the jaw and face. Once you have worked the oil into your face, head, neck, and shoulders, begin working downward, with long strokes along your arms, massaging the arm bones down toward your hands. Stroke from the outside of the arms toward the center of the body, massaging the joints of the arms and working gradually toward the wrists. You can use long strokes on your arms.

After you finish your arms, take some time and give loving attention to your upper chest, working downward toward your stomach. Because sensitivity heightens the abdominal area, take extra time in circular motions working gently through from the top of the abdomen into the lower abdomen, using circular strokes (left to right), moving energy along the digestive tract. After you've covered your entire chest and abdomen, switch strokes and rub your sternum. On the middle of your chest, rub from the top of the breastbone up and down. Use long strokes along the sides of the body, and bring both hands around to cradle the lower back and lower spine. As you rub the medicated oil into this lower lumbar area, use a gentle downward motion all throughout the back and into the lower back and upper hips.

To massage your legs, begin at your upper thighs, then work methodically down to the knees and ankles, adding oil whenever needed.

Finally, when you have reached your feet, give your arches a nice massage. (You may want to keep socks nearby so you won't slip on the floor afterward.) Finish with the toes. Observe how your toes feel. Notice places in your toes and feet where there may be sensations of stiffness or numbness. Give them some extra love by rubbing these areas.

There is no substitute for the tender kindness you can give your own body by using healing touch. It will help soothe the nervous system immediately and moisturizes your skin, giving you a radiant afterglow. This kind of self-massage will help you feel loved, well grounded, and stable throughout your day.

Aromatherapy

The volatile oils of plants in their concentrated forms—essential oils—have the power to knock out some sensitive individuals. Others absolutely adore them! Sensitives can be quickly overpowered by the strong smells of essences of lilac, jasmine, and peppermint. I have had sensitive people share how sick, lightheaded, or nauseated they feel by the strength of overly flowery aromas. Their aversion to smells may be so powerful that they must avoid places where concentrated aromas are a part of the environment. If you've ever seen signs that an area is "fragrance free" posted in schools or doctors' offices, it is because these are controlled, hypoallergenic spaces. Sensitives are often affected by strong perfumes, spices, body odors, and aromas of noxious chemicals.

Read a testimony from Billie, who remembers her first experience with markers.

BILLIE'S STORY

It was in first grade. The new scented colored markers we used for the first time gave me such a headache that I complained to the teacher. Believe me, I was not the complaining type. In fifth grade the school had been painted right before the first day of school, and the paint odor bothered me so that I could not concentrate in classes. I remember telling myself, "Look like you're paying attention. Look smart, take notes, and learn it tonight, because at this moment, nothing makes sense." I was in a daze but knew that I was not stupid. This experience repeated in my university years. The tipping point came when, in my thirties, we moved to a townhome cooperative. The policy was that every unit was sprayed with pesticides on a monthly basis. At that time I was an avid runner, running miles a day across the desert mesa. I had stopped my regular job to try to become a mother and to start my own business so I could work at home. The "bug man" came and sprayed, holding the wand in the air, and just sprayed everywhere. I was standing right there. One day, roughly three months later, I had been away, and I returned home, entered the house, and felt like I had walked full force into a brick wall. I stopped and could not move another step. I couldn't breathe. By sheer will I turned, ran out, gasping for air. Later I confirmed that the unit had been sprayed that morning. My life would never be the same. After that day I was no longer able to walk unassisted upstairs, and running was out of the picture. I had run a race a couple of weeks prior but could no longer.

Billie's sense of smell and intuition told her that she was sensitive at an early age. Like most of us, she didn't have the ability to communicate to others that her senses were working overtime and impacting her focus. As an adult her chemical sensitivity was a traumatic experience she is still recovering from. Often our olfactory sense will warn us first. The olfactory sense is one of the most primal. Closely linked with our sense of taste and regions of the brain that govern emotion, it can conjure memories, alter our moods, and help us smell fear. When we breathe we absorb the chemical molecules that produce aroma and they travel throughout our bodies. That's why aromatherapists often say "the smell's in our cells."

Some aromatherapists know how to match the molecules in the volatile oils of a plant and their therapeutic constituents with sensory treatments highly sensitive individuals need. But anyone can use the oils they like—you don't need to go to a physician or ask for a prescription. Please yourself! Therapeutic effects can be calming, relaxing, energizing, or grounding states.

Using aromatherapy as a sensory therapy is considered a form of natural medicine. Finding aromas that please and strengthen your nervous system establishes a connection between the sensory neurons in your brain and the natural healing chemistry of the plants.

Clearly, if you are hypersensitive to aromas, it is best to reduce all scents in your environment.

But if you aren't averse, try incorporating essential oils slowly into your daily rituals. Try adding a drop or two of an essential oil when you're doing an abhyanga massage. Add a couple drops to a water diffuser in your room. Put a few drops in a carrier oil and then introduce it to your bath water. Or put a few drops on a warm moist cloth that is then held on areas of your body needing support and attention.

Balance the sensory system with the seasonal essences of plants, trees, and flowers. Use cedarwood oil to nurture your heart and soul. Use Douglas fir for calming your nerves and to purify the air. For more delicate healing, essential oils made from flower petals can offer a nice alternative. Use rose oil, lavender oil, and geranium oil for emotional support, relaxation, and to brighten your mood.

You could also explore *neuro-associative conditioning*. The purpose of this process is to form a conscious connection between a specific scent, such as the scent of orange oil or the vanilla extract in your kitchen, and a specific healing response. Find the aromas that don't trigger sensory issues. Then connect the aromas to a positive feeling state, such as joy, kindness, peace, or happiness.

Mind-body medicine practitioners prefer to use guided imagery, hypnosis, and trance states to help alleviate tension and bring positive imagery with the aroma. Professional aromatherapists teach their clients to invoke these feeling states with their chosen aroma when a stressful situation arises. You can learn how to do it as well by using hypnosis, music, and meditation practice. This kind of neurological sense training can help you take control over your moods by using your sense of smell and intelligence.

Sound Therapy

There are known physiological effects from sound. Some are negative. But many are positive and even therapeutic. If you have hearing damage, it can take place gradually. Loud noises are very common in our culture. When acoustic trauma happens, there are no clear, visible signs. Hearing sensitivity is an issue that once again depends on each person. The normal range in which a human ear can discriminate sound waves is as low as 20 Hz and as high as 20 kHz (20,000 Hz). Our ability to sense the higher end of the frequency range begins to decline as we age. This explains why we often see young children cover their ears or bolt out of rooms if there is loud music, sounds, or noise. The hearing rage is far lower in the aging population, while babies and young children have more hearing capacity. According to studies, the auditory sense for higher frequencies begins to dwindle by eight years old.

Scientific research based on studies of industrial workers investigated the effects of noise on hearing. This field of research has shown that "after excessive noise has stimulated cells in the inner ear, chemical processes occur that can exceed the cells' tolerance, damaging their structure and function."[3] Typically when sound causes hearing loss, there is a temporary loss of hearing sensitivity, known as temporary threshold shift (TTS). Many of us who enjoy music, theater, and concerts have experienced this hearing sensitivity loss afterward. Being around other loud noises such as gun shots, tools, machinery, and auto racing can have similar effects. When the ear is given time to rest and recover, the TTS will repair itself. Doctors recommend 16 to 48 hours of quiet time to heal. However, if subjected to prolonged noise, TTS does not recover and instead becomes a permanent threshold shift. Studies on noise in urban environments reflect that people exposed to ongoing noise pollution are more likely to suffer from repeated stress and lowered immune function.

Sound therapy, sometimes called *acoustic therapy* or *vibrational medicine*, can help if you have high auditory sensitivity. At holistic health centers, sound baths are popular. During these events people lie on the floor and are surrounded by acoustic instruments. Drums, harps, gongs, and crystal bowls are struck and played rhythmically to bathe the participants in sound vibrations and induce trance states. According to Fulbright scholar Flicka Rahn (one of the authors of *The Transformational Power of Sound and Music*), sound healing happens through a process that activates inner healing because it stimulates and balances both sides of the brain. Through a healing interaction between sound frequency and the human biofield, this interaction harmonizes frequencies within the mind and body. For example, drums are vital to the experience. They change the brain waves to theta, one of the deepest states of healing. In some healing communities, massage therapists place their hands on the sound bathers so they can also receive nurturing touch during the experience.

One of the most popular instruments of vibrational healing is the metal Tibetan singing bowls, which produce different resonant notes when they are struck by a mallet. The history of these bowls dates to the era of Buddha in the 5th century B.C.E. In Asia and elsewhere, they are often found in sacred spaces, temples, and shrines. They can be used to evoke relaxation, calm, and inner peace while meditating. Different frequencies produced by the bowls impact different areas of the body and help to open stagnation and rebalance energy in the body.

Their historical use for vibrational sound medicine goes back even further to India. Renowned 8th-century B.C.E. tantric master Padmasambhava brought the bowls with him from his homeland of India to Tibet.

Singing bowls are also crafted out of crystal. Whether metal or crystal, they produce deep, resonant, and tranquil sounds that induce different states of centering, calm, positivity, and relaxation. Their historical usage reportedly helped meditating monks during their long hours of immobility. The bowl's sounds assisted their focus and attention for guided travel into continually held meditative states of peacefulness. They are used for meditation, stress reduction, vibrational therapies, and pranic healing. The healing response to frequencies of sound is partly due to the synchronization of the brain waves in the left and right hemispheres of the cerebrum. Yoga practitioners use singing bowls, harmoniums, gongs, bells, drums, and chanting to attune the inner self to the sound of the cosmos, Om.

Om (or Aum) is comprised of three Sanskrit letters, *aa*, *au*, and *ma*. When combined these letters make a sound that serves as a mantra or prayer. If repeated with the correct intonation, the sound resonates throughout the body so the energy penetrates to the center of your being, your *atman* (soul).

Yoga and its medicinal cousin, Ayurveda, both use mantras for sound healing. *Mantra* comes from the root words *manas* (mind) and *trai* (to protect, to free from). Freedom from the mind can be attained through the repetition—either aloud or silently in your mind—of the same sounds over and over. It is helpful to receive instruction if you are new to the practice. The mantra carries a vibration that contains the intention for healing and wholeness.

There have been some exciting studies showing proof of the positive therapeutic effects of sound healing on the mind-body. I have mentioned a few already. One of the most impressive is the effect of sound on patients waiting for surgery. Using music before treatment was more effective in reducing symptoms of stress and anxiety than medication. Even so sound therapy is still considered an alternative therapy. Some doctors remain open-minded, like Dr. Vijay B. Vad, a sports medicine specialist at the Hospital for Special Surgery in Manhattan and doctor for the Professional Golfers' Association tour. According to his hypothesis, those who try sound healing feel their pain diminish because pain is entirely subjective. Dr. Vad was quoted in the *New York Times* on sound healing that may distract the mind and help break stress cycles: "Even if it breaks your cycle for fifteen minutes, that's sometimes enough to have a therapeutic effect."

Taste

The sense of taste is *gustatory perception*. A tasteful sensory experience relies upon the different flavors and sensations of the foods and beverages we prefer. Imagine cutting open a ruby red pomegranate and sipping at the sweet, delicious, dark red juice encasing its seeds. Or cracking open a coconut and slurping the refreshing water and munching on the creamy white flesh. Dig your spoon into a bright green avocado and smash it into a smooth guacamole infused with lime and garlic. The human sense of taste is closely linked with our other instincts, evolutionary imperatives, and pain/pleasure responses.

Cro-Magnons (early modern humans) learned that the berries, leaves, roots, fruits, and seeds that were safe in their environments depended on tastes of acidity, sourness, bitterness, saltiness, savoriness, or sweetness. The current Paleo eating movement relies upon this foundation. Adherents believe many diseases and the obesity epidemic are directly related to the introduction of sugar and gluten into the modern diet and veer away from traditional ways of eating.

In *Food of the Gods*, Terence McKenna hypothesized that the early humans' ingestion of hallucinogenic mushrooms might have been a contributing factor in *Homo erectus* evolving into *Homo sapiens*. He calls this hypothesis the "stoned ape" theory. He argues that psilocybin, the psychedelic ingredient in this type of mushroom, gave primitive humans the ability to reason, plan, and organize, and says it might have helped them generate spoken language. McKenna fostered the idea that we humans "ate our way to higher consciousness."[4]

Ayurveda categorizes food into six tastes: sweet, sour, salty, pungent, bitter, and astringent. According to its nutritional guidance, each taste has a unique effect on the mind-body. Mental outlook, emotions, physiology, and spirit are balanced through the six tastes and help balance the five elements. Practitioners recommend including the different tastes in every meal to harmonize and balance the presence of the elements in your body and ensure you receive nutrients that are essential for your dosha.

In terms of soothing your senses, satiation is another factor. When you incorporate the six tastes with every meal, you feel full, satisfied, and content. If individual tastes are neglected or restricted, you can feel low energy, foggy, or hungry. But it is also known that the pursuit of pleasure through taste can bring about imbalances. Regularly combining the six tastes in the palate creates harmony and balance and good health. This advice is based on a 5,000-year-old science of holistic health. One's specific needs are determined by many factors, and nutrition is one of the primary needs.

Ayurveda philosophy teaches that our sense of taste affects all levels of the body: physical, emotional, mental, energetic, and subtler senses (chakras are the subtle energetic centers of the body). The sense of taste is treated through dietary nutrition, plants, and herbs. For example, someone with a Pitta (fire-water combination) temperament and constitution would limit spicy foods as spices aggravate the inherent heat of the Pitta's fiery element. Pitta consists primarily of fire (*agni*) and a smaller amount of water (*apas*). *Pitta* comes from the root word *tapas*, which translates to *heat*. The water of Pitta is seen as a hot, steamy, humid water element rather than a cool waterfall. Pitta people can be courageous, driven, directed, fiery, sharp, penetrating, and transformative. They usually have strong, sturdy constitutions with an excellent metabolism, and when in balance they exude their transformative elements. Pittas are blessed with great digestion and can convert their food into absorbable nutrients easily. If they choose to eat foods that are highly acidic, oily, spicy, or enflaming (this includes fried foods), they will experience bouts of painful inflammation, skin rashes, irritability, and anger—all signs that their predilection for strong, intense flavors has swung dangerously out of proportion, affecting their mental, emotional, and physical life.

Each element has cravings for the tastes and flavors that soothe their element. There are more serious cravings that create addictive imbalance. The addictive tendencies of Pitta are using alcohol, tobacco, and marijuana/cannabis. Pitta people also have a tendency toward workaholism and taking on too many activities. Since Pitta dosha has an excess of heat, they can find balance with foods that are nourishing, cooling, and calming. They need to reduce salt intake, add plenty of ghee (considered the medicine of Pitta) as a fat, and incorporate sweet, bitter, and astringent tastes. For each dosha Ayurveda recommends specific treatments with nutrients designed to heal the palate with tastes, spices, and herbs to balance and heal the sense of taste. If you're interested in this philosophy find an Ayurvedic health counselor near you. They will do a diagnostic assessment of your specific dosha. The National Ayurvedic Medical Association (NAMA) have clear guidelines and academic standards to attain NAMA health coach certification.[5]

Sight

Our visual perception brings the imagery of the outside world inward, informing us in vivid detail about our surroundings. Vision is a basic survival mechanism. It perceives patterns, helps us find our way, and enables us to scan for danger. One of the visual influences in our culture that is most disturbing to the senses is the violence on television. Violent images—both real, as in the news of wars and terrorist attacks, and fictional, as in dramatic series about police and crime, doctors, hospitals, and soldiers—can provoke fear and activate hypervigilance. We are becoming desensitized and habituated to violence. But we are also being damaged by the repeated and constant exposure to it. It overloads the central nervous system through evoking the fight-or-flight response.

By contrast using imagery as a healing modality involves evoking a positive thought process through the senses of vision, hearing, smell, taste, movement, position, and touch. Because we can imagine so clearly with our mental visual field, visualization is a clear communication channel for healing disconnection between mind and body. Using visually stimulating imagery also helps heal disruptions in perception.

The imagination is the storehouse containing images, pictures, and sensory perceptions that filter inward and influence our biology. As energetic messengers, our own imaginal thoughts can transform our energy, cells, and makeup by shifting neurotransmitters, quelling CNS activation, and smoothing out turbulent emotions.

Visual imagery is a wordless thought process. When our internal mental images are infused with negativity, worry, and sadness, they have been shown to be an early indicator of illness. When our mental images are infused with positivity, love, and gratitude, they have been shown to heal. We could think of it as an imaginary attitude of gratitude! The influence of the imagination on health has been researched by pioneering doctors like Bernie Siegel, M.D. (author of *Love, Medicine, and Miracles* and *The Art of Healing*). His books have included case histories, philosophy on guided imagery, and a teaching approach that educates patients, doctors, and medical students on the relationship between imagery, perceived stress, and modern disease. Along with meditation and self-realization, Dr. Siegel promotes guided imagery as a tool for self-healing.[6]

Guided imagery uses visualization in conjunction with the active imagination for therapeutic purposes by creating mental images using every kind of sense perception to recreate states of attentional awareness to our healthier moods (awe, interest, joy, admiration, amazement, and gratitude), an external environment, or an action. If this is done in the presence of a therapist, the practitioner guides the listener into a creative headspace where the listener can experience different scenarios that go beyond memories, intrusive thoughts, or fearful experiences.

Guided imagery is one of the most extensively studied contemporary mind-body therapies. It has been used as an intervention for conditions such as PTSD, depression, and anxiety. Using images as a form of art for healing also may be one of the earliest forms of mind-body medicine. Prehistoric images are depicted in petroglyphs, rock art circa 70,000 B.C.E., in cave paintings circa 37,900 B.C.E., and on the sides/faces of cliffs. Indigenous tribes preserved their cultural traditions through rock carvings and paintings.

Symbolic visual storytelling is an ancient and well-established means of representing a way of life, depicting routine events (like hunting, planting, and ceremony), tribal communication (maps and messages), and spiritual journeys (travel and religion). The placement of symbols and context of the petroglyphs were important to determine symbolism and meaning.

Carl Jung popularized the term *primordial image*, which refers to any image that possesses an archaic character. The primordial image eventually gave way to the more well-known *archetype*. Primordial images and archetypes are distinctive patterns and images inherent to the collective unconscious of all humankind. Jung considered archetypes the intrapsychic counterpart to instincts. In *Living Archetypes*, Anthony Stevens explains, "They are inherited potentials which are actualized when they enter consciousness as images or manifest in behavior on interaction with the outside world."[7]

Jung's work on archetypes as images transformed psychoanalytic theory. Archetypal images provided a new cultural perspective on dream analysis, intrapsychic conflict, and neuroses. Jung believed working with personal archetypes, which are hidden in symbolic forms, can help heal and transform us once we uncover them. When a hidden archetype finally bursts through to our conscious mind, it is assigned an individual meaning. This capacity to assign meaning is what makes images such powerful healing tools.

Online you'll find my series of guided imagery recordings that incorporates the specific kinds of visual imagery lessons for sensory healing. I have designed each recording for helping to ease sensitivity overwhelm. Included in these recordings are meditations, hypnoses, and guided imagery exercises. The titles and descriptions can be found in the Resources section at the back of the book. They are located on my website. My favorites are "The Healing Garden," "Samskara," "The Mansion," and "The Lamp of Illumination" (see Resources).

SENSITIVITY BRINGS POWERFUL EMOTIONS

To be able to freely employ your gifts of sensitivity without feeling harmed by them, it is important to release any emotions you are holding in your physical body. Emotional interventions are also necessary at times when you are feeling intense waves of emotion as they move through you. You can consciously direct your attention any place you observe a habitual patterning of storing emotion.

Our senses are the barometers of the intensity of different sensations and emotions. They measure the level of our internal turmoil or peace. Our senses give us moment-to-moment feedback from the outside environment. Our emotions give us feedback on how we are personally interpreting what we are sensing.

Emotions are fluid and wild. Like white water rapids, they can turn suddenly turbulent. And then we pass through that patch of life and we're back to relative calm. Within moments we can feel the extreme intensity of anger and rage and then the extreme comfort of being peaceful. The body is where all this emotion takes place. With a self-care practice that uses breathing, sensory therapies, and routine healing, these emotions take on less intensity and become more like clouds drifting by. You can learn to recognize your powerful emotions and transform them into action-taking, as a sensory guidepost when an environment has too much stimulation, or for listening to your gut instincts.

A major breakthrough for most sensitives—and perhaps it will be for you too—is the discovery that a perception of powerful *sensations* is not actually a perception of their own *emotions*. That is what sensitivity teaches us. We can perceive intense sensory information from our environment because we literally *feel more information* than other people. Confusion immediately sets in because we also *respond faster emotionally.* Learning how to distinguish between *sensations* and *feelings that arise in response to sensations* can be transformational for a sensitive.

Yes, your sensations do *influence* your emotions. When you make this powerful connection, you can take control over how you feel. You have the power to change your interpretation, which can help you change ongoing patterns of feeling that might have forced you into withdrawal, shutdown, distraction, self-soothing, or, in dangerous environments, disassociation.

Emotions can feel disrupted and unstable. When we feel worn down, it doesn't take much sensory stimulation to provoke us to feel aggression, anger, or sadness. If we've had a long day, we might lose it when someone looks askance at us or an aggressive driver cuts us off in traffic. Our volatility increases. While the offenders may have no idea how deeply they have offended us, *we take it personally.*

One of the easiest ways to determine whether you are a sensitive person (if you are still in any doubt) is to summon the courage to go to a busy shopping mall. A sensitive person will max out quickly due to the vibrant colors, the powerful odors wafting from the perfume counters, the proximity to many people, and from feeling muscular tension build up from forcing oneself to be there against instincts to be elsewhere. While the majority of the population can undergo simple tasks, like taking harmless shopping trips, and walk away feeling fine, sensitives often will feel as though they were assaulted.

We judge ourselves—*a lot.* It takes immense energy to cope with having intense emotions, reflecting on them, and enduring a judgmental mind-set. As empaths, intuitives, visionaries, and expressives, at times when we feel challenged, we may ask ourselves why we can't pull it together. "What's wrong with me? Why am I feeling exhausted? Why is that person looking at me?!" Our anger will likely get triggered by feeling we have failed in some way, and then we may lash out at friends and family members who are with us. While our friends and family surely love us, if they aren't sensitive themselves, they won't understand why we can't just go hang out with them without losing our cool. In comfy kitchens and living rooms where we are protected and safe, we are completely different people. Sensitive people can be introverted, extroverted, and process sensory information at different speeds.

If you are someone who experienced early-life trauma, you will have more difficulty stabilizing and addressing your emotions. If there is a history of abuse or neglect (attachment disruption), you must address any residual hidden feelings about that history and heal your old wounds for the emotions to be released.

In this section on emotions, I will show you how to observe your mental attitudes as they connect with your feelings. I'll walk you through a meditative exercise called *vipassana*. It is an ancient technique, and the word *vipassana* literally means *insight*. Insight translates as clear seeing into the true nature of reality. Vipassana is drawn from the earliest form of Buddhism, which teaches us how to still our rapidly fluctuating thoughts and emotions. When we can calm our turbulent thoughts and emotions, we can bring mindful attention to them and learn how to modify these states and feel safer in our own mind and body.

In the method we'll use two categories of vipassana, or *insight meditation*. The first uses *concentration* for calming the mind by focusing on and observing our own thoughts about emotions. This lessens emotional restlessness and irritability. The second uses *awareness* by paying mindful attention to reality as it is.

Since we have used body scanning, effective breathing, and learned new sensory therapies, we can shape old wounds with a new light. There may be strong fears about letting these survival energies go. They can be transformed with vipassana through new insights. The body will protect itself by building up tissues, strength, and compensation patterns where it feels it has been viscerally wounded. We cannot separate the mind from the body. We can understand how bodily sensations affect both. Vipassana helps us surrender by seeing our true nature with clear attentional focus that energizes old wounds. Vipasssana teaches self-transformation through self-observation. Through cultivation of higher awareness, we can reshape early trauma using movement and embodiment.

VIPASSANA

Every sensory experience you have has three aspects: *reactions*, *emotions*, and *degree of overwhelm*. These levels of every experienced moment flow into a single feeling. If the degree of our overwhelm increases beyond a certain threshold of tolerance, we begin feeling overwhelmed, which leads to more sensitive reactions, which then impact our emotions. Vipassana helps us break up this pattern through observation of reactions that are active in the present.

Vipassana operates under the idea that one's thoughts, feelings, judgments, and sensations can become clear. By directly observing our own nature and how we have translated our experience, we transform the past through increased awareness, self-control, and peacefulness. Since largely unconscious defense mechanisms shield our vulnerable inner selves from unpleasant sensations and overwhelm, we armor ourselves with physical tension to avoid the possibility of experiencing reality too intensely. Body armoring can sometimes feel like the only option we have to stay safe. Body armoring is only a physical instinct and we have more healthy internal resources than we realize. Vipassana helps detach from these old patterns of reaction.

Your emotions may be running wild because a past issue that hasn't been resolved is still locked inside your body. If anger or grief or impressions from a traumatic event have been held in for long periods, it doesn't take much sensory stimulation to trigger them to emerge again. In psychology there is a colloquialism: "Depression is anger turned inward." It is a catchall phrase that does not do justice to the complexity of one of the most diagnosed emotional disorders in the world.

What is revealing about this phrase borrowed from Freud's work is the "turned inward" part. When you turn your anger inward without assessing its reason for being, the situation can become dangerous. It can be self-destructive. Blaming yourself for how you are feeling could lower your self-esteem. It increases your tension and leads to chronic disease—or to making poor lifestyle choices in an effort to gain some relief. When we find calm and transform the past, we are literally reshaping our mind and body into a new self.

Trauma has a way of encoding the mind and body with intense emotions, like anger and grief, so they resurface automatically anytime we perceive we are reexperiencing the same type of event (or reimagining it if we are triggered). These are reflexive responses. Emotional processing can help us avoid the long-term adverse effects of strong, passionate feelings. By doing our best to understand what our sensations are showing us, even as they are creating physiological stress markers in our bodies, we can intervene and stop this progression. We also can change our emotional states by releasing emotions regularly.

Vipassana Concentration Meditation

Alan Watts once said, "Once you learn to start thinking, you never stop." He's capturing the Zen Buddhist idea that the nature of our mind is to keep generating thoughts. The observing mind also creates meaning and stories behind thoughts as they relate to our emotions. Like how the ocean builds waves that wash up onto shore, our mind builds thoughts that crash upon our body. Vipassana recognizes a separate nature of the mind. It is meditation that teaches us how to pierce through their illusory nature with clear awareness. The vipassana concentration meditation allows us to observe the breath as it rises and falls. With practice using concentration to observe the breath, we can learn to watch thoughts become conscious, into a specific thought pattern, and then allow them to pass.

During meditation when we realize and observe the thoughts that automatically arise, we also find there may be discomfort related to specific thoughts or ideas. Through vipassana we learn how to recognize a story behind our thoughts. When we feel pain, our mind may not have enough sophisticated resources to handle it, so it generates more thoughts about it. The mind is always trying to achieve *coherence*, or to understand and reconcile sensory stimulation with present reality. When we witness a story about any uneasiness, we simply observe and regulate the breath. Then we can appreciate how thoughts can pass, just like the breath, and we let them go. By paying mindful attention to watching what exactly happens as it is happening, we become highly conscious of our pain and fear cycle. This is called restlessness, and the idea behind vipassana is to focus on only one thought.

Find a restful position and sit with your eyes closed. If you have any knee issues and cannot sit on the floor, you can sit in a chair. You don't have to be uncomfortable while doing vipassana. Have your back straight as you sit. This position will help you support your spine, head, and neck. Start by inhaling and exhaling. As you pay attention to your breathing, you notice a pattern. Where does the breath arise from? Your chest or deeper in the belly? Watch the pattern of your breath in and out. If you have any difficulty focusing, soften the focus on a point of your nose, or on the space just in front of the tip of the nose. Feel the air as you breathe in your nose. Glue your awareness to this sensation and simply feel the breath as it comes out your mouth. After a while you will notice thoughts that float up with your breath. These might have a pattern. The idea is to resist the tendency to combine them into a story. Just track the individual thoughts and watch them pass. That is all. Watch repetitive thoughts come and let them go.

As you continue doing a vipassana concentration meditation, you observe your own mind's thought process and learn not to engage it. It builds the mental skill and functioning of consciousness. In Buddhists texts vipassana was written about with a similar concept called *samatha*. Samatha can be translated as concentration or tranquility. Together, vipassana as insight and samatha as concentration, bring the mind into a state of focused rest to experience states of serenity. By focusing on one thing, the breath, the mind is not allowed to wander into restlessness or agitation. During the meditation a meditator focuses on one thought or perception from her consciousness to the exclusion of all others. By chipping away at mental thoughts that connect to emotions, the meditator becomes aware of the nature of his own thoughts as an illusion. With practice this meditation brings states of tranquility and harmony.

Vipassana Awareness Meditation

This meditation increases cultivation of awareness so we may see into the different sensations affecting our reality. Attention is carefully drawn to the different aspects of our being. It is a gentle training of the mind to become more aware of the patterns (thoughts and emotions) of our life.

Sit quietly and breathe freely. Close your eyes and bring your fixed gaze inward. Softening your inner gaze, play with the quality of your focus. Soften any intensity you feel around your eyes by allowing the muscles in your eyes, temples, and forehead to release any tension. Turn your attention to your breath. As you freely inhale, notice the air as it flows inward through your nose. With gentle awareness pay attention to the exhale. As the breath leaves your lungs, feel it release and let go. Follow the breath as you breathe in and expel breath out. You will notice a rhythm building. Once you feel easily focused on this breath cycle, you can bring partial awareness to the sounds your breath makes. What quality do you experience? Is it peaceful or difficult? Listen to the sounds around you. What do you hear? As you listen for the sounds around you, draw your attention to what you feel. Feel your clothing against your skin. Feel the textures of these fabrics. How does your skin feel? Can you feel any sensations on your head? Are they weightless or is there some pressure? Now focus farther down your head and extend your awareness throughout your body. Feel the weight of your body in the chair where you sit or on the floor. Rest your attention here. Be present with the sensations you feel. As you feel your awareness to these sensations of sound, weight, and touch, draw your attention to them and simply observe them. Breathing in and exhaling out when you're ready, you can expand your consciousness outward into the environment beyond the body. Then bring your focused awareness back, just in front of your nose. Breathe in and breathe out. Notice how you can embrace your environment through your perception.

Using Vipassana to Release Emotions Safely

Many sensitive people are kind, caring, and thoughtful, although they do experience a fair amount of anger in response to their sensory overload. Anger is a symptom of stress linked to frustration, irritability, and exhaustion. Sensitive people get tired of others in their environment who are (you name it!) abrasive, cruel, inconsiderate, hypocritical, mean, rude, sloppy, and disorganized. That is because when sensory overwhelm hits, we feel we don't have enough internal resources to cope, so we connect stories to our thoughts. If we're on a hair trigger emotionally, thoughts may focus in on one person, find fault through a story, and get angry—just to blow off steam. It's not done consciously. Think of it as a heated tea kettle that starts whistling as it lets out steam. This list of complaints about people's character sounds a little arbitrary. When it comes down to anger finding a reason, it doesn't need a strong association. It will get discharged. God help the person on the receiving end of it. A friend and doctor with whom I worked realized she was sensitive. When processing her anger, she had this to say: "It's hard to believe I can be a healer and at the same time feel such immediate rage."

Anger and its extreme, rage, would seem counterintuitive for most sensitive individuals to express because of their inherently empathetic and kind natures. It's not their first choice of how to be. You may not experience anger as a one-time blowup or unleashed tirade; it likely comes up regularly during a constant stream of uncomfortable interactions with life and people. Sensitive people are often highly aware of the social demands of their environment, whether due to conditioning by their parents or due to having a keen eye for social norms. If such a person expresses outrage, he will quickly recognize it as inappropriate and feel guilty for crossing a line. Sensitives have a chameleonlike faculty for adapting to environments by responding to the moods, energy, and feelings of those who are present.

If you are always emotionally available and providing what others need, you could habitually neglect your own needs and feelings. Resentment over this self-imposed neglect may give rise to anger. You can use vipassana to track your breathing as it connects to your thoughts. This simple gentle method guides the release of old thought patterns as they connect to emotions. By becoming consciously aware of how they form, you can use vipassana as a tool for gathering insight into a thought process to inform how to release it. As your meditation practice grows and you become aware of thought patterns, you can then add a positive statement. Express it aloud, verbally, as you witness a negative thought forming. For example, the thought connected to a boss or co-worker sounds like this: "It's upsetting that my boss gave me that assignment so late yesterday afternoon. He's always dumping on me." As you watch these thoughts unfold, you say out loud a corresponding positive statement: "I realize he's usually very responsible and under a great deal of stress." Another negative thought might interject mentally: "He gave me a bad performance review and doesn't deserve my loyalty." Transform it with another equally positive statement: "The work I did on my last case was highly regarded by my team, and I really came through." If you find yourself feeling more positive thoughts, or a cascade of positivity, allow them to flow freely. For example: "I really liked working on that last job. It was fun and I found myself enjoying it." As you work with using positive statements to transform negative thoughts connected to emotions, you may notice energetic boundaries that keep coming up in your meditations. This is a sign that your emotions are being affected by someone who you may feel infringed upon. Watch these important clues about boundaries and how they influence what you feel. Establishing energetic boundaries could be your first necessary step in reducing feeling others' emotions.

THE IMPORTANCE OF ENERGETIC BOUNDARIES

To reiterate: When sensations flood in from the outside environment, they stir up your inner feelings. If you do not have the language to describe this invisible process to yourself, or your having trouble identifying it, you may not know that you are picking up on the subtle feeling states of others. When a flood of emotions suddenly hits you, you are then likely to feel confused, lost, disoriented, and overpowered because you have no explanation for what you are experiencing. After a while you may finally say, "I know it's not me!"

Managing outside influences, such as the emotions of others, is a taxing job. Empaths especially must develop a strong sense of self-awareness to discern the difference between their own emotions and those of others. Dealing with other people's feelings requires a large storehouse of personal energy to heal, repair, and recover from the emotional intrusion. As a result the processing of feelings exhausts the sensitive's own energy reserves. When their energy is depleted, they will feel there is nothing left for themselves. This exhaustion leads to despair, low self-worth, and chronic fatigue.

Identifying when emotions are simple sensations versus toxic sensations is another important self-awareness tool you will want to add to your emotional tool kit. Because we are all human and have emotions, staying in balance when we're in mixed company is not as simple as merely identifying other people's emotions as we encounter them. There is a sensory and energetic influence we get from meeting them as well. Our identity has personal meaning. When we encounter another person, their identity has personal meaning too. It is through these two reference points, through the encounter, that we must filter the emotional complexities we suffer from.

The critical distinction of *me* and *not me* in the individual-system theory of psychology developed by psychoanalyst Harry Stack Sullivan is a super-relevant one. In terms of the individuated self, we think, feel, and relate according to our own ideas and interpretations of self. When we meet others, through emotional insight, we can also feel qualities of the personality, identity, and feelings of others. If these feelings are toxic to us, they will immediately shift us out of our own state of balance as we focus on the intrusion.

Discernment of the dynamic that emotions are not always ours comes to us by virtue of education and experience and cultivating mindfulness. If you are in a room with other people and feel an overwhelming or overpowering emotion, often the very best thing to do is to leave the room. If you can walk out in the hallway, or even better, take a walk outside in nature or sit in a garden, you will quickly feel the intensity of the feelings dissipate. This is a classic sign of transference.

Nature is a place of healing, rest, and recovery. Because sensitive people respond so quickly to beauty, serenity, and tranquility, you should feel your equanimity return immediately when you place yourself in environments that are calm, pleasing, and low in stress.

Once the sensations and energetic forces connected to an experience dissipate, you should also be able to clearly name the feeling that you felt. Being able to label it means that cognitive processing has been done. It can be stored in memory and put at a distance. If you can also identify from whom or from where those increased sensations were felt, this should help you forge clear energetic boundaries after processing. Once you know the source of a sensation, you can avoid attachment to it by using vipassana, mindfulness, or movement to transform the intense emotional charge you felt.

By concretely naming the emotion and connecting it to their own mind-body system, empaths tease external influences out of their energy fields and learn how to detach from them mentally and emotionally. This process mostly involves energetic grounding. In the psychotherapeutic style known as bioenergetics there are several sensory exercises used to help sensitive people ground energy. The first is running energy from the sacrum (tailbone) down into the ground and feeling it connect like tree roots into the floor beneath the feet. This visualization can be done in a chair with both feet flat on the ground and the back supported. Breathing slowly in and out, the sensitive individual feels his connection to the earth and the strength within this connection.

ENERGETIC GROUNDING

This sensory exercise for establishing boundaries is doing visualization plus saying your name. You connect your feet to the ground in a relaxed state and feel your energy grounding into the earth. This is best done sitting down so you can relax and use focused concentration. Once the energetic grounding has been established through your feet, you say your name out loud or silently. Repeat your name. While you listen to the sound of your name imagine your energy coming back to your body from wherever it has become scattered throughout your daily activities—some might be left in a phone call, some in a place you had a meeting. This practice is a visual meditation using the name as a mantra to call back energetic pieces of yourself. Practice boundary-setting daily to discern and detect where emotional patterns are being held energetically in your own body.

If there are complications with weak boundaries, difficulty discharging emotions, or complex relationship connections, you can deepen your visualization by focusing on your seven main chakras, one at a time, while picturing their corresponding colors. The color of the root chakra is red. The color of the sacral chakra is orange. The solar plexus chakra is yellow. The heart chakra is green. The throat chakra is light blue. The brow chakra is indigo. And the color of the crown chakra is violet.

By mentally visualizing the energy centers and also discerning their qualities interoceptively while saying their names out loud, you can strengthen your connection to your energetic system and affirm your body's structure.

Many empaths have described how these easy visualization exercises were critical in helping them establish healthy boundaries. While doing either exercise, if the energy of a partner, parent, child, or friend comes into your energetic grounding space, it is a sign that you have *energy leakage*. If this happens to you, continue doing energetic boundary work to strengthen your sense of individuality by energetically restoring your being.

Martial arts, such as tai chi and qigong; yoga; and other practices are also useful for cultivating and managing your subtle energy. This energy can be perceived via the felt-sense. The aim of these practices is to achieve self-mastery through self-cultivation; to be self-aware and self-regulating. Bruce Lee once said about listening through the senses, "Can you hear the birds singing? If you can't hear the bird sing, you can't hear your opponent." Applying Lee's philosophy to sensory awareness, we must hear and know our true inner self to accurately relate and sense the intentions of others.

THE PHYSICS OF EMOTIONAL HEALING

Receiving energetic bodywork from a trained Reiki energy healer, or a Quantum-Touch, Rolfing, or shamanic healer has emotional benefits too. Energetic body therapy is a very effective way to release deeply held emotions. Often tension builds in the body as a result of repressed feelings. The muscle memory of those stored feelings can run counter to our current emotions. This creates a psychological split in us. Sometimes healing and reframing traumatic past experiences can only be done with the aid of another healer or compassionate person who can witness any suffering and help us consciously release it. We all have blind spots, and there is no shame in seeking support from a highly trained therapist.

In terms of energy healing, modern theorists on quantum energy believe our universe is intelligent, creative, and evolving. They propose unique subtle energies are nature's healing information at the quantum level. An example of this theory is quantum holography. This philosophy is predicated on nature's basic system of information exchange through molecules of energy.

Quantum holography works through the organization, management, and utilization of energy through patterns of light and of energetic information. When we give meaning to these energetic patterns, it is a form of human interaction with nature's intelligence. Quantum holography is often misunderstood as the entire universe being a hologram. That idea is a misinterpretation. The actual root of quantum holography is that nature and the earth exist as they are. Theoretically nature has a holistic energy system within it that uses a unique process information exchange to communicate to all of life. It is how we humans know what we know living within this intelligent system, nature. Holography's philosophy draws on a fundamental property of physics, information is delivered between energy and matter.

There are different viewpoints about quantum healing effects. All of them are rooted in the absorption and emission phenomenon. In absorption all matter emits and reabsorbs quanta of energy. *Quanta* means "a little packet of something." We know this from quantum mechanics, a branch of physics that studies small particles such as amounts of light (photons) and energy. In quantum mechanics we find fascinating principles such as *entanglement, resonance, coherence,* and *nonlocality,* which are specific characteristics of particles. These were derived from the standard quantum formation of the Heisenberg principle. In the Heisenberg principle, emissions from quanta are coherent and carry information.[8] All matter has quantum properties, such as waves and particles. This applies to quantum healing because when properties of two resonances connect, like waves, they run together but stand in resonance with each other. They form a new wave. The energetic information carried in the phase between the two resonances form a *phase relationship.*

In energy medicine this theoretical phase relationship has been used to validate transactional healing between physical matter (like the body) and quantum attributes (like healing effects). By obeying the rules of quantum energetic exchange at the subatomic level, it is hypothesized that quantum healing is possible due to interactions between electrical and electromagnetic effects and being in resonance with objects, animals, and other human beings. When a healer uses their self-awareness, it is believed they can interact between mind and matter, and influence healing through subtle energetic actions of psychokinesis (PK). There are alternative ideas on how this process happens. Let's start with the healers.

Healers use a form of reflective self-awareness to enhance their perception to influence information exchange between themselves and others. Healers may be able to narrow in on moment-to-moment healing sensations and magnify these energetic states for others to receive them. Magnification of these energetic states make others conscious of them by feeling their creation (from the healer) and participating in this exchange. This is predicated on the notion that there is no separation between the healer and others. In this regard a healer is a conduit for transference of nature's healing force or energy.

Another perspective is that an individual can heal themselves and the healer is simply an amplifier. The healer taps into a healing energy field and runs this energy. The healer doesn't do the healing, they provide a field where healing can be produced. The healer and the participant go into a synchronistic wave pattern and have the same pattern or wave. The participant then shifts their former perception of illness and generates a new faith or belief that they can heal. Scientist and researcher Dean Radin studies phenomena between healers and others at the Institute of Noetic Sciences (IONS) in Petaluma, California. I anxiously await their newest publication on healers and possible quantum effects in the IONS research study.

This notion runs against the Cartesian system of separation. Most theories on why healers can increase healing effects in others run against the grain of modern medicine. As sensitives we already know that we perceive more than others in our environments. It is not too hard for us to suspend disbelief and open our minds to the idea that healers may have more capacity to enhance nature's healing states. Oftentimes sensitives who are gifted (like the sensitive-empath healer) have learned how to channel these higher states of healing in their own lives. Healers are almost always highly empathic and have deep compassion to help others find their own healing resonance.

If it is a participatory universe and we are involved in the observation and interaction with nature's intelligence creation, then healing may be related to "nature's healing intelligence" as an attempt or evolution to heal itself. In the next chapter, we'll learn how to bolster the gifts, including healing mechanisms, through routine self-care that will build resilience through inner strength.

CHAPTER 8

BUILDING YOUR INNER STRENGTH AND RESILIENCE

*When, like the tortoise which withdraws its limbs
on all sides, he withdraws his senses from the
sense-objects, then his wisdom becomes steady.*

— BHAGAVAD GITA

Since we can't eliminate our sensitivity, living life successfully as a sensitive person involves building internal strength. Resilience. We must be vigilant in protecting ourselves (and our senses) so we may live life to the fullest and be at peace. Self-care that accomplishes these objectives is a matter of devising or identifying routine healing strategies we can employ. Each of us needs to ask: "What works best for me? What am I willing to do to heal myself?"

Once you move out of sensory overwhelm, you can begin practices that build inner strength. If you are a sensitive-empath, this might be joining a Bliss Flow yoga class so you can feel the energetic states of joy and bliss from tapping into the healing energy of the five energetic sheaths, or *koshas*. If you are sensitive-intuitive, you'll find power poses like warrior, which strengthens your connection of core energy to mental clarity, refreshing. If you're a sensitive-visionary, power positions like inversions immediately ground you while also resetting your nervous system. If you are sensitive-expressive, you can use different movement therapies like the Feldenkrais Method, dance, and performance art to release your pent-up creative energy.

Remember, when our senses shut down, when we feel we must draw back, we are not truly living. We are hiding, avoiding, and shutting out the world to survive. There is a huge difference between living, engaging, and participating in life, and fleeing in fear of life. By shifting this drive for avoidance into a healthy practice that restores and rejuvenates the senses, by turning inward and gathering strength, we can transform fear.

We can use *pratyahara*, one of the eight limbs of yoga, for *sense withdrawal*. It is an advanced practice that can provide sensitive people deep sensory healing. Pratyahara connects both inner and outer aspects of yoga. Yoga has both inner work, such as meditation and development of higher consciousness, and outer aspects such as self-care and vitalization of the mind-body energy system. In pratyahara the senses link both the body and the mind. In this philosophy they both need to be observed and developed properly. This is where pranayama breathing and pratyahara become assets for sensitive people. When we take conscious control of the breath while also sustaining focus on our vital energies, impulses, and sensations received through the senses, we gain mastery over external influences.

If there is one surefire combination that works to build resilience while also restoring sensory health and balance, that combo is restful sleep and restorative physical activity—whether that's doing yoga, dancing, walking, running, or another type of movement. Anything that raises our heart rate, gets us breathing heavily, and releases tension from our muscles is beneficial. When we take on too much and don't get a chance to move to reduce stress throughout the day, the first thing we sacrifice is our valuable sleep time. Poor sleep can result from a failure to discharge energy and being too wound up.

THE VALUE OF SLEEP

When we feel maxed out from our senses, sleep is often the first thing to go. But we need to do better because sleep is one of our primary ways we restore our physical and mental well-being. Truly restorative sleep must be deep enough (and last long enough each night) to achieve several REM cycles—the phase of sleep when we dream. This is essential especially when we've experienced hypersensitivity.

Neurotransmitters involved in our cycles of sleep and wakefulness are adenosine, norepinephrine, serotonin, glutamate, orexin, acetylcholine, and histamine. When sleep is needed, the waking functions of the brain gradually diminish.

When any of these functions are interrupted and it becomes difficult to sleep, many people reach for sleep medication. I do not advocate this approach if you are sensitive. These kinds of substances only help us deal with a superficial problem. Drug-induced sleep won't heal your nervous system in the way you need it to as a highly sensitive person. Our brains need a chance to replenish their stores of neurochemicals naturally without introducing other chemicals.

In fact we have the important chemical and physical processes we need within us to heal and repair our minds and bodies. It is only because we push ourselves too far and disrupt these normal rhythms that we interrupt our regular daily healing mechanisms. Pushing too hard is an especially troublesome matter for sensitive people who are not yet aware they are sensitive. They are prone to overloading their normal homeostatic patterns. If you are exploring whether you are sensitive or not, try reducing your stress level by finding restful sleep. The healing effects from deep, restorative sleep will be felt immediately.

NATURAL REMEDIES FOR SELF-CARE

We are powerfully influenced by modern drugs, even mild pain killers such as Tylenol. Similarly we are influenced by nature's medicine, plant-based ingredients. The medicine of nature, for example, a tonifying herb, when used in moderation and with common sense, can promote resilience, strength, detoxification, and cellular renewal. If our neurotransmitter function has been impeded through activities such as traveling, excessive consumption, or living in extreme environments, we can take nutritional supplements to activate their replenishment and mimic normal neurochemical processes.

Let's look at several nutrients you might want to supplement your diet with.

Melatonin. Taking a melatonin supplement can nudge the awake-inhibition sleep cycle along.

Magnesium. A nutrient that may help balance sleep functions is the mineral magnesium. It also promotes calm in the nervous system. It is good for stress relief, reducing muscular aches and pains, and as a natural laxative. You can use Epsom salts, which have a high concentration of magnesium, in the bath, where it will be absorbed through the skin. Or you can take an oral supplement or eat foods high in magnesium. Most health experts believe a large portion of the U.S. population is low in magnesium. Not having enough in the diet creates inflammation. Inflammation is a serious condition, especially if it is ongoing or chronic. Low magnesium and high inflammation together may be a risk factor for heart disease, diabetes, and some cancers. Taking the proper amount of magnesium has been shown to stabilize blood pressure, keep bones strong, and help healthy bowel movements. Because it is one of the essential minerals our body needs and one of the macrominerals our body doesn't produce on its own, we must make sure we eat enough foods enriched with magnesium. Magnesium helps regulate many functions in the body. It promotes enzyme production and function, activates ATP (an energy molecule that fuels cells), helps cells transport calcium and potassium, balances heart rhythm, regulates cortisol levels, and can level blood glucose.

One of the symptoms of magnesium deficiency is insomnia. When we run low on magnesium, we may experience fitful sleep and restless legs, and wake up throughout the night.

What does this have to do with being a highly sensitive person? So much! One of the most important reasons for sensitive individuals to get adequate amounts of magnesium is for the sleep-promoting, stress-reducing, and disease-preventing benefits. Foods that are high in magnesium include dark-green leafy vegetables, sunflower seeds, almonds, cashews, squash, broccoli, legumes (beans), meat, and unprocessed whole grains.

Rhodiola rosea. This herb known commonly as arctic rose has been extensively studied and has been shown to reduce symptoms of anxiety by 50 percent. It is an adaptogenic herb used to increase energy, endurance, and mental resiliency. It also helps protect metabolic health and stabilize mood. This herb benefits sensitive people who are experiencing any kind of sensory overwhelm connected with anxiety. Rhodiola provides the strength and energy needed to cope and manage stress.

GABA (gamma-Aminobutyric acid). This is the chief inhibitory neurotransmitter in the central nervous system. Use herbs and natural supplements that directly target this neurotransmitter. GABA helps us feel relaxed. Our brain's neurotransmitters can be inhibitory or excitatory. GABA has both properties. GABA has also been detected in other areas of the body where GABAergic mechanisms function outside the brain, including the intestines, stomach, kidneys, urinary tract, lungs, and liver. One of the main actions of GABA's inhibitory properties is that it reduces neuronal activity in the nervous system. That means it helps calm the nervous system by regulating nerve signals. Sensitive people who experience ongoing anxiety may benefit from adding herbs and supplements into their diet that target GABA for increased relaxation.

Electrolytes. These are liquids that contain ions that are needed for brain health. A winning combination for highly sensitive people is electrolytes and brain health–boosting supplements. Using supplements to support neurotransmitters like dopamine and serotonin helps optimize nervous system function. The right combination will depend on the person. Good general supplements that will help include:

- curcumin
- tryptophan (an amino acid)
- SAM-e (S-adenosylmethionine)
- L-theanine
- Omega-3 oils
- St. John's wort
- vitamin D
- magnesium
- zinc
- vitamins B6, B9, and B12

For sensitive people who have hypersensitivity in their gastrointestinal tract, reducing sugar and increasing electrolytes may help the absorption of these vitamins and mineral supplements. Electrolytes are substances that produce an electrically conducting solution when dissolved in water—essentially positive and negative ions. They are also known as salts such as sodium, chloride, potassium, calcium, phosphates, and magnesium. When we don't have enough electrolyte ions in the body (through proper intake of these salts), the ion channels in our body that regulate the positive and negative ions force water to one side of the ion channel or the other. Without the proper balance of electrolytes and water, our cells shrivel up and die or burst from being too full. Electrolytes help control and conduct the electrical impulses of our body. When our body doesn't have enough electrolytes, our nerves won't work properly, which can affect the heart, blood pressure, and breathing. You can drink adequate amounts of water and still not have enough electrolytes. There is a big difference between drinking water and absorbing it. If you don't have the essential minerals, like electrolytes, you won't absorb water properly. The food and drinks that replenish electrolytes are milk, yogurt, bananas, coconut water, watermelon, and avocado.

Also adding foods with calcium, potassium, magnesium, sodium, and phosphorus will help build the proper nutrients for alkalinity versus acidity.

AVOIDANCE OF SUGAR

Sugar is one of the most dangerous ingredients for the highly sensitive person's mind and body because of insulin sensitivity. Insulin sensitivity is a resistance to the hormone insulin, which results in increasing blood sugar. When we consume too much sugar, we get insulin sensitivity. Nutritionists say sugar is hidden in plain sight because we are so accustomed to having it in our diet as a preservative and flavor enhancer in our food as fructose, sucrose, and high-fructose corn syrup, and we may not realize its influence. Natural sugars are also commonly added to health foods through mediums such as agave nectar, barley malt, beet sugar, rice syrup, and maple syrup.

Our body needs glucose to function normally. When we have enough glucose, the additional sugar we take in gets stored as fat. This process is a metabolic one. When our metabolic processes are functioning normally, sugar is a positive source fueling our body, giving us the energy needed for activity. Our metabolism incorporates anabolism, the buildup of substances, and catabolism, the breakdown of substances. It is a process our body uses to make energy from the food we eat. Sugar has been studied extensively as an active contributing factor in metabolic disorders. A metabolic disorder occurs when abnormal chemical reactions in our body disrupt the normal metabolic process. Diabetes is an example of a metabolic disorder. When breakdown of metabolic processes occurs, it may disrupt the normal ability to metabolize amino acids, carbohydrates, lipids, or mitochondria. Breakdowns in the metabolic process affect the organs such as the liver, pancreas, and kidneys. When sugar consumption is too high, it affects insulin, which directly impacts the heart, cardiovascular system, hepatic function, and liver. The only way to repair metabolic functions is with immediate diet interventions through proper nutrition and increased physical activity.

For sensitive individuals who have an environmental vulnerability to substances, sugar may be a causal factor in metabolic diseases. There are usually early warning signs if there is a sensitivity to sugar. Symptoms like dizziness (feeling light-headed or shaky), irritability, mood fluctuations, tingling in the extremities, and hunger after eating may all be subtle warning signs of insulin resistance. Insulin resistance is also considered prediabetes. It is a condition where the cells in the muscles, fat, and liver don't respond normally to insulin, which is made in the pancreas. Insulin acts as a regulator and helps glucose enter the cells in the muscles, fat, and liver, where it can be drawn upon later for energy. When there is insulin resistance, the pancreas produces more insulin (or not enough) than is needed and blood glucose levels rise. Without enough insulin, extra glucose stays in the bloodstream rather than being absorbed by the cells. When this condition worsens, it becomes diabetes.

Most studies on the effects of excess energy and intake of refined sugars have linked insulin resistance to a wide range of disorders. The physical signs of insulin resistance are weight gain, especially around the belly, bloating, flatulence, infections, diarrhea, fatigue, and obesity. Some of my sensitive clients have told me they found cinnamon helpful in reducing sugar cravings. I recommend a small amount of cinnamon mixed with probiotic yogurt as a good starting place. Apple cider vinegar is another natural solution for sensitives who may be insulin resistant. You can add a few drops into mineral water, hot water, or tea to balance alkalinity and reduce sugar cravings.

HERBAL MEDICINE

We can use natural medicine to heal and repair our nervous system. Learning about herbs and their constituents will help us understand their healing actions. Herbal constituents are the phytochemical compounds found in medicinal plants. Nowhere do we see the popularity of these more than in the wide usage of essential oils. Sensitive people must be careful with them. We are impacted powerfully by environmental substances, including herbs, plants, and flowers. The medicine they offer is no exception.

The simplest way to start using medical herbs is to study their actions. These begin straightforward but become more complex when you begin to analyze their synergistic effects with other plants.

Medicinal plants can be used topically, internally, or vibrationally. Generally they have certain chemical actions: they may be *adaptogenic* (help us adapt while under stress), *aromatic* (have a strong aroma), *alterative* (build natural defenses), *astringent* (drying), *bitter* (stimulate and restore digestion), *calming* (also known as nervine), *carminative* (expel gas), *demulcent* (protect mucus membranes), *diaphoretic* (regulate body temperature), *diuretic* (support urinary tract function), *emollient* (soothe mucilaginous cells), *expectorant* (expel mucus of the lungs), or *tonic* (strengthen organs and systemic health). From their use as natural pain relief, an antibacterial, or as a digestive, medicinal herbs offer a natural health solution that is gentle, effective, affordable, and easily accessible.

As a sensitive person, your nervous system may benefit most from calming, nervine, and tonifying herbs and essences.

Calming herbs. The most common calming medicinal herbs are passionflower, valerian, chamomile, lavender, lemon balm, and kava.

Nervine herbs. Nervines act upon the nervous system and can be used as relaxants, stimulants, or tonics. Some serve as sedatives and bring relief of systemic stress and anxiety, as well as promoting the repair of damage to the nervous system.

Safe nervine relaxants—which, even so, should be used with extreme caution—are lavender, hops, lemon balm, wood betony, chamomile, and skullcap.

Nervine stimulants activate the nerves if there is depression or a shutdown, or if you have a sluggish nervous system. They help stimulate the body and its innate ability to adapt during stress.

Good, safe nervine herbs are blue vervain, brahmi, oats, St. John's wort, and gotu kola. Each of these plants has a long list of medicinal actions as well as synergistic effects when used with other plants. For example, skullcap is a tasty mint herb. Its light flavor doesn't mean it's a lightweight. There are two common varieties: Chinese skullcap and American skullcap.

Traditionally skullcap has been used as a calming nervine that helps tone, support, and strengthen the nerves. For sensitive people it provides specific treatment of conditions such as insomnia and nervous tension. Skullcap can be used effectively during periods of stress or illness when repair of the immune system is needed. It has beneficial qualities useful to those sensitives who have anxiety; it is good for reducing anxiety, insomnia, and has sedative effects. Sensitive people should use skullcap in moderation as its side effects are light-headedness, irregular heartbeat, sedation, and confusion. American skullcap has been studied for its important properties such as anxiolytic action (anxiety reduction).

While research on its effects have shown some promise for anxiety disorders, scientists believe the sedative effects of skullcap work synergistically because of its effects on the neurotransmitter GABA. Through the interaction of certain pain receptors in the brain, its clinical effects may be due to the neuromodulating action of GABA by increasing the opening of chloride channels on cellular membranes. As more chloride flows into the cell, neuronal firing is inhibited. It can be used for treating serious inflammation along with acetaminophen. For example, acetaminophen inhibits brain inflammation, especially in headaches. When combined with skullcap, this combination can significantly reduce brain inflammation along with strong antioxidant effects.[1] Used together this is a prime example of the synergistic effect skullcap can have when used with other medicines. I realize this is tricky because you'll have to find the right combination for your type of sensitivity. By understanding the medicinal action of these potent herbs, you'll be able to understand what may work for you.

Tonifying herbs. In Chinese medicine some herbs are used to strengthen and others are used to tonify. Tonifying herbs enhance the organs' capacity and function. For example, nervine tonics strengthen the nervous system. They tone and strengthen the soft tissues and boost energy. They can also reverse the damage of modern stress. Tonifying herbs promote health by their medicinal actions to restore and repair, and then boost function.

When using herbs to tonify, energy is being added to the body. Herbs that are tonifying are usually considered adaptogenic too, including:

- ashwagandha
- Cordyceps
- Chinese, American, and Siberian ginseng
- maca
- shilajit
- pine pollen

RESTORATIVE MOVEMENT PRACTICES

We've looked at the many ways mental and emotional stress create bodily distress. Like sleep, restorative movement enables us to re-balance the physiological processes needed for relaxation. Among other things it can help us use calm agitation and allow release of stress. Then we can relax. And relaxation is one of our best allies in healing sensory stress and overload.

Movement that is accompanied by focused attention allows sensitives to observe the vivid internal currents of heat, vibration, and energy that are running through their bodies. Because healing is intricately related to the same brain regions that are involved with mapping the sensory organs of the body, as soon as we can create a physically relaxing state, we can restore our sensory balance. It is interesting to note that when trauma reactions still exist in the body, they often remind us of their presence through sudden shifts in temperature, like feeling immediately cold in the hands and feet (thereby shivering or trembling).

The body is usually on autopilot. Restorative movement is mindful, meditative, and attentional. Meditative and mindful movement (like walking meditation, yoga, or Pilates) help us stay present and observe the body's unique language when it responds to sensory stimuli. When we pay attention, we don't push our sensations aside or attempt to avoid them. We create an opportunity to safely acknowledge what happens in the body and learn new coping mechanisms.

From yoga, Pilates, and swimming to martial arts, sensitive people benefit from consciously moving and releasing their physical energy. One recent Japanese study found that when HSP college students with depressive tendencies walked as their form of exercise, their depressive symptoms were lessened.[2] The researchers attributed the positive therapeutic effects of walking to students gradually habituating to increased sensory stimulation. This may be due to endorphin release as well. While the positive effects of endorphins are well known, they can't be understated. Endorphins are our bliss hormones. They stimulate us to feel positive feelings, from mild euphoria to ecstasy. They interact with the receptors in the brain to uplift our moods and reduce our feelings of physical pain. Because their effects are so powerful, they have been likened to opiates, such as morphine. A lot of our suffering comes from the subjective experience, or internal perception, of pain.

Sensitive people are *more reluctant* than others to use public gyms, bathrooms, and communal spaces. As sensitives we may need to rethink the concept of exercise. Exercising does not have to mean buying a gym membership and working out six times a week to loud music with a group of strangers. This has no appeal to many of us. It can mean physical movement that takes place outdoors, relieving stress, and inducing relaxation. The benefits of movement done with the conscious intent to explore the dimensions of our inner space and sensations for certain types of sensitives are astronomical.

Sensitive-empaths may enjoy Pilates. Pilates is excellent for developing deep muscular strength, which can help an empath achieve the grounded sense they need to root the core of their being into the earth. Additionally exercise can help sensitive-empaths feel their internal core as being more physically present when emotions arise unexpectedly in their environment. Core strength helps them build their reserves of energy through development of muscles and soft tissues that hold the abdominal girdle together.

Similar physical results can be achieved by doing yoga postures like downward dog, bridge, and tree pose on a yoga mat. Combined with proper breathing, you can find core stability by focusing on complementary opposite stretching, like pressing into your hands and lifting your tailbone while doing down dog.

Once again sensitive people do not need to buy a membership to a big gym to achieve significant results from movement for body, mind, and spirit. It sometimes is far better for a sensitive individual to contact a local instructor for private one-on-one training so they can reduce distracting sensory stimulation and focus on the physical tasks at hand—muscular movement, building strength, and relieving stress.

Bliss Flow is a style of vinyasa yoga that allows sensitive-empaths and intuitives to feel expansive states of energetic bliss through *Anandamaya*. In yoga and Ayurveda, Andandamaya kosha is considered the innermost energetic layer of the five koshas or "sheaths" that protect the inner self or atman (soul). This series of yogic asanas warms up the body through grounding and restorative physical movements. As it progresses into more complex rhythmic sweeps of the arms and legs, and expansion of the chest (and the heart), it releases the flow of bliss energy from within. Since sensitive-empaths and intuitives are super in tune with this energy, they will feel it internally as it flows through the heart, downward into the solar plexus and then outward into an expansive full-bodied force. I highly recommend finding a Bliss Flow yoga class in your area. It is energizing and immediately connects you with a deep sense of inner peace and self-love.

Sensitive-intuitives tend to develop physical tension in their shoulders, necks, jaws, and upper backs. These are areas where there is a large concentration of nerve endings, so blocking movement enables them to avoid feeling the emotions of distress. Beneficial exercises for the physical release of stored emotions are child's pose, gentle upper-back bend, cat/cow stretch, forward bend, and cobra pose.

Sensitive visionaries will benefit from concentrated movements that harness stress energy downward, away from their heads and faces, and into the lower trunk of the body. Visionaries spend an inordinate amount of time in their heads. They are the quintessential thinkers who think about thinking. Sometimes they can get stuck in analysis paralysis. They need to counterbalance this energetic stagnancy with more release, toning, and spreading of energy through to the upper thighs, legs, and feet. Working with the feet as a major source of grounding will be a good starting place. Yogic positions such as mountain pose, forward bends, lunges, and cat/cow stretches help sensitive visionaries make direct contact with the ground with both hands and feet.

Sensitive-expressives are usually familiar with forms of expression that incorporate movement, like dancing. Dancers particularly understand how to use movement to release physical stress. They also tend to appreciate the aesthetics of movement and love working to attain a high standard, such as a precise turnout of the leg, or achieving a full extension of the pointed toe at the end of a musical phrase, or the fluidity and special flair they give to a gesture, or how well they communicate and meld with a partner. Striving for excellence and grace—an optimum flow where they can be lost in the moment—refreshes their souls.

Once again physical movement practices used for stress relief should be relatively stress free and without expectation. It would be better to allow the physical movement practice that is best for the sensitive-expressive to be found intuitively. They need their workouts to be something they love. This selection strengthens their confidence in their skills.

An excellent posture for sensitive-expressives who do yoga is eagle pose, as it resets the circulatory system, restricts blood flow in an intentional way, and then releases it safely. They will also benefit from the warrior series (1 to 3), which is good for finding energetic balance between the hips, thighs, and head. Triangle pose, reverse warrior, and temple pose will help them find a safe extension of the upper back and lower back, and stabilizes the hips. Hip openers can be a powerful restorative practice for sensitive-expressive as this gives them an opportunity to release their emotions and enjoy deep communication with the body while offering therapeutic rehabilitation to the hip flexors.

In general yogic inversions are also excellent physical tools for resetting the nervous system of an expressive. Inversions are downward facing dog, wall T stand, bridge pose, supported shoulder stand, and dolphin pose. Movement experts believe that what a living organism senses and perceives is a function of *how it moves*. Through exploration of these movements and how they transform our sense of self, we can strengthen our sensory awareness. Only through high-level discernment can we learn from the subtlest levels of movement, whether internal or imagined, how our life force could most effectively be directed. In the next chapter, we will discuss the highest level of self-discernment transcendent states, that shifts sensitives into higher consciousness.

CHAPTER 9

SOUL MEDICINE AND TRANSCENDENCE

I know, somehow, that only when it is dark enough,
can you see the stars. And I see God working
in this period of the twentieth century in a way
that men, in some strange way, are responding.[1]

— MARTIN LUTHER KING, JR.

Our sensory intelligence helps us communicate with an elevated aspect of our being—the soul or the enlightened intelligence. Like a heavenly twin, this inner being gives us access to higher wisdom. When this occurs it is as if a spiritual light, call it the light of the Divine, has shone upon us and illuminated our soul's purpose. All the sensitive types can receive divine, spiritual, and inspirational insights using their unique form of sensory intelligence through "higher" awareness or expanded consciousness. I call this the *higher self.*

Higher self-consciousness reveals itself to us in different ways, among them synchronicities, signs or omens, and prophetic dreams. Prophetic dreams are messengers that give us advice. They may remind us to turn away from attachment to worldly things and encourage a visit to the inner divine kingdom, where our spiritual instincts remain intact. Or they may instruct us in something immediate that we must do for our well-being. Or they may be insights about a probable future event.

A few paranormal psychologists have theorized people who have extreme hypersensitivity that perceive spiritual intelligences such as angels, ghosts, spirits, or deities are interpreting one continuous field of anomalous phenomena, but in different ways. The explanation behind the different sensory perceptions depends on a sensitive's analytical overlay. For example, during Carl Jung's NDE from a heart attack, he separated from his body and floated above the earth. With the guidance of his doctor's spirit, Jung was given directions to an ancient temple, called an Asklepion. In another NDE example, doctor Eben Alexander felt a similar separation from his body. While unconscious from a meningitis infection, he first found himself in primitive jelly-like world. Then he was lifted up by a beautiful woman (who turned out to be a sister he never knew) with large butterfly wings. She flew him through a cosmic gateway of butterflies. Why is it that both of these powerful NDEs describe common thematic elements such as a separation of consciousness (spirit), help from a specific guide, and transportation to another world?

Sensitive people are like divining rods. You can activate your sensory intelligence to channel, find, and discern information from the quantum field around you. Some sensitive people are attuned to humanity's existential crisis in the quantum field. Studies have shown that sensitives experience non-ordinary states, mystical experiences, and anomalous events more often as a result of their sensory processing sensitivity.[2] Many sensitives have reported feeling the immediate impact of a faraway catastrophic event in mind and body. Einstein called this quantum phenomenon "spooky action at a distance."

Your insights and reactions to events do not have to be local. We now know that due to the phenomenon of entanglement, subatomic particles can be affected by what happens to their counterparts at great distances. Everything material in the universe is at some level entangled. While we can point to the more obvious physical and mental aspects of sensitivity and their impact on our health, we are also vulnerable psychically and spiritually if we pick up on mass casualties and trauma, such as earthquakes, terrorist attacks, or other atrocities.

When I worked at a homeless school in Seattle, Washington, I provided support to children who needed a mental, emotional, and social "brain break" from the high intensity of the classroom. A recent transfer to the school was a girl in Ms. Lencioni's second-grade class. The girl lived with her mother in an emergency shelter in downtown Seattle. As we drew pictures on a side table outside her classroom, I noticed a certain motif taking shape: An image of a beach with people on the sand. They were all running away from a huge blue wave with white crests on the top of it. It was a childlike version of the Japanese painter Hokusai's *The Great Wave*, except the massive wall of water was about to make landfall. There were fish escaping the wave, diving outward from the water and suspended in the air, as if about to fly headlong into the shore.

In art therapy we prefer to ask about the artist's perspective of the rendering rather than applying our own meaning to the art. So I asked the little girl what was happening in her drawing. She replied, "They're running 'cause they're scared."

The next day, December 26, 2004, I learned that a tsunami had struck Sri Lanka due to the megathrust of a 9.2 earthquake off the coast of northern Sumatra. After I heard the news, the image of the girl's drawing sprang to mind. I knew her trauma somehow was connected to perceiving the incoming terror of this event from across the globe.

Like the Italian study based on Sandor Ferenczi's work tracking ESP through dissociation, I witnessed the same invisible phenomenon of advanced perception that the researchers described. The ability to see or connect visually with future events may be a sensory defense mechanism during periods of increased traumatic stress. In this case the young student was already homeless and coping with transitioning to a new school. Her central nervous system was heightened and highly sensitized through this turbulent change. Her ESP may have been acquired as veridical (nonlocal) information about reality. When hypersensitivity is activated, we use veridical perception through heightened perceptual states, like empathy, intuition, and vision to avoid reexperiencing the painful occurrence of terror.[3]

Being emotionally and intuitively attuned to the whole of humanity's experience through our advanced intuitive perception makes us vulnerable, psychically and spiritually. We live within an invisible field of consciousness that connects us all. Ecologist and systems theorist Fritjof Capra calls this the web of life.[4] Biologist Rupert Sheldrake believes there are larger and smaller fields of consciousness that take shape (morph) through repetition of thought or feeling. They undergo *genesis*, or becoming.[5] Whether it is through psychic inheritance from our DNA, cellular memories, or imprints of some kind, we are a part of an intricate network of consciousness because we reside within it. As sensitives who are processing the environment deeply all the time, it is no wonder that precognition, like the little girl's sensing of an impending tsunami, would occur.

To feel strong with our sensory awareness when we are awakened to events that bring vulnerability, we can use different forms of spiritual wellness.

SPIRITUAL WELLNESS

In the tradition of yoga, it is taught that the mind can come to a place of rest with a physical practice (asanas), mantras (sounds), and meditation. Through the stilling of the mental agitation, also known as cessation of inner chatter (ego), consciousness may elevate and reveal *pure awareness*. Using higher awareness, an adherent eventually experiences the difference between thinking and pure energy or pure consciousness. Zen Buddhism is similar in that meditative practice helps an individual align with "beginner's mind." This is a place of *attentional presence* within the moment, where the observation of thoughts, transcendent thinking, and pure awareness channels through an ebb and flow of consciousness. These beginning states of being, which help an individual learn how to be awake and lead to higher awareness, are the beginner's mind. When we become attuned to different states of consciousness as an observer, we can witness our divine intelligence through transcendental states of bliss, joy, serenity, and peace. Many wisdom traditions have helped the modern mindfulness movement take shape for stress reduction, healing, and staying attuned to the current moment.

In the book *Transformative Imagery*, Gerald Epstein used the term *visible reality* as a concept for encompassing the shared visible human experience as opposed to a spiritual matrix that he considers an *invisible reality*. He also shares that others have called this invisible reality Cosmic Consciousness, Divine Consciousness, God, the Absolute One Mind, or Macrocosmic Reality. Finding spiritual wellness can be defined by a search for the meaning of life within the self. When our life has certain meaning, it can be found within the soul's journey through divine consciousness.

Wise teachers inspire us to reach for personal and spiritual freedom, respect the human soul, and diminish reliance on external dependencies (attachments). Living a life free of cultural dependency and freedom from attachments can be a form of spiritual emergence for sensitive people. The symptoms come in the form of loss of relationships (freedom from unhealthy attachment), distinctive pressure to do something, guidance, instructions, or questioning one's existential meaning. These awakening experiences include lucid dreams, visions, inner knowing, or hearing the voice of a deity. Such increases in sensory anomaly or unusual perception force the sensitive to confront their assumptions about mundane existence.

THE NEED FOR A NEW SOUL MEDICINE

Many ancient systems of health recognized the spirit and worked to ameliorate spiritual illness. They are based on the understanding that we are more than our physical bodies; we are spiritual beings having a human experience. Spiritual wellness has been left out of the modern Cartesian system of diagnoses, mechanistic models of care, and reductionist treatment. This scientific disconnection of the mind, body, and soul may be one of the primary reasons we are seeing such catastrophic levels of greed, destruction, and violence on the planet today. Sensitivity was valued in ancient and indigenous cultures. Ancient people developed strategies to take advantage of this trait and supported its development.

For example, in ancient times, the Greeks used the temple of Asclepius, which provided healing for spiritual illness. The famed healer Hippocrates studied at the Asclepeion before becoming the private physician of the Roman emperor Marcus Aurelius. The Asclepeion was a Greek healing temple devoted to Asclepius, the god of medicine. The healing temples were a source of solitude where individuals who were experiencing different illnesses could take refuge and receive physical and spiritual healing. Through dream divination, priests would offer prescribed treatments based on the symbolic communication with the soul.

Hippocrates was one of the first physician-scientists to recognize natural factors that we call bacteria and viruses contributed to illness. He evolved medicine and science through his understanding that illness was not just the whim of erratic gods. Hippocrates became a famous influential healer whose pledge of "primum non nocere," or "do no harm," became the oath that guides the practice of medicine today.

We can still see the symbolic influence of this powerful healer through hospitals and the symbol for medicine. The American Medical Association symbol has the ubiquitous staff with a snake wrapped around it. This is a representation of Asclepius himself with his arm resting on a large piece of wood with a snake coiled around it. Asclepius came from a long lineage of healers who included spiritual practice in their lives.

Modern medicine has forgotten its deep roots in Asclepius's rod where ancients lived according to this symbol. It was a representation of many ideals. One of the most important virtues was taking quiet time needed for contemplation and accessing inner wisdom for healing. The Asclepius rod is very similar in visual makeup to the nadi yoga meridians and the lunar and solar energy channels that crisscross the spine. Their central channel is called the *sushumna*. The *ida* and *pingala* cross the chakras, bringing our life force (the serpent of the kundalini) up to the pineal gland in the center of the head. As discussed, the pineal gland is connected to the regulation of the endocrine system. As I hypothesized before, the release of the pineal gland magic elixir (maybe DMT) might allow us to "see" with more spiritual eyes.

Modern science shuts out our earliest spiritual teachings along with their wisdom and knowledge. Today's medicine treats our body with its various symptoms and ills. Many integrative health practitioners believe we have taken this method too far, treating only physical illness. The spiritual reality has been banished to the point of extinction. The notion of spiritual health may be outdated today. We see the vestiges of this type of healing in hospitals, meditation centers, and retreats, where personal work can be accomplished away from societal influences. In Hippocrates time it was interwoven through all aspects of life. The spiritual world and the physical could not be separated. In his time there was an inner spiritual world invisible to the naked eye that was as vitally important to overall health as treatment of the physical body. Through the passage of time we have forgotten the language of the soul. It has been lost or buried like the ruins of the ancient temples where Greeks once took healing shelter and listened to the inner language through dreams, omens, signs, and inner visions.

Just because our culture has largely forgotten its own soul language doesn't mean it has vanished. When we enter into more intuitive states of awareness, we can become more receptive to the symbolic language of our dreams, synchronicities, and our inner life, where divine intelligence informs us. It is our birthright as spiritual beings. When we heal our sensory channels and contact the divine within, life takes on a mystical quality. This experience stems from the dimensions where our rich imagination and intuition live. Here we find the symbols that are not just images but are the psychic counterparts to our divine instincts. We can access this soul language through symbolism and our own artistic impulses. The following sections outline how to use the soul's unique style of language in the *divine wheel*, which is a process used to access higher consciousness for opening up to transcendent or awakening experiences. As a simple starting point, let's look at how dreams naturally use this soul language to awaken our higher consciousness.

TRANSCENDENT DREAMS AS THE SOUL'S MEDICINE

We intuitively walk between different states of consciousness in our dreams. As Jung taught there is a delicate balance between the intellect, liminal space, and rich symbolic imagery, which is our archetypal inheritance. Archetypes are spiritual messengers. It is like any muscle or foreign language. One must travel through the archaeology of the soul and practice to hear, speak, and translate the archetypal language. The mystical union between the self and the totality has a profound influence on the sensitive person. Ancients have been explaining this connection through traditional wisdom in stories and through rituals such as shamanic journeys, song, dance, prayer, meditation, and union with nature.

Through different spiritual traditions, it is said that the creator, universe, source, God, or Goddess is perfection, serenity, and blissful once encountered. This divine presence has also been described as cosmic consciousness. We expand easily into higher states of consciousness through our dream states, which reflect our thoughts and feelings. Lucid dreaming is the primary mechanism for these advanced states of consciousness. Lucid dreams manifest latent images, content, and patterns. Lucid dreams break down into three different categories: physical, emotional, and spiritual. Spiritual dreams feel less like dreams and more like intense psychic visions. These different types of dreams explore, through comparison and contrast, how we feel about life through personal, cultural, and archetypal symbols.

Personal symbols. These are the most important, as we give personal meaning to these individual symbols. They take priority over cultural symbols and archetypal symbols because they have importance that translates specifically to us. For example, I might dream of a Toyota truck. This has specific meaning to me because I've owned two. The first I bought in college. It represents freedom, prosperity, and wildness. My second truck was a little different. I bought it when I was in a serious life change and needed more room. My husband and I were growing our little family. In this case my second truck stands for growth, reliability, and protection. Same brand of truck. Big differences in meaning.

Cultural symbols. Cultural symbols can be found everywhere. The Statue of Liberty, Eiffel Tower, White House, American flag, and on and on. Our cultural symbols represent ideas about the community, country, and world we live in. They go beyond personal meaning to define the current era or society.

Archetypal symbols. These spiritual messengers enlighten us. Through visions of angels, God, or spirit-beings, we meet divine intelligence. Archetypal dream content is unforgettable, and the quality of the images feels supernatural and otherworldly. You might meet an old hermit or a wise woman by a lakeside. If you are traveling to an unknown destination, who is your guide? Archetypal symbols have been described by vivid dreamers, and there are many catalogs of these spiritual entities.

As we have discussed, Jung furthered the notion of a primordial image, which is now known psychoanalytically as an archetypal image. Archetypes are the psychic connection point to instincts like intuition, which often contain spiritual perception as well.

They can feel overwhelming and often break up entrenched ways of thinking. They transform our thought process. Many sensitives describe heightened sensory awareness after a profound prophetic or precognitive dream. When a sensitive experiences a transcendent dream state that imparts information, they are often unsure how to interpret it. We find ourselves being confronted with the same questions Descartes and Jung grappled with in their eras. They both searched relentlessly for truth and meaning within science and spirituality.

As Descartes examined it is easy for sensitive people to get lost in their senses. For Jung it might have been getting carried away by his senses through his own soul-searching for the cultural imagery that brought on psychosis, or maybe it was inborn. Either way his persistence with the psychic processes of healing and the language of symbolism made intuitive sense to him. He proved their efficacy in psychoanalytic therapy. Whether he knew it or not, Jung birthed a new treatment modality that included art and spirituality for healing in psychiatry.

The sensory awareness thread that weaves both these progressive leaders together is *discernment*—between illusion and truth. Getting lost in the senses is a problem. When we feel the sudden onset of anxiety, the thoughts, feelings, and ideas about the immediate future feel real, although they may not be true. Conversely our lucid dreams do not occur in our waking reality but can express our truth. To find solutions to this intrinsic problem of illusion versus truth, we can use artful, scientific, and spiritual methods. I don't think we need to completely remove the wheat (science) from the chaff (spirituality). Using imagery as a medical intervention can bridge all these effective sciences together and show us the way. Sensitive people can use imagery for healing to help understand dreams, find blissful states of feeling, and even surrender into the unknown.

IMAGERY

Imagery can be thought of as a graphic, symbolic, or pictorial analogue of an emotional state. It has been used to gain extraordinary insight into the personal experience of what discomfort feels like. While imagery has been used therapeutically as a means for coping with pain, stress, and discomfort it has also been used to help our soul transcend earthly boundaries. This capacity for change is within each of us. We all have learned limitations. Things we believe hold us back or stop us from becoming who we might truly be if we were able to tap into our full potential.

Using imagery we can go into relaxed, deep modes of focus with concentration and discern what specific imagery can help our own physiological states. The science of imagery shows that we can use it to impact our physiology. Mental states can affect biological processes, including our susceptibility to illness.[6]

People who use imagery successfully for healing do so when they are in altered states or hypnotic trances, which is a necessary condition for them to be able to sense and generate mental images that create a context for healing. Gross absorption on these images must include all the senses and emotions.[7] New research using fMRI devices has shown that while in a hypnotic state, using guided imagery, the areas involved in cortical processes, including the senses that are active, light up on the fMRI when activated. Internal healing imagery allows healing responses to happen.[8]

In traditional medicine images are used with ancient diagrams that have symbolic meaning, such as the yantra (Hinduism), mandala (Tibetan Buddhism), and medicine wheel (Native Spirituality). Imagery provides clues used to reveal perceptions, inner attitudes, and behaviors. Using these circular structures, guided imagery is highly effective as a therapeutic intervention for sensitive individuals because it uses all the senses. It is a full-sensory, somatic, mind-body experience. Using a mandala as a physical representation of the psyche helps bring the symbols, images, and inner attitudes into a concretized space. Using a gentle meditative process to perceive images that are exploratory in nature, we can gain insight, hindsight, and foresight. This wisdom can lead to clear action.

Using the imagination coupled with guided imagery can be an evocative, relaxing, and therapeutic healing process. Psychoneuroimmunology has shown prelinguistic symbols and imagination are a process driven by implicit memory.[9] PET scans show that imagery affects neurology. Where attention goes, neurofiring goes. Where neurofiring goes, neuropathways light up. With our most advanced technology, we can now reflect how ancient techniques like meditative thought, imagery, and the imagination can influence our biophysical processing through our senses.

TRANSCENDENCE

If we believe we have a soul, spirit, or divine intelligence, we can connect to it through higher consciousness. The soul uses our specific sensory intelligence to communicate with us through visions, intuition, sudden insights, knowledge, and sensing wisdom by feeling certain truth or a "knowing." Visions can be thought of as a prelinguistic language balancing the energetic forces of the body be they physical, mental, or emotional. *Prelinguistic* means the visual languages we used before we learned verbal communication. Our early communication is through sensory awareness, facial expression, body language, gestures, and vocalization (cooing and laughter). Additionally when any part of our sensory system is damaged, the brain recognizes this deficit and strengthens other areas to help cope. We might see a strong visual sense or inner vision from someone who has hearing difficulties or communication delays, or if they suffered an accidental injury.

I believe our sensory awareness does inform us with sensory intelligence through the soul's symbolic language. It is found in the balance between these two different phases of language development: prelinguistic and linguistic. Prelinguistic uses sounds, vocalization, and word play. Linguistic language development is the emergence of words and symbolic communication. Imagery for transcendent medicine uses symbolic communication through healing visions, symbols with energetic information, and transpersonal perceptions of space, movement, and sensory information through the visionary sense. Sensitive visionaries will understand this faculty quite well as their gift of inner vision, spatial imagery, and visual sensory intelligence solves problems routinely.

Images for transcendence are portals into a different reality. The journey inward to the hidden terrain of the psyche, which is the job of an artist or visionary, involves self-discovery, mastery, and illumination. Joseph Campbell called this inner quest, the hero's journey.[10] He labeled the process of personal mythmaking because it involves herculean strength, requires navigation of mystical realms within the psyche, and leads us to uncover a special gift. We also see this journey as a recognizable framework in popular stories going back thousands of years, such as the tale of Hercules, or more recently through Luke Skywalker in *Star Wars*, or Neo in *The Matrix*.

Every individual has the capacity to make an artistic journey via a process I call the *intuitive language of the soul*. Sensitive people may already be more receptive to this spiritual symbolic code. They have a higher faculty for sensing symbolic prelinguistic language of imagery. We all have it, although we might have neglected it through modernization of technology. As sensitives we have a strong susceptibility for this language, which we can experiment with through play, creativity, and art. Our imaginations are active. Our minds are a storehouse for symbolic reasoning because we have stayed in touch with our full capacity for expression.

Soul language is embedded within our psyche. It includes the phenomenal realm of our cultural imprinting and contains the imagery we need for healing the soul. We can strengthen our physical mind and body with our innate desire to be united with God, Goddess, or Cosmic Consciousness. Soul healing is a natural by-product of this work. When someone goes through a physical or psychological wounding, this language is more persistent and available through the psyche as the mind-body-spirit seeks to gain energetic equilibrium. The soul's influence is by nature a healing mechanism for fusing the higher self's knowledge and perfection of self-love with the physical material self. This is spiritual integration at its finest.

Spiritual trauma occurs when there is a "metastasizing" of traumatic energy from any source—mental/emotional or physical—within the mind-body-spirit. Metastasizing in this context means growing or stagnation of energy into areas where it doesn't belong. We are integrated beings, whole beings, so spiritual life is a vital part of our lives when we are healthy. Treating our energy is as vital to restoring our overall health as the treatment of our physical and psychological selves.

We all have patterns of thought, emotions, and images that depict our personal story and influence our behavior. Jung was drawn to the mandala and labyrinth as a symbolic tool for undergoing artful therapeutic work because their circular structure allows for a container to integrate the hidden aspects of the psyche. Going through an artistic symbolic process activates the language of the soul. This activation brings it forward so it may be interpreted by the self. I have developed a process using the divine wheel, an energetic force embedded within the soul. Through sensory intelligence, using the mandala as a physical, concrete representation of ourselves, we can contact the divine intelligence of our soul using intuitive symbolic language as the means for communication.

Whatever is buried in the memory by the collapse
of meaning under an inadequate or lying language—
this will become, not merely unspoken, but unspeakable.

— ADREINNE RICH, *ON LIES, SECRETS,*
AND SILENCE: SELECTED PROSE, 1966–1978

THE DIVINE WHEEL

Once we understand our own sensory gifts, we can use them to find our story, symbolic imagery, and thematic life events to realize our life's purpose. This form of soul medicine is a transcendent experience into the union between our self and the divine. By using imagery the sensitive person can travel through the imaginal realm, using imagery as a portal, and find meaning in their personal experience.

During trance states perception of the time-space continuum distorts. As we have discussed, through guided imagery, hypnosis, and other forms of trance meditation, consciousness is an inherent intelligence. Sensory intelligence is the only mechanism for accessing the divine wheel and understanding the deep aspects of the self that are hidden in it. The divine wheel concretizes the sacred connection between the human mind-body and the divine sacred aspects of the soul. It is not healing work to be undertaken lightly. The human experience contains turmoil, pain, traumatic memory, and emotionality. As you integrate this symbolic meaning into your reality, you can feel powerful shifts of consciousness through the transcendent function of spiritual awareness.

Symbolic images can be thought of as an illustrative analogue of an emotional state. These images are more than flat, one-dimensional pictures; they are the counterpart to psyche, our subtle instincts that offer solutions to intrapsychic spiritual conflict. They become enlivened through guided imagery. Characters may speak, act, and portray specific themes.

The divine wheel contains the entirety of your human existence. Similar to a dream, creative content that springs forth will not raise imagery, concepts, or themes you have already dealt with or healed. It will bring forth what remains psychically energized and needs immediate attention. This is the function of the psyche, which balances the forces between conscious/unconscious thoughts, right/left hemispheric perception, and equilibrium/disequilibrium.

We cannot perceive the entirety of existence through our waking consciousness. What the subconscious does perceive are our own images, symbols, and memories (including from preexistence) embedded within a nexus of the conscious mind. Take Jung's NDE as a prime example. In 1944 Jung had a heart attack and then an NDE. He described his encounter with a force both real and *eternal*. During his NDE he saw his much larger self. In *Visions/Life After Death* he describes what transpired: "I had the feeling that everything was being sloughed away; everything I had aimed at or wished for or thought, the whole phantasmagoria of earthly existence fell away, or was stripped from me—an extremely painful process. Nevertheless something remained."[11]

Jung experienced what he determined was a surrender and acceptance of his life's purpose. He traveled outside the earth and saw an expanded reality, had inherent knowledge from a universal truth and order. He felt a profound disappointment at having to go back into his pained body: "It seemed to me as if behind the horizon of the cosmos a three-dimensional world had been artificially built up, in which each person sat by himself in a little box."

If we use such powerful realizations for our spiritual health and healing, anything is possible. Even though we may have forgotten the soul's language it can still be a vital salve for self-healing. Magnificent healing dreams and visions are how we first experience it. We can further expand on these themes in the daytime by undergoing a journey into the self. Envisioning where this energy streams from through a concretized form opens us up to new realizations. How might we process divine information? We know this world exists within and outside of ourselves due to lucid dreams, visions, and out-of-body flight. After his intense healing, Jung believed he had completed a part of his own individuation: "It signified detachment from valuations and from what we call emotional ties. In general, emotional ties are very important to human beings. But they still contain projections, and it is essential to withdraw these projections in order to attain to oneself."

In Ayurveda sensory withdrawal is a part of healing the senses, balancing the turbulence of the mind, and restoring spiritual health. The divine wheel helps us use this pratyahara sensory withdrawal to draw inward. It gives inner breath and energy to creative imagination. It is a sensory-energetic journey. By reducing the inputs from the outside world and turning our conscious attention inward, we divine transpersonal and transcendent experiences. We must vibrationally clear any lingering or agitated energy in the mind through breath work to help aid our resolve during this process. Advanced breath work and sensory withdrawal give us strength to travel inward. I have included a short pratyahara exercise for you to try in my description of how to make your own divine wheel. You can find this link in the Resources section on page 283.

When a sensitive person undergoes such a journey, it helps open up a new understanding and value of their life. If we realize the purpose to our soul journey, there is less of a human struggle. As we continue to shape and define the soul's meaning within our life, we can attach to emotions less and spiritually evolve more.

Make Your Own Divine Wheel

Creation of the divine wheel is an intuitive process. You document what is discovered through divine sensing by bringing symbols, imagery, and pictures from this inside world outward. You might receive a flash of insight about a job, life direction, or soul partner. Many times clients have told me when completing this exercise, they had a hypnagogic image or heard their inner voice magnified. It will depend on you and your processing style. You can use the divine wheel for any burning questions you have about your life. It works as a journey, and while you may not understand any specific detailed imagery, try not to judge what you see, hear, or feel. My specific intention behind this guided travel was for healing spiritual issues (like feeling loss of energy, depression, or grief).

If sensitivity truly is a meaningful connection to the soul's perception, we are already tuned into this information through dreams, intuitions, and visions. All we need to do is take conscious control over this process. We tap into it and use the spiritual energy, divine insights, and self-healing as a form of self-mastery to reach personal enlightenment. Buddha teaches us that a healthy mind, body, and spirit are by-products of such enlightenment.

Perceived exclusively through sensory awareness, our divine consciousness goes beyond the individual's personal pain process. Expanded sensory awareness taps into the expanded state of the universal mind/soul/creator. This transition or transcendence allows a sensitive greater perception and acknowledgment of the inner truth, life destiny, divine purpose, or soul connection. This feeling of ecstatic bliss feeds the senses with supernatural wonderment that enlivens the sensitive soul.

Materials. You will need to gather some materials. You'll need a large piece of paper, a pen and crayons or markers, and a recording device, like a voice memo app on your phone. I have prepared several recordings you can listen to online as well during the visioning portion of this exercise. Grab a comfy blanket and a mat to lie on. You can lie on your bed if you'd like. You might also like an eye pillow, towel, or something to block out the light.

Step 1. Draw a circle. Start by drawing a circle. Inside it create four equal quadrants, like four big pieces of pie. View these quadrants as a map, and on the outer edge of each put a label. In the top right-hand corner, write *Physical*. On the lower right corner, write *Spiritual*. On the lower left corner, write *Emotional*. On the top left-hand corner, write *Past Life*. Then set the paper aside.

Step 2. Prepare for pratyahara (sensory withdrawal). You can prepare for pratyahara by sitting in a restful position. Sit however works for you: in a chair with both your feet on the floor or cross-legged on the floor.

Close your eyes. Use your thumbs to close your ears. Then use both ring fingers or pinkies to close your nostrils.

Take in a large, expansive breath in. Seal your lips and make the humming sound of a bee buzzing. When your held breath becomes slightly exhausted, exhale, then inhale again, and start over, buzzing and humming while holding your breath.

Go through five cycles of buzzing breath, then rest.

Now that you're warmed up, you can travel to your inner world. If you want to use your phone, you'll need it now so you can listen to my instructions while traveling inward. Once your body is ready, you'll need a quiet place to lie down.

Step 3. Travel into the divine wheel. In this exercise you'll need to access the Divine Wheel Guided Imagery online (see Resources). When you're ready, get comfortable. Lie down with a blanket. Cover your full body up to your chest. Make sure your head rests easy. Use a pillow or towel to shut out the light over your eyes. Play "The Divine Wheel Guided Imagery."

Use your inner senses and relaxed breathing as you travel inward.

Step 4. Make notes. As you come back and open your eyes, you'll write on the paper that you drew a circle and quadrants on. Without communicating with others or taking a break, record the imagery from your divine wheel journey on the circle.

In the upper right-hand quadrant, put symbols that represent any sensory information you felt physically. Depict what you felt inside your body with a symbol, color, or image on the upper right corner.

In the lower right-hand quadrant, draw a picture of any deity, entity, or divine intelligence (including angel, guides, or spirits), or something from the natural world like a tree, flower, or nature spirit (fairy, tree spirit/goddess, or water spirit) that you encountered.

In the lower left-hand quadrant, describe whether there were any images that felt emotional. If there were, depict what you encountered in the form of a symbol. Use color with this symbol if you perceived it as a vivid picture.

In the upper left-hand quadrant, draw any archetypal or spiritual symbols you encountered. These images take on thought forms and feel like memories. If you had any recollections of the past, record them in the upper left corner.

Step 5. Create a symbolic key. Now you will create a short symbolic key, which you can build on to create a larger soul symbol library. List out what was discovered to the right or left of your circle. For example, if it was a train, you would draw or write *train* and then list three of your immediate meanings for this symbol below it. Don't think long and hard about this. Go with your gut instinct. Train equals *engineer, old form of travel,* or *an old-timer.* Farmhouse equals *country, renovation,* or *old world.* Tractor equals *farmer, back to the land,* or *agriculture.*

Since personal symbols are more important than cultural meaning, the description you give your symbols provides further insight into the soul connection. When you unlock a symbol's meaning, it will come with a sudden realization. Sometimes the meaning of a symbol is not metaphorical; it is perfectly concrete (exact or specific). Any appearance of a person you know should also be recorded. If it is a mother, father, sister, brother, or other contact, list them in the corresponding corner.

For example, when I guided a client through this meditation the first time, she saw her mother on the land near her family's farm. As she explored the familiar landscape of their farm, her mother appeared near the barn where she used to play. She started to cry, and while I didn't know why, I continued to guide her into having a conversation with her mother. When she came out of the guided imagery, she was completely astonished. In the deep inner space where she visually created her divine wheel, she was able to receive a message from her mother who had passed away several years earlier. She even received a message for her sister. It was powerful and she felt like there was a message given to pass on. When she started processing her emotions, she realized she missed her mother more than she realized, and having this conversation with her mom allowed her to process these feelings.

After a guided imagery session, clients have told me they encounter direct messages from ancestors, clear healing information, or directions from a spiritual guide. One time a young man I was working with saw a large grizzly bear in his symbolic scene. As he approached the bear and spoke with it, the massive animal stretched out its claws fiercely in a defensive posture. The young man spoke with the grizzly and asked why it was gesturing. He couldn't understand. The bear literally said, "You need better boundaries. You're trying too hard." The man told me the bear's claws in the imagery represented a physical defense mechanism. He realized he had been too open with new acquaintances. This led to them borrowing his stuff, asking for favors, and sometimes lending money.

While this is certainly possible, many times we receive sensory information that doesn't come with such direct guidance. At times it can be very precise; we often need to enter a dialogue with the soul. We must translate the meaning through symbolic expression. This symbolic expression continues to ebb and flow through consciousness. As you grow your own soul symbol library, you will learn to discern this language and translate symbolic meaning as it filters into your consciousness through your own sensory intelligence.

TO WHOM MUCH IS GIVEN, MUCH IS REQUIRED

The gifts of sensitivity are a human trait that, at least on some level, is intended to restore balance. As change and healing occurs, sensitive people can lead the way for others.

Gary Swanson once told me, "I want to be alive, awake, and aware during the most volatile times we have ever faced on Earth."[12] I found that perspective interesting, for it doesn't really matter what we want. If we are alive, this is the reality we must contend with. Turning our faces away and refusing to confront the truth is not sustainable. Yes, it takes courage, resilience, and a strong sense of self to look the rapid and unwelcome changes facing humanity head on and not buckle. That is why we must make the commitment to heal our mental and emotional wounds and engage in a daily regimen of self-nurturing. This is the only way we will have the resiliency and strength needed to positively impact the world around us. When it comes to sensitivity, I believe: to whom much is given, much is expected. We have been gifted with our sensory abilities. We must use their wisdom to help heal our communities. Through healing sensitives learn to channel energy, stabilize through emotional resiliency, and achieve a spiritual outlook.

To summon the strength and courage needed to confront such profound shifts in our shared reality, let's explore the gifts of our divine intelligence. In her book *End of Days*, psychic Sylvia Browne predicted "a severe pneumonia-like illness will spread throughout the globe, attacking the lungs and bronchial tubes and resisting all known treatments."[13] While many of the technological medical advances she also predicted have not been invented yet, the respiratory illness she described with explicit detail a decade earlier has appeared with catastrophic deadly force.

Healthy sensitive people who are attuned to their own inner divinity are desperately needed right now. We have entered a global health crisis with COVID-19. The infectious disease has spread throughout the world, expanding like a wildfire. At the date of this writing,[14] there have been over 7.5 million cases of COVID-19 diagnosed. Almost half a million have died from this new type of coronavirus. Right now we are experiencing a collective trauma. It is my hope that sensitive people will provide solutions during this crisis. If we raise our consciousness together, with the power of spirit, anything is possible. We can lead the way. Sensitives who have already experienced extreme trauma and undergone an intensive healing process can share through their perseverance and strength what helped them survive, build resilience, and restore hope. With enforced isolation we've seen dramatic increases in mental health issues, violence, and despair.

Most sensitive people have learned through their self-imposed isolation and separation how to restore, balance, and find equilibrium. Now is the time for sensitives to step up and share their insights and make an impact by using their sensitivity to help humanity.

Sensitive-visionaries are often the people who caution, warn, and guide humanity. One of the most famous is world-renowned physicist Stephen Hawking. He was an articulate, outspoken critic of degradation of the earth from human impact, and a sensitive-visionary leader. Before his death in 2018, he warned about potential dangers associated with the rise of artificial intelligence, the devastation of global resources due to overpopulation, and the proliferation of nuclear arms. His warnings about these catastrophes were explicit. Experts believe we are beginning to see his prophetic warnings come true.

Some prediction specialists, including corporations such as RAND, have projected our possible extinction by the year 2040. In April of 2018, RAND corporation, a global think tank, warned of future events in which artificial intelligence could influence human decision-making, weakening the current equilibrium measure of mutually assured destruction to deter global war using nuclear weapons. The catastrophic mistakes outlined in their report detailed how humans could create machines that generate processing errors that lead to mass destruction. In terms of sensitivity, we have discussed human processing errors that occur from receiving too much sensory information. As humans we can self-correct, and we have due to the horrible costs of past errors in judgment such as using the nuclear bomb.

This is the kind of cognitive and emotional dissonance that sensitive people feel intuitively with the very fiber of their being. One of the chief complaints of sensitive people is they can see the signs of impending disaster and crisis while others choose to remain blind. Several of my close friends have witnessed possible futures including nuclear attacks wiping out the entire East Coast, a foreign superpower invasion of California, and strikes by mysterious black helicopters over the United States. They have seen a reality that is even more disturbing than what we are capable of dealing with psychologically. This gap often leads to existential angst, frustration, and exhaustion. When other people refuse to make the changes needed to make our world a better place, sensitive people can lead the way.

As sensitives we have also foreseen the future as we wish it to be. Reflect on Martin Luther King, Jr.'s 1968 speech when he once famously said, "I've been to the mountaintop." In his empowering and unifying speech, he emphasized humanity's ability to confront injustice and create change. We must step up and take our place in society as peacemakers and healers who can help spiritually direct humanity. Sensitive people have the sharp discernment to reach out without coercion. Spiritually we know we are on the brink of disaster and sensitive people might help create the reparative functions to mitigate such catastrophes.

Sensitive people often receive warnings through sensory channels such as the visual sense tied to intuition. Edgar Cayce, prophet, healer, and teacher, was called the "sleeping prophet," as he received his psychic information through visionary lucid dream states. Caroline Myss, a modern medical intuitive, perceives health information from other people through her felt-sense, or physically embodied sensations. All the way back to biblical times we find examples of the metaphysical sensory gifts. The individuals who were sensitive to spiritual undercurrents were called prophets, teachers, leaders, and healers. There is a rich biblical history of the human-spiritual potential to see, hear, and feel warnings that served as allegories to steer humanity into spiritual holism.

The story of Moses from the Old Testament is one of the earliest. Moses was an Israelite prophet who received spiritual information through visions and hearing sacred messages. Also called *Moshe Rabbenu*, "Moses, our teacher" in Hebrew, he rose to spiritual prominence when the Israelites were enslaved by the Egyptians. Moses was a spiritual leader who freed his people from slavery after receiving direction from his higher power. He had several life-changing transpersonal experiences. Most memorably he witnessed, through an intense vision of the light, a "burning bush" in which the presence of a spirit who called itself an "angel of the Lord" appeared. The angel instructed Moses to lead his brethren out of Egypt. Eventually he interpreted the 10 Commandments, a system of spiritual laws that laid out the specific rules of God.

His influence as a spiritually gifted leader is still firmly held in his allegorical legend.

Similar historic transcendent lineages can be found cross-culturally in the lives of Buddha, Jesus, Muhammad, Dionysius the Areopagite, Teresa of Ávila, Hildegard of Bingen, Ibn'Arabi, and Sufi mystical poet Rumi. Through these individuals' lives, we see a pattern of translation, interpretation, and deep connection to the divine invisible world, which has helped shape human morality, ethics, and individual freedoms. In all these cases there is a thread of divinity running through the human experience guiding the sensitive through the power of the soul. These themes reflect their own spiritual emergence. Through their individual spiritual expression, we see a process that bridged human awareness to the development of divine intelligence.

There is a predictive pattern that we can use to intuit the spiritual calling. A spiritual gift is present from a young age (such as a visionary experience, healing, or prophetic dreams). A healing crisis occurs, causing a profound transformation of beliefs, ability, or inner strength. This predictive pattern is grounded through an underlying spiritual hunger, a search for meaning, a felt destiny, or through a higher awareness of the human soul/spirit. The underpinning with most spiritual callings is a deep drive for spiritual wellness. Spiritual wellness has been described by many wisdom traditions as an idea of destiny or fate.

LIVING WITH SPIRITUAL AWARENESS AS A HIGHLY SENSITIVE PERSON

You can do it! You don't have to be the new Jesus or Buddha with such a heavy burden on your shoulders. Accept who you are. As I have pored over everything on sensitivity, I've seen us called backward, awkward, odd; labeled manic, hysteric, or mentally ill. Let's just call it what it is: a difference. Our differences don't have to separate us anymore. The label hangers don't know we're also the game changers, rule breakers, and love makers. Providing your own routine spiritual wellness is enough to maximize your spiritual awareness. Hopefully you've tried some of the suggestions in this book. If you have increased spiritual awakening or awareness from practicing the self-healing techniques outlined, you're on the right track. When you immerse yourself in healing communities like church, yoga centers, or meditation retreats, you can get more support on your spiritual journey.

Living with spiritual awareness as a highly sensitive person is not only possible, it's enlightening. We live less for ourselves and more for humanity. If these intelligences are the next phase of spiritual evolution, nature is guiding sensitives to adopt a new reality. We've learned that the sensitive's survival strategy is an inherent defense mechanism nature built in for self-protection to help us serve our tribe, or community. When we excel with the gifts through a divine capacity, we need to trust in our intuition and let our visionary abilities guide us into a new future. We must help build a world where all humans are treated as equals and can live without fear. The profound states of awakening that come with being sensitive will invariably lead sensitives to find a way to create an existence in which every life is cared for, regardless of the current illusion of separation. When we respect every living human being, we can heal past and current traumas through reconciliation. This is the only way to restore our hope. Many spiritual healers, teachers, and gifted ministers use their sensitivity to feel whole during transitional states of growth in spiritually. From spiritual teacher Mahatma Gandhi: "When helpers fail and comforts flee, I find that help arrives somehow, from I know not where."[15] Have faith and let us go forth and bear witness to the magnificent power and beauty in ourselves. When we can see the beauty in ourselves, we see it in others. We can be the helpers and the change. Listen to the wisdom of your heart, dear sensitive, and it will guide you.

ENDNOTES

Chapter 1

1. Cliff Smyth, Ph.D. (Mind-Body Medicine practitioner at Saybrook University) in discussion with the author, January 23, 2020.

2. Malcolm Gladwell, "Dangerous Minds," *The New Yorker*, accessed November 12, 2007, https://www.newyorker.com /magazine/2007/11/12/dangerous-minds

3. Sarah Wiedersehn, "The Aboriginal trackers who saved an abducted schoolgirl will finally have told their story." SBS, accessed January 24, 2019, https://www.sbs.com.au/news/the-aboriginal-trackers-who-saved-an-abducted-schoolgirl-will-finally-have-their-story-told

4. Kylie Boltin, "Missing: The Abduction of Wendy Pfeiffer." SBS, 2019, https://www.sbs.com.au/nitv/feature/missing-abduction-wendy-pfeiffer

5. "London 'Hamlet' star loses star to illness," *The New York Times*, September 16, 1989, https://www.nytimes.com/1989/09/16/theater/london-hamlet-loses-star-to-illness.html.

6. Douglas R. Gere, Steve C. Capps, D. Wayne Mitchell, and Erinn Grubbs, "Sensory sensitivities of gifted children," *The American Journal of Occupational Therapy* 63, no. 3 (2009): 288–295.

7. Li, S., Jordanova, M., and Lindenberger, U., "From good senses to good sense: A link between tactile information processing and intelligence," *Intelligence* 26, no. 2 (1998): 99–122; Wolf, M., Sander Van Doorn, G., and Weissing, F., "Evolutionary emergence of responsive and unresponsive personalities," *Proceedings of the National Academy of Sciences* 105, no. 41 (2008): 15825–15830; Helmbold, N., Troche, S., and Rammsayer, T., "Temporal information processing and pitch discrimination as predictors of general intelligence," *Canadian Journal of Experimental Psychology/Revue canadienne de psychologie expérimentale* 60, no. 4 (2006): 294; Ian J. Deary, "Intelligence and auditory discrimination: Separating processing speed and fidelity of stimulus representation," *Intelligence* 18, no. 2 (1994): 189–213.

8. Elaine N. Aron and Arthur Aron. "Sensory-processing sensitivity and its relation to introversion and emotionality," *Journal of Personality and Social Psychology* 73, no. 2 (1997): 345.

9. Edward Zagha et al., "Motor cortex feedback influences sensory

processing by modulating network state," *Neuron* 79, no. 3 (2013): 567–578; Adam Gazzaley and Anna C. Nobre, "Top-down modulation: bridging selective attention and working memory," *Trends in Cognitive Sciences* 16, no. 2 (2012): 129–135; Jeffrey Moran and Robert Desimone, "Selective attention gates visual processing in the extrastriate cortex," *Science* 229, no. 4715 (1985): 782–784; Cristopher M. Niell and Michael P. Stryker. "Modulation of visual responses by behavioral state in mouse visual cortex," *Neuron* 65, no. 4 (2010): 472–479; John H. Reynolds and Leonardo Chelazzi, "Attentional modulation of visual processing," *Annual Review of Neuroscience* 27 (2004): 611–647.

10. Zaidel, E., Zaidel, D., and Sperry, R., "Left and right intelligence: Case studies of Raven's Progressive Matrices following brain bisection and hemidecortication," *Cortex* 17, no. 2 (1981): 167–185.

11. Elaine N. Aron and Arthur Aron. "Sensory-processing sensitivity and its relation to introversion and emotionality," *Journal of Personality and Social Psychology* 73, no. 2 (1997): 345.

12. David Jay Brown and Rupert Sheldrake, "The anticipation of telephone calls: A survey in California," *Journal of Parapsychology* 65, no. 2 (2001): 145–156; Grinberg-Zylberbaum, J., Delaflor, M., and Sanchez Arellano, M.E., "Human communication and the electrophysiological activity of the brain," *Subtle Energies & Energy Medicine Journal Archives* 3, no. 3 (1993).

13. Stuart Hameroff, "Consciousness, microtubules, & 'Orch OR': A 'space-time odyssey,'" *Journal of Consciousness Studies* 21, no. 3–4 (2014): 126–153.

14. Elsevier, "Discovery of quantum vibrations in 'microtubules' inside brain neurons supports controversial theory of consciousness." ScienceDaily (January 16, 2014). www.sciencedaily.com /releases/2014/01/140116085105.htm.

15. Satyajit Sahu et al., "Multi-level memory-switching properties of a single brain microtubule," *Applied Physics Letters* 102, no. 12 (2013): 123701; Idem., "Live visualizations of single isolated tubulin protein self-assembly via tunneling current: effect of electromagnetic pumping during spontaneous growth of microtubule." *Scientific Reports* 4 (2014): 7303.

16. Russell Targ and Harold Puthoff, "Information transmission under conditions of sensory shielding," *Nature* 251, no. 5476 (October 1974): 602–607.

17. Giuseppe Scimeca et al., "Extrasensory perception experiences and childhood trauma: A Rorschach investigation," *The Journal of Nervous and Mental Disease* 203, no. 11 (2015): 856–863.

18. Judith Dupont, ed., *The Clinical Diary of Sándor Ferenczi* (Cambridge, MA: Harvard University Press, 1988).

19. Booth, C., Standage, H., and Fox, E., "Sensory-processing sensitivity moderates the association between childhood experiences and adult life satisfaction," *Personality and Individual Differences* 87 (2015): 24–29.

20. Smolewska, K., McCabe, S., and Woody, E., "A psychometric evaluation of the Highly Sensitive Person Scale: The components of sensory-processing sensitivity and their relation to the BIS/BAS and 'Big Five,'" *Personality and Individual Differences* 40, no. 6 (2006): 1269–1279.

21. John-Dylan Haynes and Geraint Rees, "Decoding mental states from brain activity in humans," *Nature Reviews Neuroscience* 7, no. 7 (2006): 523–534.

22. Li Zuo, "Creativity and aesthetic sense," *Creativity Research Journal* 11, no 4 (June 8, 2010): 309–313.

23. Garry Nolan in discussion with the author, May 5, 2020.

24, Daniel J. Felleman and David C. Van Essen, "Distributed hierarchical processing in the primate cerebral cortex," *Cerebral Cortex* 1, no. 1 (1991): 1–47.

25. L.J. Cauller and A.T. Kulics, "The neural basis of the behaviorally relevant N1 component of the somatosensory-evoked potential in SI cortex of awake monkeys: evidence that backward cortical projections signal conscious touch sensation," *Experimental Brain Research* 84, no. 3 (1991): 607–619; Andreas K. Engel and Wolf Singer, "Temporal binding and the neural correlates of sensory awareness," *Trends in Cognitive Sciences* 5, no. 1 (January 2001): 16–25; Roelfsema, P., Lamme, V., and Spekreijse, H., "Object-based attention in the primary visual cortex of the macaque monkey," *Nature* 395, no. 6700 (1998): 376–381.

26. Adam Gazzaley and Anna C. Nobre, "Top-down modulation: bridging selective attention and working memory," *Trends in Cognitive Sciences* 16, no. 2 (2012): 129–135.

27. James F.A. Poulet and Carl C.H. Petersen, "Internal brain state regulates membrane potential synchrony in barrel cortex of behaving mice," *Nature* 454, no. 7206 (2008): 881–885; Bilal Haider et al., "Enhancement of visual responsiveness by spontaneous local network activity in vivo," *Journal of Neurophysiology* 97, no. 6 (June 2007): 4186–4202; Kenneth D. Harris and Alexander Thiele, "Cortical state and attention," *Nature Reviews Neuroscience* 12, no. 9 (August 2011): 509–523. Andreas K. Engel, Pascal Fries, and Wolf Singer, "Dynamic predictions: Oscillations and synchrony in top-down processing,"

Nature Reviews Neuroscience 2, no. 10 (2001): 704–716. Michael Goard and Yang Dan, "Basal forebrain activation enhances cortical coding of natural scenes," *Nature Neuroscience* 12, no. 11 (October 2009): 1444; Stephan L. Marguet and Kenneth D. Harris, "State-dependent representation of amplitude-modulated noise stimuli in rat auditory cortex," *Journal of Neuroscience* 31, no. 17 (April 27, 2011): 6414–6420.

28. Camil Correia et al., "Global sensory impairment in older adults in the United States," *Journal of the American Geriatrics Society* 64, no. 2 (February 2016): 306–313.

29. Harriet Allen and Katherine L. Roberts, "Perception and cognition in the ageing brain: a brief review of the short- and long-term links between perceptual and cognitive decline," (2016).

30. Pamela J. Meredith et al., "Sensory sensitivity and strategies for coping with pain," *American Journal of Occupational Therapy* 69, no. 4 (2015): 6904240010p1–6904240010p10.

31. David E. Evans and Mary K. Rothbart. "Temperamental sensitivity: Two constructs or one?" *Personality and Individual Differences* 44, no. 1 (January 2008): 108–118; Laura A. Thomas et al., "Development of emotional facial recognition in late childhood and adolescence," *Developmental Science* 10, no. 5 (September 2007): 547–558; Arthur Aron et al., "Temperament trait of sensory processing sensitivity moderates cultural differences in neural response," *Social Cognitive and Affective Neuroscience* 5, no. 2–3 (2010): 219–226. Jadzia Jagiellowicz et al., "The trait of sensory processing sensitivity and neural responses to changes in visual scenes," *Social Cognitive and Affective Neuroscience* 6, no. 1 (2011): 38–47. Bianca P. Acevedo et al., "The highly sensitive brain: an fMRI study of sensory processing sensitivity and response to others' emotions," *Brain and Behavior* 4, no. 4 (July 2014): 580–594. Hauke R. Heekeren et al., "A general mechanism for perceptual decision-making in the human brain," *Nature* 431, no. 7010 (2004): 859–862.

32. Red Pill Film Knowledge and Tinfoil with Jon Lippe, "The 3rd Insight - A Matter of Energy - The Celestine Prophecy - by James Redfield," November 17, 2018, https://www.youtube.com/watch?v=r7LTH-9OC9c.

33. David Luke, "Anomalous phenomena, psi, and altered consciousness," *Altering Consciousness: Multidisciplinary Perspectives: History, Culture, and the Humanities; Biological and Psychological Perspectives* (2011): 355–374.

34. William Booth, "Huichol 'cosmic portal' peyote ceremonies threatened by silver mine," *Washington Post* (February 13, 2012), https://www.washingtonpost.com/world/the_americas/cosmic-portal-threatened-by-silver-mine/2012/02/04/gIQA7iB0BR_story.html

35. Jayson Gaddis, "The Shamanic View of Mental Illness," *Uplift*, February 26, 2019, https://upliftconnect.com/the-shamanic-view-of -mental-illness/.

36. Oberman, L., Rotenberg, A., and Pascual-Leone, A., "Use of transcranial magnetic stimulation in autism spectrum disorders," *Journal of Autism and Developmental Disorders* 45, no. 2 (2015): 524–536.

37. Terry Gross, "Electric currents and an 'emotional awakening' for one man with autism," *Fresh Air,* (April 2016) NPR; https://www.npr.org/ sections/health-shots/2016/04/21/475112703/electric-currents-and -an-emotional-awakening-for-one-man-with-autism.

38. John Elder Robison, *Switched On: A Memoir of Brain Change and Emotional Awakening,* (New York: Random House, 2017); Terry Gross "Electric currents and an 'emotional awakening' for one man with autism," *Fresh Air,* (April 2016) NPR; https://www.npr.org/sections/ health-shots/2016/04/21/475112703/electric-currents-and-an -emotional-awakening-for-one-man-with-autism.

39. Catherine E. Kerr et al., "Tactile acuity in experienced Tai Chi practitioners: evidence for use dependent plasticity as an effect of sensory-attentional training," *Experimental Brain Research* 188, no. 2 (June 2008): 317–322.

40. Ton de Jong, "Cognitive load theory, educational research, and instructional design: some food for thought," *Instructional Science* 38, no. 2 (August 27, 2009): 105–134.

41. John Sweller, "Cognitive load during problem solving: Effects on learning," *Cognitive Science* 12, no. 2 (1988): 257–285.

42. Jeffrey W. Sherman et al., "Stereotype efficiency reconsidered: Encoding flexibility under cognitive load," *Journal of Personality and Social Psychology* 75, no. 3 (1998): 589.

Chapter 2

1. Jen Viegas, "Elephants Added to List of Animals That Show Empathy," Seeker, last modified February 18, 2014, https://www.seeker.com/ elephants-added-to-list-of-animals-that-show-empathy-1768309442. html.

2. Gavin deBecker, *The Gift of Fear: And Other Survival Signals That Protect Us from Violence* (New York: Dell Publishing, 1998), 13.

3. ETH Zurich, "Hereditary trauma: Inheritance of traumas and how they may be mediated," ScienceDaily, last modified April 13, 2014, https://www.sciencedaily.com/releases/2014/04/140413135953.htm.

4. Vincent J. Felitti et al., "Relationship of childhood abuse and household dysfunction to many of the leading causes of death in adults: The Adverse Childhood Experiences (ACE) Study," *American Journal of Preventive Medicine* 14, no. 4 (May 1, 1998): 245–258; https://www.aap.org/en-us/Documents/ttb_aces_consequences.pdf.

5. Garry Nolan, in discussion with the author, May 5, 2020.

Chapter 3

1. Gary Morning, *The Complete Idiot's Guide to Understanding Einstein* (Alpha, 1999), 286.

2. Garry Nolan, "Can genetic differences in intuition and cognition drive success in space?" lecture, Harvard Medical School Symposium on Space Genetics, November 30, 2018.

3. James Iandoli, "Is the caudate-putamen an antenna for anomalous information?" *Terra Obscura* (blog), January 8, 2018, https://www.terraobscura.net/blog/is-the-caudate-putamen-an-antena-for-anomalous-information.

4. Andrea Brovelli et al., "Differential roles of caudate nucleus and putamen during instrumental learning," *NeuroImage* 57, no. 4 (August 2011): 1580–1590.

5. Ibid.

6. Ibid.

7. Ibid.

8. Ibid.

9. James Iandoli, "Is the caudate-putamen an antenna for anomalous information?" *Terra Obscura* (blog), January 8, 2018, https://www.terraobscura.net/blog/is-the-caudate-putamen-an-antenna-for-anomalous-information.

10. Alejandro Rojas, "Dr. Eric Davis Investigating and Experiencing the Paranormal Interview Transcript," OpenMinds, accessed on April 30, 2019, http://www.openminds.tv/dr-eric-davis-investigating-and-experiencing-the-paranormal-interview-transcript/42351.

11. St. Francis College, "Gavin de Becker, The Gift of Fear," September 19, 2013, video, 52:44, https://www.youtube.com/watch?v=zNtXjIiJ0PU.

12. Ibid.

13. TED, "How do you explain consciousness? | David Chalmers," July 14, 2014, video, 18:37, https://www.youtube.com/ watch?v=uhRhtFFhNzQ&vl=es.

14. Louis Jolyon West et al., "Space Perception," *Encyclopedia Britannica*, accessed April 16, 2019, https://www.britannica.com /science/space-perception#ref488146.

15. Russell Targ and Jane E. Katra, "Remote Viewing in a Group Setting," *Journal of Scientific Exploration* 14, no. 1 (2000), 107–114; Caroline Watt and Ian Tierney, "Psi-related experiences," *Dissociation, trauma, memory, and hypnosis series. Varieties of anomalous experience: Examining the scientific evidence* (2014): 241–272.

16. Walter Blanco and Jennifer Tolbert Roberts, *The Histories: Herodotus*, (New York: W.W. Norton, 1992).

17. Gilbert Clotaire Rapaille, "The Culture Code: Why People Around the World Really Are Different, and the Hidden Clues to Understanding Us All," Microsoft Research, last modified on June 13, 2006, https://www.microsoft.com/en-us/research/video/the-culture-code-why-people-around-the-world-really-are-different-and-the-hidden-clues-to-understanding-us-all.

18. Katherine Stangret, "Code of Conduct: Bayesian Predictive Coding," *Grey Matters Journal*, last modified on June 12, 2019, http:// greymattersjournal.com/code-of-conduct-bayesian-predictive -coding/.

19. Carl G. Young, *The Collected Works of C. G. Jung* (Princeton, NJ: Princeton University Press, 1983).

20. Saul McLeod, "Carl Jung," Simply Psychology, last modified 2018, https://www.simplypsychology.org/carl-jung.html.

21. Edutopia, "Martin Scorsese on the Importance of Visual Literacy," video, 10:43, https://www.youtube.com/watch?v=I90ZluYvHic.

22. Thomas G. West, *In the Mind's Eye: Creative Visual Thinkers, Gifted Dyslexics, and the Rise of Visual Technologies* (Buffalo, NY: Prometheus Books, 2010).

23. Linda Kreger Silverman, *Upside-Down Brilliance: The Visual-Spatial Learner* (Denver, CO: DeLeon Publishing, 2002).

24. Michele Root-Bernstein and Robert Root-Bernstein, "Einstein On Creative Thinking: Music and the Intuitive Art of Scientific Imagination," *Psychology Today*, last modified on March 31, 2010, https:// www.psychologytoday.com/us/blog/imagine/201003/einstein -creative-thinking-music-and-the-intuitive-art-scientific-imagination.

25. Benaroya, H., Nagurka, M., and Han, S., *Mechanical Vibration: Analysis, Uncertainties, and Control* (Boca Raton, FL: CRC Press, 2017).

26. Fred Child, "Aldo Lopez-Gavilan: Emporium," *Performance Today*, last modified on June 16, 2018, https://www.yourclassical.org/programs/performance-today/episodes/2018/06/16.

27. Mary A. Carskadon, *Encyclopedia of Sleep and Dreaming*. (New York: Macmillan Publishing Co. Inc, 1993).

28. Pat Ogden et al., "Sensorimotor psychotherapy: One method for processing traumatic memory," *Traumatology* 6 no. 3, 149; Pat Ogden, Kekuni Minton, and Claire Pain (2006). "Trauma and the body: A sensorimotor approach to psychotherapy." (New York: W.W. Norton & Company, 2006).

29. Stumbrys, T., Erlacher, D., and Malinowski, P., "Meta-awareness during day and night: the relationship between mindfulness and lucid dreaming," *Imagination, Cognition and Personality* 34, no. 4 (2015): 415–433, https://journals.sagepub.com/doi/abs/10.1177/0276236615572594.

Chapter 4

1. Ashlee Vance, *Elon Musk: Tesla, SpaceX, and the Quest for a Fantastic Future* (New York: Ecco, 2017).

2. Ibid.

3. Ibid.

4. Wikipedia. "Spatial Intelligence." Last modified August 19, 2020. https://en.wikipedia.org/wiki/Spatial_intelligence_(psychology) #cite_ref-Gardner_1-0.

5. Andrew Newberg. "How do meditation and prayer change our brains?", http://www.andrewnewberg.com/research.

6. R. Nisha Aurora et al., "Best practice guide for treatment of nightmare disorders in adults," *Journal of Clinical Sleep Medicine 6 no.* 4 (2010): 389–401.

7. Ibid.

8. Ibid.

Chapter 5

1. William Shakespeare, *As You Like It Act II, Scene VII.*

2. Alan di Perna, "Interview: Carlos Santana Discusses His New Album, 'Shape Shifter,'" *Guitar World*, last modified on July 20, 2012, https://www.guitarworld.com/features/interview-carlos-santana -discusses-his-new-album-shape-shifter.

3. Oscar Wilde, *Decay of Lying* (London: Alma Books, 2018).

4. Gary Swanson, in conversation with the author, May, 2014.

5. Truman Capote, "The more sensitive you are the more certain you are to be brutalized," *The Guardian*, last modified on September 10, 2007, https://www.theguardian.com/theguardian/2007/sep/11/ greatinterviews.

Chapter 6

1. Mariella Frostrup, "Rhys's pieces," *The Guardian*, last modified on September 1, 2002, https://www.theguardian.com/film/2002/sep/01/ familyandrelationships.

2. Del Giudice, M., Ellis, B., and Shirtcliff, E., "The adaptive calibration model of stress responsivity," *Neuroscience & Biobehavioral Reviews* 35, no. 7 (2011): 1562–1592.

3. Jonsson, K., Grim, K., and Kjellgren, A., "Do highly sensitive persons experience more nonordinary states of consciousness during sensory isolation?" *Social Behavior and Personality: An International Journal* 42, no. 9 (2014): 1495–1506.

4. Batool Ahadi and Sajjad Basharpoor, "Relationship between sensory processing sensitivity, personality dimensions and mental health," *Journal of Applied Sciences* 10, no. 7 (2010): 570–574.

5. Lucy Jane Miller et al., "Concept evolution in sensory integration: A proposed nosology for diagnosis," *American Journal of Occupational Therapy* 61, no. 2 (2007): 135–140.

6. Grant Benham, "The highly sensitive person: Stress and physical symptom reports," *Personality and Individual Differences* 40, no. 7 (2006): 1433–1440.

7. Chunhui Chen et al., "Contributions of dopamine-related genes and environmental factors to highly sensitive personality: a multi-step neuronal system-level approach," *PLoS One* 6, no. 7 (2011).

8. Kaitlyn Bakker and Richard Moulding, "Sensory-processing sensitivity,

dispositional mindfulness and negative psychological symptoms," *Personality and Individual Differences* 53, no. 3 (2012): 341–346.

9. Lucassen et al., "Stress, depression and hippocampal apoptosis," *CNS & Neurological Disorders-Drug Targets (Formerly Current Drug Targets-CNS & Neurological Disorders)* 5, no. 5 (2006): 531–546.

10. Grant Benham, "The highly sensitive person: Stress and physical symptom reports," *Personality and Individual Differences* 40, no. 7 (2006): 1433–1440.

11. Hanne Listou Grimen and Åge Diseth, "Sensory processing sensitivity: Factors of the highly sensitive person scale and their relationships to personality and subjective health complaints." *Comprehensive Psychology* 5 (2016): 2165222816660077.

12. Warren Jones and Ami Klin, "Attention to eyes is present but in decline in 2–6-month-old infants later diagnosed with autism," *Nature* 504, no. 7480 (2013): 427–431.

13. Ellie Lisista, "The Four Horsemen: Stonewalling," The Gottman Institute (blog), May 20, 2013, https://www.gottman.com/blog/the-four-horsemen-stonewalling/.

14. Maté, Gabor. *Scattered Minds: The origins and healing of attention deficit disorder.* (Vintage Canada, 2011).

15. Britta K. Hölzel et al., "Neural mechanisms of symptom improvements in generalized anxiety disorder following mindfulness training," *NeuroImage: Clinical* 2 (2013): 448–458.

16. Luciano Bernardi et al., "Effect of rosary prayer and yoga mantras on autonomic cardiovascular rhythms: comparative study," *BMJ* 323, no. 7327 (2001): 1446–1449.

17. Mona Lisa Chanda and Daniel J. Levitin, "The neurochemistry of music," *Trends in Cognitive Sciences* 17, no. 4 (2013): 179–193.

18. "Parinama," Yogapedia, accessed April 26, 2019, https://www.yogapedia.com/definition/5722/parinama.

Chapter 7

1. Translated by D.C. Rao. "Yoga sutra 1.3." https://yogainternational.com/article/view/yoga-sutra-1-3-translation-and-commentary.

2. McGlone, F., Wessberg, J., and Olausson, H., "Discriminative and affective touch: sensing and feeling," *Neuron* 82, no. 4 (2014): 737–755.

3. To, Your Guide. "Prevention of hearing loss from noise," Better Hear-

ing Institute, http://www.battlegroundhearing.com/wp-content/uploads/2017/05/BHInoiseGuide.pdf

4. Terence McKenna, *Food of the Gods: The Search for the Original Tree of Knowledge, A Radical History of Plants, Drugs, and Human Evolution* (New York: Bantam, 1993).

5. National Ayurvedic Medical Association, "NAMA recognized ayurvedic health counselor programs," https://www.ayurvedanama.org/ayurvedic-health-counselor-programs

6. Bernie S. Siegel, *The Art of Healing: Uncovering Your Inner Wisdom and Potential for Self-Healing* (Novato, CA: New World Library, 2013).

7. Anthony Stevens, *Archetype Revisited: An Updated Natural History of the Self* (Routledge, 2015).

8. Walter Schempp, "Quantum holography and neurocomputer architecture," *Journal of Mathematical Imaging and Vision* 2 (1992): 383–467.

Chapter 8

1. Lesley Braun and Marc Cohen, *Herbs and Natural Supplements, Volume 2: An Evidence-Based Guide* (Elsevier, 2015).

2. Kosuke Yano and Kazuo Oishi, "The relationships among daily exercise, sensory-processing sensitivity, and depressive tendency in Japanese university students," *Personality and Individual Differences* 127 (2018): 49–53.

Chapter 9

1. Martin Luther King, Jr., "I've been to the mountaintop,"(speech, Church of Christ Headquarters, Memphis, Tennessee, April 3, 1968).

2. Jonsson, K., Grim, K., and Kjellgren, A., "Do highly sensitive persons experience more nonordinary states of consciousness during sensory isolation?" *Social Behavior and Personality: An International Journal* 42, no. 9 (2014): 1495–1506; Irwin, H., Schofield, M., and Baker, I., "Dissociative tendencies, sensory processing sensitivity and aberrant salience as predictors of anomalous experiences and paranormal attributions," *Society for Psychical Research* (2014).

3. Judith Dupont, ed., *The Clinical Diary of Sándor Ferenczi* (Cambridge, MA: Harvard University Press, 1988).

4. Fritjof Capra, *The Web of Life: A New Scientific Understanding of Living Systems*, (Anchor, 1996).

5. C.O. Scharmer, "Morphic fields interview with Rupert Sheldrake," *Presencing Institute,* last modified on September 23, 1999, https://www.presencing.org/aboutus/theory-u/leadership-interview/rupert_sheldrake.

6. Cohen, S., Tyrrell, D., and Smith, A., "Negative life events, perceived stress, negative affect, and susceptibility to the common cold," *Journal of Personality and Social Psychology* 64, no. 1 (1993): 131.

7. Belleruth Naparstek, *Staying Well with Guided Imagery* (Grand Central Life & Style, 2008).

8. Tusek, D., Church, J., and Fazio, V., "Guided imagery as a coping strategy for perioperative patients," *AORN Journal* 66, no. 4 (1997): 644–649.

9. Daniel J. Siegel, *The Developing Mind: Toward a Neurobiology of Interpersonal Experience* (New York: Guilford Press, 1999).

10. Joseph Campbell, *The Hero's Journey: Joseph Campbell on His Life and Work* (Novato, CA: New World Library, 2003).

11. Carl G. Jung, *Visions/Life After Death* (na, 1996).

12. Gary Swanson, in conversation with the author, March 2018.

13. Sylvia Browne, *End of Days: Predictions and Prophecies About the End of the World* (Berkley Press, 2008), 210.

14. COVID-19 Coronavirus Pandemic, Worldometer, accessed, June 12, 2020, https://www.worldometers.info/coronavirus/.

15. Mahatma Gandhi, *Autobiography: The Story of My Experiments with Truth* (North Chelmsford, MA: Courier Corporation, 1983),153.

RESOURCES

Anodea Judith, *Eastern Body, Western Mind: Psychology and the Chakra System As a Path to the Self* (Random House Digital, Inc., 2004).

Carl Gustav Jung, *The Collected Works of CG Jung: Symbols of Transformation*, Vol. 5. (Routledge, 2014).

Carl Gustav Jung. *Memories, Dreams, Reflections* (Vintage, 1989).

Gabor Maté, *Scattered: How Attention Deficit Disorder Originates and What You Can Do About It* (Penguin, 2000).

Gavin de Becker and Thomas Stechschulte, *The Gift of Fear* (Boston: Little, Brown, 1997).

———. *Protecting the Gift: Keeping Children and Teenagers Safe (and Parents Sane)* (Dell, 2013).

Grant Cameron and Desta Barnabe, *Contact Modalities: The Keys to the Universe* (Independently published, 2020).

Linda Kreger Silverman, *Upside-Down Brilliance: The Visual-Spatial Learner* (Denver, CO: DeLeon Publishing, 2002).

Russell Targ and Jane Katra, *Miracles of Mind: Exploring Nonlocal Consciousness and Spiritual Healing* (Novato, CA: New World Library, 1999).

Peter A. Levine and Ann Frederick, *Waking the Tiger: Healing Trauma* (North Atlantic Books, 1997).

Walter Isaacson, *Einstein: His Life and Universe* (New York: Simon and Schuster, 2008).

Thomas G. West, *In the Mind's Eye: Visual Thinkers, Gifted People with Dyslexia and Other Learning Difficulties, Computer Images and the Ironies of Creativity*, (Buffalo, NY: Prometheus Books, 1991).

Mind Body Method Audio Files

Body Scan, visit www.inspiredpotentials.com/bodyscan

Vipassanā Concentration, visit www.inspiredpotentials.com/vipassanaconcentration

Vipassanā Relaxation, visit www.inspiredpotentials.com/vipassanarelaxation

Vipassanā Awareness, visit www.inspiredpotentials.com/vipassanaawareness

Guided Imagery

The Healing Garden, www.inspiredpotentials.com/healinggarden
Samskara, www.inspiredpotentials.com/samskara
The Mansion, www.inspiredpotentials.com/mansion
The Lamp of Illumination, www.inspiredpotentials.com/lampofil-
lumination

Meditations

Empath Boundary-setting meditation, visit www.inspiredpoten-
tials.com/boundarysetting
Chakra meditation, visit www.inspiredpotentials.com/chakra

Divine Wheel

Pratyahara, visit www.inspiredpotentials.com/pratyahara
The Divine Wheel, visit www.inspiredpotentials.com/divine-
wheelimagery

ACKNOWLEDGMENTS

Thank you to my sister Heather and mom, Chris, who loved me unconditionally over the years. Dad, I am forever grateful for you. I know you were overseeing the writing of this book in heaven.

I'd like to thank all my teachers, friends, and supporters who believed in me before this book was a twinkle in my eye. Dr. Silvia Jimenez-Krause listened with the patience of a saint. Thank goodness her husband, Garrison, could put up with my meanderings. He shared his own story, which reinforced my ideas about a possible book. Thank you to my soul sister, Maria Benavent-Diaz, whose kindred spirit I have always felt. You are my trusted consigliere. Maybe, I'll finally be able to come visit you.

Long, long ago, one Berkeley, California, energy teacher, Lynda Caesara, came to Seattle monthly to teach a bunch of energy students bioenergetics. Lynda taught me a great many things. Some of the most valuable were the tenets of energy. Thank you to Leigh Shambo, who guided me safely through my first awakening process on an Olympia, Washington, farm. I'll never forget the "four-leggeds" who held space for us. Many thanks to all of my co-workers at Mental Health and Addiction Services at Harborview, including Candace, Nancy, Francine, and Christy. I'd like to especially thank my former office mate Rena Elkins.

Gary Swanson you are a true artistic visionary and as your father once said, "you guys are going to do great things." Your level of mastery informed everything in this book.

Thank you to these superb editors Stephanie Gunning, Lisa Cheng, and Sally Mason-Swaab. Stephanie, you will always be my editor extraordinaire. Finally, thank you to my nearest and dearest family Tom, Luca, Jacob, and Maia. You have continued to support me despite the dirty laundry, cobwebs, and other unfinished chores. The cause for all of our celebrations has finally materialized. To my daughter Bailey, you have helped me in countless ways. I will always give you the last word and you will always be my precious angel.

Whether I was a student or friend, sought guidance, or you lent me a book, I appreciate your immeasurable influence: Carolyn Marchesani, Mary Ann and Larry Marchesani, Mom and Pop Marchesani, the Meehan Family, Amanda Lyon and Dr. Cassandra Lidin, Jodee and Matt Zunker, Sara Hospador and Hugh Geenen, Ken and Beth Zerone, Dr. Nabil Haddad, Marie Polito, Sara Rossi, Elaine Kimbler, Joyce Netishen, Donna Ireland, Tracee Lloyd, Dr. Allison Kelliher, Lois Law, Emily O'Neill, Dr. Stuart Hall, Dr. Charles "Chuck" Langeness, Alan Brown, Georgia and Promethea, June DeYoung, Sabrina Hanan, Hilary Wheeler-Smith, Carol Anne, Karolyn McKinley, Rhonda Liebig, Kelly Turnage, Lori Fox, Katey Inman, Shasheen Shah, Sharon Litwin, Kaya Kade, Dr. Michael Aanavi, Elaine Molchanov, Denise Gonzalez-Walker, Letitia Jackson, Tonya Spivey, Steve Johnson, Dave and Elizabeth Roberts, Bob Stech, Rob Annett, Tanya Venskus Ferrell, Holly Purdy, Grant Cameron, Dr. Garry Nolan, Dr. Kirwan Rockefeller, Dr. Eric Willmarth, Susan Nader, Pamela Doerr, Dave and Jill Heimke, Liane Buck, Christianne Cook, Kimberlee and Art, Lamar Gunter, Devorah Curtis, Dr. Cliff Smyth, Deborah Bowes, Dr. Selene Kumin Vega, Posie Boggs, Lauren O', Jessica Batson, Susan Romes, Billie Urabazo, Jolene Grover, Dr. Alexandra Cope, Maureen McGavin, Penny and Chris Williams, Deborah Fachko, Lauren Roelling, Martha Eden, and last but never least, Loni McKenzie.

ABOUT THE AUTHOR

Courtney Marchesani, M.S., is a certified health coach with the Institute of Integrative Nutrition, a 200-Hour yoga teacher, herbalist, and highly sensitive person. In 2002 her passion for understanding the gifts of sensitivity came about through a transformative personal experience. She prevented a fire at her friend Rebecca's Seattle brownstone. Life would never be the same. Ever since, she's investigated the anomalous aspects of sensitivity, including telepathy, lucid dream states, and precognition. When she had her own health crisis due to sensitivity in 2005, Courtney realized the powerful effects anxiety has on the mind, body, and spirit. After healing her own symptoms from sensitivity, she focused on learning the complementary healing modalities used to treat sensitivity, such as herbalism, expressive art therapy, meditation, yoga, and guided imagery.

The core of Courtney's integrative health practice emphasizes stress reduction from sensory overload. Using the body as a barometer, she helps clients identify their unique sensory processing style with mindfulness using the senses. She teaches specialized yoga classes. Her classes are trauma-sensitive and focus on how sensitivity impacts anxiety and sensory integration processing issues such as autism.

Her love of nature is combined in everything she does, from using plants to address spiritual wellness, to her walks in the nearby Chugach mountain range where she lives in Alaska with her husband, Tom, and children, Luca, Jacob, and Maia. She enjoys lively conversations about movies and politics with her oldest daughter, Bailey, who lives in Oregon. One day, Courtney will finally write a book about spirit animals entitled *Why Do Cats Stare at You While You Sleep?* due to her little tortie companion, Katie, who has the preternatural ability to peer into a soul. This pantherlike housecat scares the holy bejesus out of Courtney when she wakes up because Katie is usually staring into her face.

Listen. Learn. Transform.

Reach your fullest potential with unlimited Hay House audios!

Gain access to endless wisdom, inspiration, and encouragement from world-renowned authors and teachers—guiding and uplifting you as you go about your day. With the *Hay House Unlimited* Audio app, you can learn and grow in a way that fits your lifestyle . . . and your daily schedule.

With your membership, you can:

- Let go of old patterns, step into your purpose, live a more balanced life, and feel excited again.

- Explore thousands of audiobooks, meditations, immersive learning programs, podcasts, and more.

- Access exclusive audios you won't find anywhere else.

- Experience completely unlimited listening. No credits. No limits. No kidding.

Try for FREE!

Visit hayhouse.com/listen-free to start your free trial and get one step closer to living your best life.

Free e-newsletters from Hay House, the Ultimate Resource for Inspiration

Be the first to know about Hay House's free downloads, special offers, giveaways, contests, and more!

 Get exclusive excerpts from our latest releases and videos from *Hay House Present Moments*.

 Our **Digital Products Newsletter** is the perfect way to stay up-to-date on our latest discounted eBooks, featured mobile apps, and Live Online and On Demand events.

 Learn with real benefits! *HayHouseU.com* is your source for the most innovative online courses from the world's leading personal growth experts. Be the first to know about new online courses and to receive exclusive discounts.

 Enjoy uplifting personal stories, how-to articles, and healing advice, along with videos and empowering quotes, within *Heal Your Life*.

Sign Up Now!

Get inspired, educate yourself, get a complimentary gift, and share the wisdom!

Visit www.hayhouse.com/newsletters to sign up today!

HAY HOUSE

HAY HOUSE online learning

Hay House Podcasts
Bring Fresh, Free Inspiration Each Week!

Hay House proudly offers a selection of life-changing audio content via our most popular podcasts!

Hay House Meditations Podcast

Features your favorite Hay House authors guiding you through meditations designed to help you relax and rejuvenate. Take their words into your soul and cruise through the week!

Dr. Wayne W. Dyer Podcast

Discover the timeless wisdom of Dr. Wayne W. Dyer, world-renowned spiritual teacher and affectionately known as "the father of motivation." Each week brings some of the best selections from the 10-year span of Dr. Dyer's talk show on Hay House Radio.

Hay House Podcast

Enjoy a selection of insightful and inspiring lectures from Hay House Live events, listen to some of the best moments from previous Hay House Radio episodes, and tune in for exclusive interviews and behind-the-scenes audio segments featuring leading experts in the fields of alternative health, self-development, intuitive medicine, success, and more! Get motivated to live your best life possible by subscribing to the free Hay House Podcast.

Find Hay House podcasts on iTunes, or visit www.HayHouse.com/podcasts for more info.